Special Physical Education:
A Resource Guide for
Professionals and Students

Meeting the Individual Needs of All Students

Barry Lavay, Ph.D.

California State University, Long Beach

"physical education for all children"

KENDALL/HUNT PUBLISHING COMPANY
2460 Kerper Boulevard P.O. Box 539 Dubuque, Iowa 52004-0539

This edition has been printed directly from camera-ready copy.

Library of Congress Catalog Card Number: 92-71474

Copyright © 1992 by Kendall/Hunt Publishing Company

ISBN 0-8403-7510-7

Printed in the United States of America
10 9 8 7 6 5 4 3 2 1

TABLE OF CONTENTS

Introduction vi

What's So Special about Special Physical Education
Benefits of Physical Education for Students with a Disability
.... 6
Now More Than Ever: Physical Education for the
Elementary School-Aged Child-Croce & Lavay.. 7-15
Special Physical Education defined 16-17
Sevice Delivery Model 18
The Special Physical Educator: Meeting Educational Goals
Through a Transdisciplinary Approach-Lavay & French 19-25
Survival Strategies for the Itinerant Special
Physical Educator-French, Lavay & Montelione 26-30
Clarity of Misconceptions Regarding the Implementation
of Adapted/Special Physical Education as Determined
by PL 94-142 31-33

Assessment in Special Physical Education   34
The Law and Assessment 35
Assuring Proper Referral Procedures in Special
Physical Education-Lavay & Hall 36-39
Assessment is Different From Testing 40
No Single Assessment Instrument Exists 41
Purpose of Assessment 42
Characteristics of Assessment Instrument 43
Appropriateness of Assessment Instrument 44
Assessment Instruments in Special Physical Education 45-48
Selected References in Assessment 49

Who is the Student with a Disability?   50
Categorical & Noncategorical Approach 51-52
The Student with a Disability as Defined by Law 53-55
The Law and the Students with a Disability 56
Adjusting to a a Disability 57-58
Sensory Systems 59

Categorical Approach

Mental Retardation 60-63

Instruction of Team Sport Strategies for the
Mild/Moderate Mentally Handicapped 64-69

Severely and Profoundly Retarded 70-71

Behavior Disordered 72-74

Help! Class Out of Control 75-80

Take A Lap-French, Lavay, & Henderson 81-88

Learning Disabled 89-92

Visually Impaired & Blind 93-95

Hearing Impaired & Deaf 96-98

Postural Deviations 99-100

Overweight & Obesity 101-103

Cerebral Palsy 104-106

Seizure Disorders 107-108

Diabetes 109-110

Asthma 111-112

Muscular Dystrophy 113-114

Orthopedically Impaired 115-116

Developmental/Individualized Instructional Approach   117

Instructional Program Implementation 118

Movement & Curriculum Guide Suggestions 119-121

Related Fitness Components & Modifications 122

IEP Development 123

Writing the IEP 124-130

Task Analysis 131-133

Combining Students with Different Ability Levels
in Games & Sports-Arbogast & Lavay 134-140

The Mainstreaming Process   141

Attitudes Toward Mainstreaming 142

Is Mainstreaming in Physical Education, Recreation
and Dance Working? 143-144

The Least Restrictive Environment is not Always
Mainstreaming 145-147

Factors to Consider to Assure Proper Physical
Education Placement 148

Student Mainstreaming Profile 149

Teacher Mainstreaming Profile 150

The Harbinger Helper: Why Mainstreaming in Physical
Education Doesn't Always Work-Lavay & DePaepe 151-156

Advantages and Disadvantages of Mainstreaming 157

Teaching Suggestions for Mainstreaming... 158-159

Strategies For Modifying Games & Sports 160

Mainstreaming into Action 161-164

Modifying Games to Meet Individual Needs 165

A Bibliography of Mainstreaming in Physical
Education-DePaepe & Lavay 166-171

References & Resources in Special Physical Education

A Reference Guide for Special Physical Educators
-Lavay & Dart 172-180

Adapted/Special Physical Education References 181-183

Motor Development References 184-185

Professional Organizations 186-187

Journal Publications 188-190

Sport Organizations for Athletes with Disabilities 191

Special Physical Education Terminology 192-193

Appendices

Appendix A Course Syllabus

Appendix B University Student Activity Assignments

Introduction

Today, many excellent textbooks and resources exist in the area of special physical education. This resource guide was developed as a supplement to these textbooks as well as a guide to professionals and students providing instruction in physical education to children with disabilities.

The guide is divided into seven major areas: (a) what's so special about special physical education provides an introduction and overview of the discipline of special physical education; (b) assessment in special physical education discusses the assessment process specific to children with special needs; (c) who is the student with a disability identifies both the categorical and noncategorical approach; (d) The categorical approach provides the reader with a definition, classification system, etiology, and developmental and programming considerations for 14 different disabilities, (e) the developmental/individualized approach provides strategies for individualizing instruction to meet the unique needs of all children, (f) The mainstreaming process discusses strategies practiced in the field for successfully integrating special needs children into regular physical education and; (g) references and resources in special physical education provides the reader with information regarding the availability of references, professional organizations, and journals specific to the discipline of special physical education. In addition, an appendices section includes: (a) a course syllabus used in an introductory class; and (b) a description of 22 activities that have been effectively used to assist university students to gain experiences with regard to physical activity and individuals with disabilities.

A unique feature of this guide is the majority of the pages are designed to be easily used as overheads for professionals conducting classroom instruction and or inservice programs. In addition, the spacing between lines of the pages are designed to allow students to easily add written notes.

The resource guide is based on the strong conviction that physical activity is beneficial and should be provided to all children. Each child is unique and should be afforded opportunities to reach full learning potential. All students deserve the very best instruction we can offer!

Barry Lavay

Special thanks to Elgerine Gross, Regina Monarez, and Tammy Walsh for their help with typing an earlier version of this manuscript and to my wife Penny for typing the articles. Thanks to Barry Miller and Gary Hefner for proof-reading the guide and Janet Romain for designing the cover.

What's So Special
About
Special Physical Education

BENEFITS OF PHYSICAL EDUCATION FOR THE STUDENT WITH A DISABILITY

The same important contributions that physical education makes toward the nondisability student can also be made toward the student with a disability. Benefits exist in all three educational learning domains.

PHYSICAL DOMAIN

Physical education makes a unique contribution to this area of learning that no other educational subject can claim.

1. Physical fitness and overall health to perform the functional skills required in daily living.
2. Physical growth and development.
3. Motor proficiency and functional skills to perform movements which have implication to the individual's play and work skills.

COGNITIVE DOMAIN

1. Develop an understanding of rules and strategies involved in various games and sports enabling the individual to appreciate the activity as both a participant and/or spectator.
2. Develop a knowledge of movement principles for safety purposes.

AFFECTIVE DOMAIN

1. Learn to move efficiently and consequently gain confidence and increase self-concept while involved in movement.
2. Learn to socially interact with others through games and sports.
3. Develop worthy use of leisure time.
4. Foster an appreciation to participate in various games and sports.

Modified from: Eichstaedt, C. & Lavay, B. (1992). Physical activity for persons with mental retardation: Infant to adult. Champaign IL: Human Kinetics.

Now More Than Ever: Physical Education for the Elementary School-Aged Child

Reprinted with permission from: Croce, R. & Lavay, B. (1985). Now more than ever: Physical education for the elementary school-aged child. Physical Educator, 42, 52-58.

Human beings are created with a natural urge for physical activity. As the child grows, this urge manifests itself in activities which progressively place greater demands on the physiological systems of the body. However, the technological progress in our modern society has reduced the amount of time the child engages in vigorous physical activity.

Nearly 30 years ago, Sullenger, Parke, and Wallin (1953) surveyed the leisure-time activities of children in working class districts of Omaha, Nebraska, and discovered that only a fraction of the children were playing in community and church recreational facilities. At that time, the first two preferences for leisure activities were listening to the radio and watching movies. In 1957, McCullough reported that television was the favored recreation of 10 to 11 year olds. In contrast, children of a comparable age in Czechoslovakia most frequently picked sports as their favorite leisure-time activity (Muradbegovic & Sarajevo, 1970).

Recently, researchers in the United States have indicated that 85% of the children 6 to 11 years of age watch television each day, and 98% watch television each week, with a weekly average of 26 hours (Cole, 1970). When one eliminates the time spent sleeping, eating, going to school and doing household chores, this becomes quite a substantial amount of time. The reduction of the time spent in physical activity has led to dangerously low scores obtained by children on basic tests of physical fitness. Based on the "abysmal" scores obtained from three large scale studies, 1957, 1964-1965, and 1975, the American Alliance for Health, Physical Education, Recreation, and Dance (AAHPERD) has strongly stressed the need for vigorous programs of physical education in our country's schools to counteract the sedentary lifestyle of today's children (Kirshenbaum & Sullivan, 1983). This need was further substantiated by a test conducted during the 1979-1980 school year by the Amateur Athletic Union and Nabisco Brands of more than four million school children, ages 6 through 17 (Kirshenbaum & Sullivan, 1983). According to the statistics obtained from this test, 57% of the youngsters failed to achieve standards which were considered to be "average" for a healthy child. Finally, based on a test administered to Michigan school children in 1979, it was reported that one or more of the common risk factors for heart disease- low levels of cardiovascular fitness, obesity, high blood pressure, and high blood cholesterol levels were found in 50% of the children tested (Kirshenbaum & Sullivan, 1983).

On the problem of weight control, researchers have recently indicated that 15% to 20% of American children are obese, and that a lack of physical activity has been found to be a serious cause of obesity as is overeating (Corbin, 1976). Children who are inactive in their youth also are more likely to develop a sedentary lifestyle as adults. Additionally, it has been demonstrated that childhood obesity is likely to develop into adult obesity (Corbin & Lindsey, 1983). For this reason, it is imperative that structured physical activity programs be introduced in the public schools so that children formulate active lifestyles that will remain with them as adults.

The purpose of this paper is to discuss the benefits derived from a sound physical education program in the public schools. The discussion is arranged into the following categories: growth and development benefits, physiological and medical benefits, cognitive and academic benefits, and psychosocial benefits.

Growth and Development Benefits

Numerous reviews have noted the effect of exercise on structural growth (Elliot, 1970; Kottke, 1966; Malina, 1969). In these reviews the authors have concluded that physical activity is an integral component of the normal growth and development of children.

According to Kottke (1966) and Rarick (1973), exercise is known to increase bone width and mineralization, while inactivity has the reverse effect; the end result being that demineralized bones are weaker and more brittle. Children in good condition tend to have stronger bones and muscles and, as a consequence, are less susceptible to injury. On the importance of exercise as an influence upon growth, Malina (1969) stated,

> Muscular exercise has a stimulating effect on growth of local bone tissue,
> skeletal muscle, linear growth of the upper extremities, and changes in body
> breadths and girths. . . . It is clear that a certain minimum of physical exercise
> is necessary to support normal human growth and to maintain the integrity
> of osseous and muscular tissue. (p. 24)

Dr. John Kimball, a noted cardiologist, has stated that there is growing evidence that bodily changes beginning early in life have a direct relationship to heart disease in later life. Clearly, the importance of proper diet and adequate exercise during the growing years should not be overlooked (cited in Bailey, 1976).

As adult health problems associated with sedentary living patterns become more pronounced, the activity patterns of both children and adults become increasingly important. One way to assure adult participation in physical activity is to make sure all young children receive positive and enjoyable exposures to physical activity. It is for this reason that physical education in our schools is important. Along with parents, it is our school administrators and educators who must play a decisive role in motivating children toward physical activity; it is in the school where motor skills should be taught and where the reasons concerning the positive benefits of physical activity should be introduced. Physical education class can give all children opportunities for fun, self-expression, discovery, creativity, and the chance to succeed. In 1964, the UNESCO Council on sport and physical education stressed that during the formative years children need a balance of intellectual, physical, moral, and aesthetic development which must be reflected in the education curriculum (International Council of Sport and Physical Education: Declaration on Sport, 1964).

Physiololgical and Medical Benefits

Various longitudinal studies have shown that children react to physical training much the same way as adults do. Compared to children of equal height, weight, and age, physically trained children at any age have a greater lean body mass (less fat), a greater maximal oxygen uptake (greater aerobic fitness), and a greater maximal cardiac output (more efficient heart) (Ekblom, 1969; Ericksson, 1972; Iliev, 1978; Parizkova, 1968). Furthermore, Astrand, Engstrom, Ericksson, Karlberg, Nylander, Saltin, and Thoren (1963) have shown that strenuous physical training has no deleterious effects on the growing child.

In programs of physical education, several authors have demonstrated that a curriculum stressing vigorous physical activity enhances a child's maximum oxygen uptake and overall physical fitness levels (Fabricius, 1964; Franks & Moore, 1969; Hilsendager, 1966; Vrijens, 1969; Wireman, 1960). Kemper (1973) reported that by increasing required physical education classes from three to five sessions per week students displayed a significant increase in hand grip strength and overall fitness performance test scores. Cumming and Cumming (1963) suggested the need for a program of specially designed endurance activities which are carefully monitored by the physical educator. These activities cannot only increase the fitness levels of the child during the school year, but also develop patterns of activity that can carry over into the child's leisure-time hours.

What about the child who has special needs, or the child who has a physical or organic limitation? According to Cumming (1976) and Eriksson (1976), there are few diseases in childhood which should prohibit the child from some type of regular physical activity. In fact, physical exercise plays an extremely important role in the medical treatment of children with diabetes (Larsson, Persson, Sterky, & Thoren, 1964; Sterky, 1963), obesity (Thoren, 1971), bronchial asthma (McElhenney & Petersen, 1963), and cerebral palsy (Lundberg, Ovenfors, & Saltin, 1967); as well as playing a significant part in the physical, social, and emotional development of the mentally handicapped child (cited in Winnick, 1979). Cumming (1976) stated,

> There are a very few medical conditions where physical activities programs
> are totally contraindicated, and the majority of school children with diabetes,
> asthma, rheumatic and congenital heart defects, and mild orthopedic problems
> can take part in regular physical education classes with their classmates. (p. 72)

Therefore, it can be stated that strenuous physical training can influence the physiological development of all children. Moreover, at present, no adverse effects have been demonstrated. Astrand (1976) concluded that, based on physiological-medical considerations, the important objectives of physical activity in the schools should be:

(1) train the oxygen-transporting system (respiration and circulation); (2) generally train the locomotive organs (especially the muscles of the back and abdomen); (3) give instruction on how to lie, sit, stand, walk, lift, carry, etc. (ergonomics) ; (4) give instruction in techniques, tactics, rules, etc., in games and sports in order to reduce or eliminate accidents (the events are eventually practiced in the student's leisure time); (5) provide physical and psychological recreation and variety; and (6) aroused interest in regular physical activity after schooling has been finished. (p. 31)

Cognitive and Academic Benefits

The importance of psychomotor learning and mental development has been stressed by several researchers. Wallon (1948), Piaget (1952), and LeBoulch (1966) all indicated a close relationship between psychomotor and mental development during the child's formative years. In Europe, the "one-third" time school experiments have indicated that the academic learning process proceeds better if one-third of the school day is devoted to physical education and other non-academic subjects, and proportionately less time is spent behind the classroom desk. This bold concept in education began in Vanves, France, in 1951. Essentially, students in the experimental classes performed their academic work in the mornings and devoted the afternoons to physical education, art, and music. The overall time devoted to academic education was reduced to about four hours per day and that devoted to physical education was raised to one to two hours per day. The results of the study clearly indicated that those students involved in the experimental school had better health, fitness, discipline, enthusiasm, and academic productivity than those children who attended standard schools (cited in McKenzie, 1974).

A correlation between academic achievement and aerobic fitness in 475 high school boys was reported by Cooper (1977). The author reported that not only were the boys who performed better on the endurance test achieving higher grades, but they were also absent from school less. Cooper stated,

Cardiovascular fitness would make these students more alert in class and more receptive to ideas, as well as giving them the mental stamina to study more effectively. . . . The students who were more fit would miss class less often, because they'd be sick less often. (p. 182)

Psychosocial Benefits

Vigorous physical activity has been successfully employed to relieve mental and emotional tension. DeVries, Wiswell, Bulbubian, & Moritani (1981) demonstrated that exercise can have a tranquilizing effect on children and adults. For some patients, as little as 15 minutes of walking had a greater relaxing effect than a tranquilizer. Griest, Klein, Eischen, Faris, Gurman, and Morgan (1978) used 30 to 40 minutes of jogging three times a week for many depressed patients and reported this activity to be more effective in reducing depression than psychotherapy. Based on reported this activity to be more effective in reducing depression than psychotherapy. Based on studies conducted by researchers at the Brooklyn Medical Center, young adults who exercised regularly demonstrated better sleep patterns than those subjects who did not engage in any type of exercise program (cited in Galton, 1980).

Researchers investigating the effects of an elementary school physical education program on a child's self-concept and body image have indicated that such a program can bring about significant gains in these measures. Folkins and Sime (1981) in a review of the literature stated that a high correlation exists between a child's self-concept and body image, and that the manner in which children perceive their body has a significant influence on their psychosocial development.

Based on the literature, relaxation techniques taught during physical education class can: (a) aid students in conserving energy and moving in a more efficient manner while performing various physical activities; (b) calm hyperactive students and enable them to focus on the task at hand; and, (c) give students a socially appropriate method to control their emotions when upset or involved in a stressful situation. Moreover, a regular program of exercise and relaxation training can significantly reduce the onset of both mental and physical fatigue. Researchers have indicated that involving a student in relaxation training can help to alleviate tension, reduce fatigue, and allow the student to study and learn more efficiently (Galton, 1980).

Physical education may also have some important ramifications in the socialization process of children. Although the research is ambiguous, participation in games and sports may allow children to interact with others in a positive manner. Cooperative skills, such as taking turns, sharing equipment, and accepting the outcome of a game, must be taught if children are to successfully engage in various activities in a socially appropriate manner.

Conclusions

A minimum of physical activity is almost certainly needed for the optimal growth and development of children. Definite reasons that support the need for physical education programs for children have been formulated by G.R. Cumming, Cardiologist, The Children's Hospital of Winnipeg (1976), and D.A. Bailey, a noted specialist in child motor development (1976) as follows:

1. Physical exercise is important during childhood for the proper development of the functional capacity of the heart and lungs, and the strength of bones and muscles.

2. Continued physical exercise is important in later life for the prevention of heart disease.

3. Physical exercise can contribute toward the mental health of children and adults.

4. Physical exercise is important in childhood as well as in the adult years for weight control.

5. Physical conditioning likely has a role in the prevention of many diseases. Physical fitness increases the body's resistance against general stress and illness throughout life.

6. The basic orientation toward adult participation in physical activity is developed at a very early age (formulating sound health habits and making worthy use of leisure time).

7. Classroom learning may be enhanced and supported via physical activity, as well as providing opportunity for creativity and expression.

8. Physical activity can increase self-concept and overall body image.

A new danger may be the shift in emphasis from public school instruction to the private sector. Kirshenbaum and Sullivan (1983) mention the following socioeconomic consequences:

The much ballyhooed growth in the number of private health clubs and employee fitness programs has been paralleled by a less widely recognized decline in the availability of traditional fitness programs in parks, recreation departments and, above all, schools. This shift in emphasis from the public to the private sector is reflected in the fitness boom demographics: Participants in it are more likely to be rich than poor, executive than blue-collar workers, white than non-white, college graduates than high school graduates, adults than children.

In conclusion, current trends in public education have focused on reading, math, science, and computer skills needed for coping in today's highly technological society. However, many educators and non-educators fail to realize that physical education also has far-reaching ramifications in how effectively our country's youth will function in society. According to Ted Grenda, Director of General Education for the New York State Department of Education, physical education is the most important subject in our school system; moreover, a child who is not healthy cannot effectively learn (Kirshenbaum & Sullivan, 1983).

REFERENCES

Astrand, P. O. The child in sport and physical activity: physiology. In J. G. Albinson & G .M. Andrew (Eds.) Child in sport and physical activity. Baltimore: University Park Press, 1976.

Astrand, P. O., Engstrom, B. O., Eriksson, P., Korlberg, P., Nylander, I., Saltin, B., & Thoren, C. Girl swimmers. Acta Paedioatrica Scandinavica (Supplement), 1963, 147, 5-75.

Bailey, D. A. The growing child and the need for physical activity. In J. G. Albinson & G. M. Andrew (Eds.), Child in sport and physical activity. Baltimore: University Park Press, 1976.

Bucher, C. A. Foundations of physical education (8th ed.). St. Louis: C. V. Mosby Co., 1979.

Carlson, G. Physical education is basic. Journal of Physical Education, Recreation, and Dance, 1982, 53, 67-69.

Cole, B. D. (Ed.). Television. New York: Free Press, 1970.

Cooper, K. H. The aerobic way. New York: Bantam Books, 1977.

Corbin, C. Being physically educated in the elementary school. Philadelphia: Lea & Febiger, 1976.

Corbin, C., & Lindsey, R. Fitness for life. Glenview, Ill.: Scott, Foresman & Co., 1983.

Cumming, G. R. The child in sport and physical activity: Medical comment. In J. G. Albinson & G. M. Andrew (Eds.), Child in sport and physical activity. Baltimore: University Park Press, 1976.

Cumming, G. R., & Cumming, P .M. Working capacity of normal children tested on a bicycle ergometer. Canadian Medical Association Journal, 1963, 88, 351-355.

de Vries, H. A., Wiswell, R. A., Bulbubian, R., & Moritani, T. Tranquilizer effect of exercise: Acute effects of moderate aerobic exercise on spinal reflex activation level. American Journal of Physical Medicine, 1981, 60, 57-66.

Ekblom, B. Effect of physical training on oxygen transport system in man. Acta Physiologica Scandinavica (Supplement), 1969, 328, 9-45.

Elliott, G. M. The effects of exercise on structural growth. Canadian Association of Health, Physical Education, and Recreation, 1970, 36, 21-25.

Eriksson, B. O. Physical training, oxygen supply and muscle metabolism in 11-13-year -old boys. Acta Physiologica Scandinavica (Supplement), 1972, 384, 5-48.

Eriksson, B. O. The child in sport and physical activity: medical aspects. In J. B. Albinson & G. M. Andrew (Eds.), Child in sport and physical activity. Baltimore: University Park Press, 1976.

Fabricius, H. Effect of added calesthenics on the physical fitness of fourth grade boys and girls. Research Quarterly, 1964, 35, 135-140.

Folkins, C. H., & Sime, W. E. Physical fitness training and mental health. American Psychologist, 1981, 36, 373-389.

Franks, D. B., & Moore, G. C. Effects of calesthenics and volleyball on the AAHPER fitness test and volleyball skill. Research Quarterly, 1969, 40, 288-292.

Galton, L. Your child and sports. New York: Franklin Watts, 1980.

Griest, J. H., Klein, M. H., Eischen, R. E., Faris, J., Gurman, A. S., & Morgan, W. P. Running through your mind. Journal of Psychosomatic Research, 1978, 22, 259-294.

Hilsendager, D. Comparison of a calesthenic and a non-calesthenic physical education program. Research Quarterly, 1966, 37, 148-150.

Iliev, I. B. Maximal aerobic power in girls and boys aged 9 to 16 years who participate regularly in sport. In R. J. Shepard & H. Lavallee (Eds.), Physical fitness assessment: Principles, practice, and application. Springfield, Ill.: Charles C. Thomas, 1978.

International Council of Sport and Physical Education: Declaration on Sport, UNESCO, Place de Fontenoy, Paris, 1964.

Kemper, H. C. The influence of extra lessons of physical education on physical and mental development of 12-13-year-old boys. In V. Seliger (Ed.), Physical fitness. Prague: Charles University Press, 1973.

Kirshenbaum, J., & Sullivan, R. Hold on there, America. Sports Illustrated, February 7, 1983, pp. 62-74.

Kottke, F. J. The effects of limitation of activity upon the human body. Journal of the American Medical Association, 1966, 196, 825-830.

Larsson, Y., Persson, B., Sterky, G., & Thoren, C. Functional adaptation to vigorous training and exercise in diabetic and non-diabetic adolescents. Journal of Applied Physiology, 1964, 19, 629-635.

Le Boulch, J. L'education par le movement. Paris: Editions Sociales Francaises, 1966.

Lundberg, A., Ovenfors, C. O., & Saltin, B. Effect of physical training on school children with cerebral palsy. Acta Paediatrica Scandinavica, 1967, 56, 182-188.

Malina, R. M. Exercise as an influence upon growth. Clinical Pediatrics, 1969, 8, 16-26.

McCullough, C. M. A log of children's out-of-school activities. Elementary School Journal, 1957, 58, 157-165.

McElhenney, T. R., & Petersen, K. H. Physical fitness for asthmatic boys: A cooperative pilot study. Journal of the American Medical Association, 1963, 185, 142-143.

McKenzie, J. One-third time physical education. Unpublished manuscript, Regina Public School Board, 1974.

Muradbegovic, M., & Sarajevo, I. O. The free activity preferences of elementary school pupils. Society and Leisure, 1970, 77-86.

Parizkova, J. Longitudinal study of development of body composition and body build in boys of various physical activity. Human Biology, 1968, 40, 212-225.

Piaget, J. The origins of intelligence in children. New York: International University Press, 1952.

Rarick, L. (Ed.). Physical activity: Human growth and development. New York: Academic Press, 1973.

Sterkey, G. Physical work capacity in diabetic school children. Acta Paediatrica

Scandinavica, 1963, 52, 1-10.

Sullenger, T. E., Parke, L. H., & Wallin, W. K. The leisure time activities of elementary school children. Journal of Educational Research, 1953, 46, 551-554.

Thoren, C. Physical training of handicapped school children. Scandinavian Journal of Rehabilitation Medicine, 1971, 3, 26-30.

Vrijens, J. The influence of interval circuit exercises on physical fitness of adolescents. Research Quarterly, 1969, 40, 595-599.

Wallon, H. Les origines du caractere chez l'enfant. Paris: Presses Universitaires de France, 1948.

Wilmore, J. Objectives for the nation-physical fitness and exercise. Journal of Physical Education, Recreation, and Dance, 1952, 53, 41-43.

Winnick, J. P. Early movement experiences and development. Philadelphia: W. B. Saunders Co., 1979.

Wireman, E. O. Comparison of four approaches to increasing physical fitness. Research Quarterly, 1960, 31, 658-666.

SPECIAL PHYSICAL EDUCATION DEFINED

PL 101-476, Individuals with Disabilities Education Act (IDEA)* mandates that all children identified as disabled receive physical education services. Recently P L 99-457, the Education of Handicapped Act ammendment of 1986 recognized the need to implement programs for at risk infants and toddlers from birth to five years. Most importantly to professionals who provide physical activity to this population, the curricular area of physical education is cited specifically in the definition of special education (U.S. Office of Education,1977).

This law defined physical education for special education students as follows:

I. The term means the development of:
    A. physical and motor fitness
    B. fundamental motor skills and patterns, and
    C. skills in aquatics, dance, and individual and group games and sport (including intramural and lifetime sports).

II. The term includes special physical education, adapted physical education, movement education and motor development (42480).

SPECIAL PHYSICAL EDUCATION

A division of physical education designed to meet the needs of individuals with movement difficulties. The intent of the special physical education program is to assist in the total development of the individual. The program is movement based, designed to enable each person to reach optimum potential while developing a positive attitude and life-time interests toward physical activity.

 * The Education for all Handicapped Children Act of 1975 (PL 94-142) was ammended (changed) in 1990 to PL 101-476, Individuals with Disabilities Education Act (IDEA)

Page 17 describes the components of special physical education, while page 18 shows a special physical education delivery system adopted from the Albuquerque Public School System.

COMPONENTS OF SPECIAL PHYSICAL EDUCATION

Special physical education consists of three component parts: adapted, corrective and developmental. Appropriate program component emphasis is determined by evaluation and student need.

ADAPTED PHYSICAL EDUCATION

Consists of the same goals and objectives as the regular physical education program, but makes modifications and "adapts" when necessary to effectively meet the needs of the individual.

For example, if a "clumsy" child is exhibiting difficulty striking a pitched ball, the instructor may modify the equipment by using a batting tee and a larger bat.

CORRECTIVE PHYSICAL EDUCATION

Designs appropriate exercises and activities to rehabilitate deficiencies in a person's body alignment and mechanics.

For example, an instructor with the physcian's permission may develop an individualized exercise program to assist in the remediation of functional scoliosis in a child who is severely mentally retarded.

DEVELOPMENTAL PHYSICAL EDUCATION

Emphasizes activities which reinforce development of fundamental motor patterns and components of physical fitness for those students who are below their age group peers.

For example, an instructor may design movement experiences which reinforce fundamental locomotor and object control skills for preschool aged children with mild mental retardation.

See: Lavay, B. (1991). Special physical education: A more appropriate term to define the profession. California Association of Physical Education, Recreation & Dance, Journal , 53 (7), 8.

SPECIAL PHYSICAL EDUCATION
SERVICE DELIVERY MODEL

<u>JOB DESCRIPTION</u>

SPECIAL PHYSICAL EDUCATION INSTRUCTIONAL DESIGN

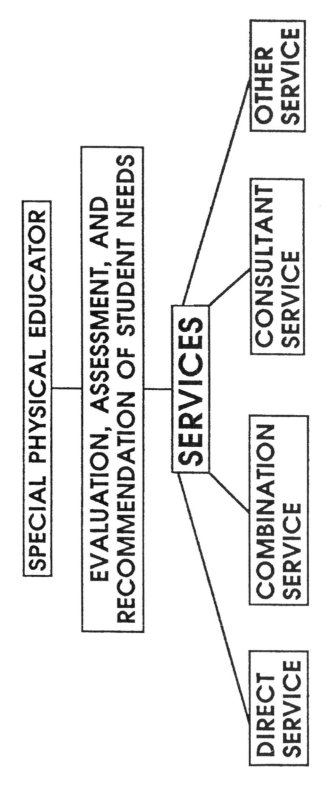

The Special Physical Educator: Meeting Educational Goals Through a Transdisciplinary Approach

Reprinted with permission from: Lavay, B. & French, R. (1985). The special physical educator: Meeting education goals through a transdisciplinary approach. American Corrective Therapy Journal, 39, 77-81.

It is clearly stated in Public Law 94-142, the Education for All Children Act of 1975, that there is a need for a cooperative team approach to provide the most effective services available to each handicapped child. For example, evaluation procedures shall be "made by a multidisciplinary team or a group of persons" (13). Results of the evaluation are the basis for the planning of the child's individualized educational program, and it is therefore paramount that input from a variety of professionals from various disciplines be made available. The term "least restrictive environment" as defined in the law has greatly broadened the scope of the child's educational environment and has identified, when needed, provisions for supplementary services must be made (19).

Wiseman (14) stated greater attention is being placed on the cooperative approach when working with the handicapped student, and professionals must not discount the expertise of other disciplines in program development. Crowe, Auxter, and Pyfer (3) believe that professionals who deal with a handicapped student cannot work independently of one another and the current trend is one of a team approach to problem solving, with experts merging their talents in the best interest of the student. Recently Dunn (4) concurred with this position by advocating the importance of sharing information and educating colleagues to the goals related to a particular profession in order to provide better student services.

Multidisciplinary, interdisciplinary, and transdisciplinary are all terms which have been used to describe this cooperative team approach among disciplines in providing a continuum of services to the handicapped student. In the past this cooperative team approach had been limited only to evaluation or assessment procedures evolving from a medical model (7). In education the team approach is relatively new and these terms are used interchangeably, causing confusion among professionals (9). Therefore, these terms are defined as follows:

The multidisciplinary approach (see Fig. 1) involves separate evaluations and prescriptions by different specialists to identify children and youth with specific problems that interfere with learning (6). The evaluations and prescriptions are generally initiated by an educator. The reports are traditionally given to the educator who requested the evaluation with little if any dialogue occurring between the educator requesting the information and the specialists. An example of a special physical educator involved in this approach would be the request of medical information regarding a student with a seizure disorder. A written report is provided by the school or the student's family physicians without any direct interaction.

In contrast, the interdisciplinary approach (see Fig. 2) not only incorporates the basic components of the multidisciplinary approach, but the specialist who conducted the evaluations and developed the prescription meets with the educator requesting the information (6). As in the multidisciplinary approach, though, the educator is left to implement the prescription.

The transdisciplinary approach is defined by Sirvis (10) as follows:

The transdisciplinary approach attempts to break the traditional rigidity of discipline boundaries and to encourage a teaching/learning process between team members. It supports the development of a staff approach that functions with greater unity. . . . further, the transdisciplinary approach advocates that team members share information and, when appropriate, skills to insure consistency in the child's program (p. 23).

In this approach, the special physical educator would not only receive a prescription from a physical therapist, for example, but class visits and individual service would also be provided with the two professionals working closely together.

The transdisciplinary approach is believed to be the most effective approach because there is a sharing of information and working together among specialists, which greatly benefit the educational program goals of each handicapped student (4,6,7,10,12). This relationship is illustrated in Figure 3.

Since the transdisciplinary approach is the most effective method, the purpose of this paper will be to discuss three major steps special physical educators can implement to use this approach: (a) have a thorough understanding of the special physical educator's own job role, (b) have a knowledge of the roles of other specialists who may work in the schools, and (c) have a variety of strategies to enable the special educator to work more effectively side by side with other specialists to meet student needs.

Initially, in order to communicate effectively with professionals from other disciplines, special physical educators must have a clear understanding of their own discipline. Many names have been given to this specialized area of physical education leading to confusion of the entire range of activities available to exceptional individuals in physical education (3). This confusion has not only existed among experts of other disciplines but professionals in the field of physical education.

In Public Law 94-142 (13), physical education was defined as the development of (a) physical and motor fitness; (b) fundamental motor skills and patterns; and (c) skills in aquatics, dance, and individual and group games and sports (including intramural and lifetime sports). The term includes special physical education, adapted physical education, movement education, and motor development.

In 1947 a committee on adapted physical education was formed by the American Association of Physical Education and Recreation, and they collectively decided the term "adapted physical education" was most appropriate to explain the functions of physical education programs for handicapped students (3). Since then the term adapted physical education has been endorsed by both the United States Office of Education and the American Alliance for Health, Physical Education, Recreation and Dance (14).

Other professionals such as Fait and Dunn (5), however, have felt the term adapted physical education is inappropriate when defining the role of the physical educator who is trained to provide services to handicapped students because it merely addresses one type of program. These authorities believe the term special physical education is the most appropriate term to define physical education for the handicapped student. This term not only includes the term adapted, but corrective and developmental physical education. These terms are defined in the following manner (6):

Adapted physical education refers to the modification of traditional physical activities to enable individuals with handicaps to have the opportunity to participate safely, successfully, and with satisfaction.

Corrective physical education refers mainly to the habilitation or rehabilitation of functional postural and body mechanics deficiencies.

Developmental physical education refers to a progressive physical fitness and/or gross motor training program to increase an individual's physical ability to a level at or near to that of peers (p. 9).

The special physical educator's role must be clearly defined and understood if successful communication with other members of the transdisciplinary team is to exist. Regardless of the program name used, most experts will agree that the basic intent of any special physical education program is the total development of the individual child.

The second step is for the special physical educator to understand the role of other professionals in providing direct and related services. Special education, of which physical education is an integral component, is clearly defined in the law as a direct service (13).

As used in this part the term "Special education" means specially designed instruction at no cost to the parents, to meet the unique needs of a handicapped child, including classroom instruction, instruction in physical education, home instruction and instruction in hospitals and institutions (p. 42480).

Related services in section 121a 13 (a) are defined as "supportive services as are required to assist a handicapped child to benefit from special education" (p. 54579). Related services are an important part of meeting total program goals and should be available to assist the special education program. Crowe, Auxter and Pyfer (3) explain the difference between direct and related services in the following statement:

Before a related service such as physical therapy, occupational therapy or recreational therapy can be implemented in the curriculum it must be determined that the limitations of the child are such that special education- or special physical education in this case- cannot effectively deal cannot make the expected progress in skill development in physical education (p. 16).

For example, in a school district in Utah and another in New Mexico the special physical educator, physical therapist, and occupational therapists developed a motor evaluation screening device which they administer together to students with suspected or actual physical deficits. Based on screening results the professionals on the team may decide that only one, two, or all three need to conduct a more in-depth assessment. The results of further testing also help the professionals determine who will provide the appropriate services. In one instance only one professional may provide direct services while the other two consult, in another situation two members or all three members may provide direct services.

As the many disciplines broaden their body of knowledge, professional boundaries can only become even more ambiguous (8), not only between professional but also to the parents of the child being served. Confusion may exist as to which services will best meet the program needs of each handicapped student. For the transdisciplinary approach to be effective, a coordinated effort must be provided by members of the team. Professionals of the many disciplines must be aware and knowledgeable of other experts' job capacities; if not, confusion during programming will cause either a vacuum and/or a duplication in the delivery of services to each child.

Finally in the third step, the special physical educator must be able to work effectively side by side with other specialists. Professionals from various disciplines will possess different training and backgrounds (1). Bennett (2) stated that varied backgrounds may cause problems regarding differences in philosophical beliefs, assessment procedures, and effective management strategies. To assure a successful working relationship, which in turn will benefit the child, these differences must be discussed and worked out.

Many times the relative importance of the information and recommendations being made by the various disciplines may depend on the individual coordinating the team. Hart (7) felt that it is possible that information from the various disciplines may only be examined and used as it relates to the coordinator's own discipline. The individual coordinating the meeting may lack knowledge or be uninformed of the importance of various disciplines. With this in mind, it is extremely important that special physical educators display a professional image and are able to communicate effectively the important contributions physical education can make to the handicapped student's total education program.

Sherrill (11) suggested that when possible, prospective educators in various disciplines begin to work together while in undergraduate college training programs. This approach may encourage students to become more flexible and willing to accept the transdisciplinary approach once becoming professionals. Special physical educators must not only be knowledgeable of their own discipline but must stay abreast of developments in other disciplines through reading, attending inservice workshops and communicating with other professionals. The special physical educators who do not understand their own profession or are unaware of the roles of professionals in other disciplines cannot be expected to communicate effectively in the transdisciplinary team approach.

All professionals, including special physical educators, must put aside territorial differences and realize it is the individual student who will benefit most from the transdisciplinary approach. In short, the student who is handicapped is not a piece of pie to be divided among various educational services. Increased communication among the disciplines will lead to a more effective delivery system with a reduced knowledge vacuum and/or duplication of services. A reduction in service duplication may in turn decrease expenses by reducing the number of professionals working with the handicapped student (19). This approach increases the probability of continuity and consistency of the program which is provided to achieve the educational goals and objectives of each student. Often various disciplines make idealistic recommendations which are not followed up after the initial assessment. The transdisciplinary approach assures that individuals in each discipline are being held responsible and accountable for their own recommendations (7). Through a coordinated effort among professionals, educational goals can be successfully met. Through the use of the transdisciplinary approach, there is a sharing of information among professionals making it more functional and consequently more effective than the multidisciplinary or interdisciplinary approaches.

The special physical educator must clearly emphasize to individuals in other disciplines the important contribution that physical education can make to the educational process. Every effort must be made to work effectively with members of associated disciplines. The importance of the transdisciplinary approach toward meeting the educational goals of the individual child is best summarized by Hart (7).

> No one person can be expected to have all the necessary skills and information. Consequently there will always be a need for some type of team approach. The better and more efficient the team, the better the services offered to the child. No matter what approach is used or the type of team involved, the better the expertise and the greater the willingness of the team members to share their information, the greater the benefits for the child (p. 396).

REFERENCES

1. Bailey, D. R. "A triaxial model of the interdisciplinary team and group process," Exceptional Children, 51: 17-25, 1984.
2. Bennett, F. C. "The pediatrician and the interdisciplinary process," Exceptional Children, 48: 306-314, 1982.
3. Crowe, W., D. Auxter, & J. Pyfer. Principles and methods of adapted physical education and recreation. (4th ed.) St. Louis: C. V. Mosby, 1981.
4. Dunn, J. M. "Current trends and new perspectives in special physical education," Proceedings of the 13th National Conference of Physical Activity for the Exceptional Individual, 13: 69-73, 1984.

5. Fait, H. F. & J. M. Dunn. Special Physical Education: Adapted, Individualized, Developmental. (5th ed.). Philadelphia: W. B. Saunders Co., 1984.

6. French, R. W. & P. Jansma. Special Physical Education. Columbus, OH: Charles E. Merrill, 1982.

7. Hart, V. "The Use of many disciplines with the severely and profoundly handicapped," In E. Sontag, J. Smith, and N. Certo (Eds.), Educational Programming for the Severely and Profoundly Handicapped. Reston, VA: Division on Mental Retardation, The Council for Exceptional Children, 1977.

8. Paulsen, R. D. Functional Activities of Related Health Disciplines. Unpublished dissertation, University of Utah, Salt Lake City, 1981.

9. Seaman, J. A. & K. P. DePauw. The New Adapted Physical Education: A Developmental Approach. Palo Alto, CA: Mayfield Publishing Company, 1982.

10. Sears, C. J. "The transdisciplinary approach: A process for compliance with Public Law 94-142," The Journal of the Association for the Severely Handicapped , 6: 22-29, 1982.

11. Sherrill, C. Adapted Physical Education: A Multidisciplinary Approach, (2nd ed.). Dubuque, IA: Wm. C. Brown Company, 1981.

12. Sirvis, B. "Developing IEPS for physically handicapped students: A transdisciplinary viewpoint," Teaching Exceptional Children ,10; 78-82, 1978.

13. U. S. Office of Education. Federal register, Public Law 94-142: The education for all handicapped children's act, 42, Author, 1977.

14. Wiseman, D. C. A Practical Approach to Adapted Physical Education. Reading, MA: Addison-Wesley Publishing, 1982.

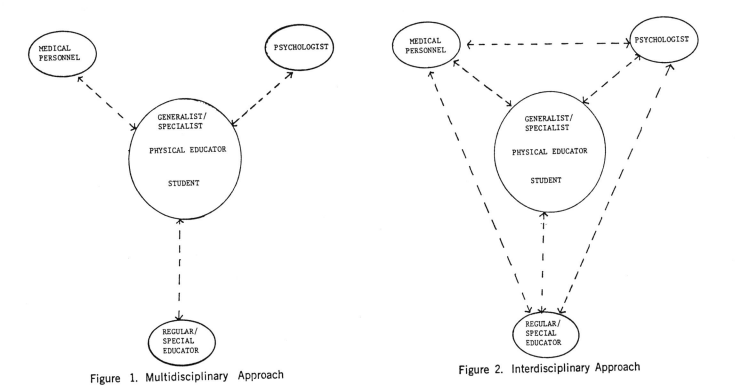

Figure 1. Multidisciplinary Approach

Figure 2. Interdisciplinary Approach

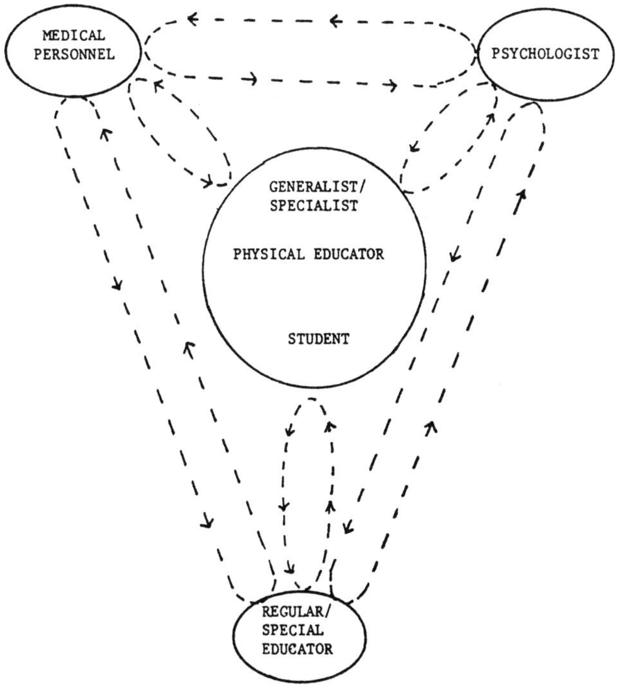

Figure 3. Transdisciplinary Approach

Survival Strategies for the Itinerant Special Physical Educator

This article is reprinted with permission from the **JOPERD** (Journal of Physical Education, Recreation & Dance), August, 1986, pages 84-86. **JOPERD** is a publication of the American Alliance for Health, Physical Education, Recreation and Dance, 1900 Association Drive, Reston, Va 22091-1599.

Numerous delivery models have been designed to provide physical education services to students who are handicapped (Auxter & Pyfer, 1985). The itinerant special physical educator is a vital link in the continuum of services for these students (Chicola & Sager, 1983). The physical educator in this delivery model travels to various school buildings providing direct instruction to students and/or consultant services to regular physical educators or special and regular classroom educators *responsible for providing physical education to handicapped students (Idol-Maestas,* 1983).

Some major administrative problems exist with the itinerant teacher delivery model (compared to the self-contained teacher delivery model) and it has been reported by some teachers to be an undesirable teaching appointment. These problems are multiplied by the number of schools to which the itinerant teacher provides services. Problems that are commonly identified are that the teacher is not regarded as a regular member of the school staff, other school personnel are confused about where the itinerant teacher will be at a specific time or day, the need for equipment and a storage area, the lack of appropriate teaching stations, time wasted traveling, and the inability to provide instruction to each student on a daily basis (Ellis & Mathews, 1982; Howe, 1981).

Strategies for survival

If these problems become chronic, they may lead to teacher burnout. In a study conducted by DePaepe, French, and Lavay (1985) an abnormally high rate of burnout symptoms were reported among the itinerant special physical educators investigated. This article discusses a variety of strategies itinerant special physical educators can use to solve problems in order to teach effectively. These strategies are based on the personal experiences of the authors, who have all taught as itinerant special physical educators, as well as discussions with practicing itinerant special physical education teachers.

The strategies are divided into the following two categories: (1) strategies for teaching in assigned schools, and (2) strategies needed to work effectively with other itinerant special physical educators.

Teaching in assigned schools

Initiate informal dialogue with regular physical educators, classroom teachers, administrators, and support personnel (Priest, 1979). For example, the special physical educator might ask the regular physical education teacher about the activities involved in that teacher's curriculum.

Provide a school inservice in which different roles are defined. Let the physical educator and special educator know that you are aware of their problems and are willing to work with them. It is also good public relations to ask their advice on specific issues.

Work with the appropriate special educators and other itinerant teachers in scheduling. Do not compete. Many times you can arrange desired schedules just by communicating and cooperating with each other.

Check the schedules of the regular physical educator and determine the time when specific teaching stations are available. If possible, become an integral part of the teaching station rotation system. This will enable you to conduct your program in a setting conducive to physical activity.

Design your schedule at the beginning of the school year to minimize the time spent traveling between schools. This will allow more time to conduct school-related responsibilities and less time traveling.

Provide teachers and administrators with your schedule so that they realize you serve other schools also.

Secure your own set of keys for facilities at the schools where you will be teaching. Nothing is more frustrating than arriving at a school a few minutes before class begins to find that the gymnasium is locked and the physical education teacher and/or custodian have disappeared.

Obtain a mailbox at each school where you provide services. This will enable the staff at each school to inform you about future assemblies, field trips, or absences.

Have the secretary of each school you serve keep you informed of any scheduling changes. It is frustrating to arrive at a school ready to teach, only to learn that because of an assembly your regularly scheduled teaching time has been moved up or back an hour. This may mean you cannot meet with that particular class.

Whenever possible, attend faculty meetings and social events to demonstrate that you consider yourself part of the school staff. In particular, attend as many departmental meetings in physical education and special education as possible. This will help keep you informed of changes that can affect your ability to meet the needs of your students. This is especially important at the secondary level or in schools with large student populations.

Earn respect. Even though you may have taught for years at other schools, you will probably have to prove yourself as a competent special physical educator at each of the schools to which you are assigned. Once you have earned respect, you can develop positive communication among the staff members.

Determine what equipment is available at each school and when it will be used by the regular physical education staff. Using what is available will alleviate the problem of carrying large pieces of equipment from school to school.

Informally observe the regular physical educator's teaching methods to determine if your teaching styles are compatible. If they are, consider team teaching during certain units or activities. This can help develop a closer professional relationship as well as initiate the mainstreaming process.

Invite the principal/curriculum specialist to observe your class and become active participants.

Plan special demonstrations for school administrators, teachers, and the student body (e.g., wheelchair basketball, beep baseball, Special Olympics).

Continually communicate with parents about their children's progress and the general program. Parents can be the itinerant teacher's greatest advocates. Communicate by telephone or letter; speak to parent groups, or publish special activities through the local newspaper or television station.

Working with other itinerant special physical educators

When working with other itinerant special physical educators, determine a system to equalize teaching responsibilities. Never dump all the problems onto the new teacher in the group. One approach is to develop a weighting system. Use a point criteria regarding such factors as distance between schools, number of students to be served, severity of the handicapping conditions of the students to be served, facilities available, and access to facilities and equipment. Another important consideration is the attitude of that particular school's staff in cooperating with the assigned itinerant teacher. For instance, if the regular physical education teacher does not want to share equipment and facilities, this can become a major irritant and should be considered in the weighting system. For example, in the Blue Lake School District there are 12 elementary schools, six middle schools, and three high schools that require the special physical education services of four itinerant teachers. Based on the use of a weighting system which involved type of school, caseload, handicapping conditions of students to be served, distance traveled, and the type of facilities and staff at each school, teaching assignments were developed (see Figure 1).

Develop a check-out system for sharing equipment. This usually involves the cooperative use of a calendar that is completed at least one week before the equipment is needed (see Figure 2).

When possible, the entire itinerant special physical education staff should pool money allocated by the district to purchase equipment based on their immediate needs.

Develop a schedule which allows time to evaluate students who are referred for testing in special physical education, to write individualized educational programs (IEP), attend various meetings, and complete all other necessary paperwork (Geren, 1979).

Plan monthly inservice training with other special physical educators in the district to discuss program successes and problems, exchange teaching ideas, and plan for future programming needs. This will allow teachers to foster a better understanding and appreciation for one another and their programs (Lavay, 1984).

As a result of the multitude of social and physical environments in which the itinerant special physical educator must function, the teacher must be flexible and able to effectively communicate with other school personnel (Masters, Mori, & Lange, 1983). Without these competencies, the itinerant special physical educator will not function efficiently, which, in turn, can detract from the quality of student learning.

References

Auxter, D., & Pyfer, J. (1985). Principles and methods of adapted physical education and recreation. (5th ed.) St. Louis: C. V. Mosby.

Chicola, N., & Sager, N. (1983). The vital link: Developing an effective continuum of intervention to meet the needs of emotionally/behaviorally disordered students. Paper presented at the Council for Exceptional Children 61st Annual International Convention. Detroit, MI. (ERIC Document Reproduction Service No. ED 203 203).

DePaepe, J., French, R., & Lavay, B. (1985). Burnout among special physical educators: A descriptive longitudinal study. Accepted by the Adapted Physical Activity Quarterly.

Ellis, J., & Mathews, G. (1982). Professional role performance difficulties of first year itinerant specialists. Research/ Technical Report No. 143. Northern Illinois University. Department of Learning, Development, and Special Education. (ERIC Document Reproduction Service No. Ed 228 802).

Geren, K. (1979). Complete special education handbook. West Nyack, NY: Parker Publishing Company, Inc.

Howe, C. (1981). Administration of special education. Denver: Love Publishing Company.

Idol-Maestas, L. (1983). Special educator's consultation handbook. Rockville, MD: Aspen Publications.

Lavay, B. (1984). Activities exchange benefits teachers, students. National Consortium on Physical Education and Recreation for the Handicapped Newsletter, 12 (3), 8.

Masters, L. F., Mori, A. A., & Lange, E. K. (1983). Adapted physical education: A practitioner's guide. Rockville, MD: Aspen Publications.

Petrie, I., & Taylor, P. (1980). Home teaching in the Northwest: A pilot survey. Child: Care, Health, and Development, 6, 57-64.

Priest, L. (1979). Integrating the disabled into aquatics programs. Journal of Physical Education and Recreation, 50 (2), 58-59.

Figure 1 Example of an itinerant teacher's weighing criteria

School serviced	Caseload	Exceptionalties include	Distance from office	Facilities staff available
Central H S (2,500)	16	LD/EMR	2.3	2 gyms, various other faclities shared with 8 teachers
Kennedy MS (685)	8	Varies	1.5	Main & Auxillary gym among 2 teachers & 1 part time teacher
Richmond (475) special EMR	15	LD/ EMR	5.5	1 gym/multipurpose room 2 P E teachers
Eugene Park (330) ED program	7	ED	3.5	Cafeteria & 2 empty classrooms 1 P E teacher
Lowell	4	TMR	11.5	Cafeteria 1 part time teacher
5 schools	50		24.2	

FIGURE 2. Equipment check out system

NAME	EQUIPMENT	DATE OUT	DUE
Charlie	12 scooterboards 8 cones, 4 ropes	1/17	1/24
Sharon	1 parachute and dozen wiffle balls	1/23	1/24
Steve	BOT Kit	1/21	1/23
Russ	flag football equipment 4 cones, 6 nerf balls	1/22	1/25
Priscilla	Floor hockey equipment 4 cones	1/14	1/25

When finished with the equipment, be sure to place it back in the proper storage area!

Clarity of Misconceptions Regarding the Implementation of Adapted/Special Physical Education As Determined by PL 94-142

Reprinted with permission from: Lavay, B. (1988). Clarity of misconceptions regarding the implementation of adapted/special physical education as determined by PL 94-142. Kansas Association of Physical Education, Recreation & Dance, 56 (2), 15-16.

Although Public Law 94-142 (The Education for All Handicapped Children Act)* was mandated in 1975, confusion among professional educators still exists regarding the intent of physical education within this law. Therefore the purpose of this paper will be to clarify these common misconceptions and provide information as to the intent of this law in providing physical education programs for the handicapped. * Now-101-476

Physical Education is a Direct Service:

Physical education is the only curricular area cited in the law in the definition of special education: The term special education means specifically designed instruction at no cost to the parent, to meet the unique needs of a handicapped child including classroom instruction, instruction in physical education, home instruction, and instruction in hospitals and institutions (p. 42480) This includes all students 3 to 21 years of age defined in the law as handicapped.

Physical Education Defined
The term means the development of:
A. physical and motor fitness
B. fundamental motor skills and patterns, and
C. skills in aquatics, dance, and individual and group games and sport (including intramural and lifetime sports) (p. 42480).

The Term Most Commonly Used is Adapted or Special Physical Education

According to the law; "the term includes special physical education, adapted physical education, movement education and motor development" (p. 42480).
According to Sherrill (1986), confusion often exists between the adjectives adaptive and adapted. Adaptive is used to describe behaviors and is notsuitable. Whereas, adapted is defined as to modify to meet needs and is therefore a more suitable term.

Difference Between Direct and Related Services

Related services in section 121a 13(a) are defined as "supportive services as are required to assist a handicapped child to benefit from special education" (p. 54579).

Related services such as physical therapy or occupational therapy can be an important part of meeting a handicapped child's educational needs, but it is not a substitute for physical education. Related service personnel are not adequately trained or qualified to properly provide physical education services as defined in this law.

When No Adapted/Special Physical Education Program Exists in the School District

As stated earlier, physical education is the only curricular area cited specifically in the definition of special education. The physical needs of each handicapped child must be considered at the IEP planning meeting.

These needs must be based on appropriate assessment procedures by qualified trained personnel in this physical education area. Regular physical education placement is appropriate when no student physical and motor problems exist. However, the child who displays special needs in this area is entitled to a specially designed program in adapted/special physical education. In fact, support for this concept is further stated in the law:

Special education as set forth in the committee bill includes instruction in physical education, which is provided as a matter of course to all handicapped children enrolled in public elementary and secondary schools. The committee is concerned that although these services are available and required for all children in our schools, they are often viewed as a luxury for handicapped children (p. 42489).

Physical Education Must be Taught by a Qualified Physical Education Instructor

According to the law, the physical education requirements for the handicapped child is not being met if taught by a special education classroom teacher. A certified physical education instructor must make every effort to meet the psychomotor needs of the handicapped. For example, Eichstaedt & Kalakian (1987), stated having trained physical educators is as important as having trained driver education instructors. While almost everyone can learn to drive a car without the aid of a trained professional, the safety and meaningful learning experiences are left to chance.

Physical Education for the Handicapped is Still Required in the School District When it is Not Required for the Nonhandicapped

A specific individualized physical education program is required for those students as defined by law as handicapped when appropriate assessment procedures by trained personnel in physical education have determined special needs in the physical domain. Handicapped students assessed with no special needs are governed by the same requirements as those used for other nonhandicapped students at the same grade level (Eichstaedt & Kalakian, 1987).

Placement of a Self-contained Class of Handicapped Children into a Regular Physical Education Class

The indiscriminate placement (wholesale dumping) of handicapped children into regular physical education is one of the most often cited abuses of the law. Placement of each handicapped child into regular or special physical education must be based on an individual basis and appropriate assessment procedures. Not every student will be successfully mainstreamed into a regular physical education program. According to the law, student placement must be within the Least Restrictive Environment. The environment in which each handicapped child's individual needs are satisfactorily provided and safely met.

Trained Personnel in Adapted/Special Physical Education

Excellent teacher preparation programs in higher education exist around the country to train personnel in the delivery of physical education services to the handicapped. Requirements vary from state to state. The reader is encouraged to check with their state department office of education to learn more about the compentencies and necessary reguirements to teach special physical education.

For more information regarding this subject the reader is referred to the following:
Eichstaedt, C.B & Kalakian, L.H. (1987) Developmental/Adapted physical education: Making ability count. New York: MacMillan.

Lavay, B. & French R. (1985) The special physical educator: Meeting educational goals through a transdisciplinary approach. American Corrective Therapy Journal. 39, 77-81.

Sherrill, C. (1986) Adapted physical education and recreation. Dubuque IA: Wm. C. Brown.

U.S. Office of Education. (1977) Federal register, Public Law 94-142. The Education for All Handicapped Children s Act.

Assessment in Special Physical Education

ASSESSMENT IN SPECIAL PHYSICAL EDUCATION

Assessment is the first step in program planning which is based on testing and measurement. Qualifications for special physical education services depend upon appropriate screening, referral and evaluation procedures. Standardized (norm-referenced and criterion-referenced) assessment instruments are paramount in determining the student's present level of performance to assure proper placement in the least restrictive environment. Proper assessment is also important in determining the student's needs and strengths to individualize instruction (IEP). Student-centered program planning can only be implemented through sound assessment procedures.

No single test is adequate. A variety of areas in the physical domain must be considered to justify adequate test selection.
Consider the following areas:

(1) Reflexes
(2) Motor and physical fitness
(3) Motor ability and development
(4) Perceptual motor development
(5) Body alignment and posture
(6) Individual, dual, and team sports
(7) Aquatics
(8) Dance
(9) Leisure/Recreation activities

THE LAW AND ASSESSMENT

All children with disabilities are entitled to a free and appropriate education.

Assessment of the child is at no cost to parents. With this law, children and their parents are provided certain guarantees during the assessment process:

1. Administered in the child's native language and preferred mode of communication.

2. Each test must be administered by trained personnel who follow instructions provided. Each test must be used for the intended purposes only.

3. No single test item can be used to determine the child's needs and IEP. Rather multifaceted testing must be used that includes a battery of test items in areas of educational needs and/or to determine placement.

4. A test can not be used that will be a disadvantage to the child's particular impairment.

5. Evaluation must be by a multidisciplinary team with at least one expert in the child's suspected disability.

6. Evaluation must deal with all areas of the individual's suspected disability.

Assuring Proper Referral Procedures in Special Physical Education

Reprinted with permission from: Lavay, B. & Hall, A. M. (1987). Assuring proper referral procedures in special physical education. Physical Educator, 44, 369-371.

Critical to the learning of all special education students is proper educational placement. Public law 94-142 was designed to assure that each child's educational placement be in the least restrictive environment, one in which that particular child can best reach his or her own maximum potential for learning. Proper procedures are often made to provide these children with the most appropriate classroom placement. However, proper decisions in physical education placement are often overlooked, or worse, are made only with regard to administrative convenience or financial constraints (Wessel & Kelly, 1986). Special physical educators are partially to blame because they do not take an active role in student placement procedures in physical education, rather leaving these decisions to other professionals. The special physical educator can take a critical first step to help establish proper placement procedures by using a proper referral request form. The purpose of this paper is to discuss both the importance of procedural guidelines and the construction of a referral request form. This will help alleviate the problem that special physical educators are faced with in receiving inappropriate referrals which may subsequently lead to inadequate student placement in physical education.

Procedural Guidelines

In physical education, the referral form is usually completed by the special education classroom teacher or the regular physical educator, but it could be completed by others such as the school nurse, speech pathologist or a concerned parent(s). The form should include a request for the student to be tested, the reasons for requesting the evaluation, as well as observations regarding the nature of the problem (Morsink, 1984).

Developing proper referral procedures in physical education is important to the special physical educator for a number of reasons (Lathen, 1983):

1. It helps alleviate the problem of receiving inappropriate referrals.

2. Addressing the specific nature of the student's problem before testing helps assure the special physical educator of proper direction during subsequent evaluation procedures. For example, a different assessment device would be selected for a student in a wheel chair opposed to one with a behavioral disorder.

3. Testing students can be a very time consuming process. The precis identification of the problem areas of concern will help to save time during evaluation for both the special physical educator and student involved. For example, if it is stated on the referral form that the child displays problems judging the flight of an object, then the evaluator will be aware of this and look for this problem during testing.

4. Time saved by the teacher can be used in program development and student instruction.

The observation of the students' movement performance in regular physical education class often provides the most common basis for making a referral request regarding special physical education evaluation (Werder & Kalakian, 1985). However, during any given school day, the regular physical educator often teaches as many as 150 to 250 students. Students who display movement difficulties may go unnoticed. This situation is further compounded by the problem of the student's classroom (regular and special education) teacher who may only observe the child in the confines of the classroom. If by chance the classroom teacher does observe the student during play, he or she may not be trained to properly identify movement difficulties which may exist.

Construction of the Referral form

A number of examples of written referral forms in physical education exist (Arnheim & Sinclair, 1985; Auxter & Pyfer, 1985; French & Jansma, 1982). However, missing from many of these referral forms is a section which can be used to easily identify movement difficulties. Most critical to the referral form is a checklist consisting of movement problem areas which can easily be scanned and checked off by the individual making the referral. This information will prove useful in the pre-referral period when the special education classroom teacher and/or regular physical educator are collecting and reviewing student information in order to decide whether or not to make a referral in special physical education (Lathen, 1983). Moreover, a form of this type is a convenience to the busy regular physical education teacher. It saves time and aids the classroom teacher who is untrained to observe movement difficulties.

Another important step in assuring smooth referral procedures is to have the special physical educator work closely with the classroom teacher as well as the regular physical education teacher. To assist the regular physical education teacher and classroom teacher as well as other professionals in making proper referrals and to alleviate the problem of the special physical educator receiving inappropriate referrals, an example of the physical education referral form, which has been effectively used by the Albuquerque Public School System follows. This referral form is made available throughout the school year to all school personnel and, in addition, special physical educators in the district conduct inservice workshops for all interested parties. Teacher and parent comments have been favorable regarding the form, as they are easy to fill out and take no longer than 10 to 15 minutes to complete.

Summary

To assure proper physical education placement for the student, carefully designed referral request procedures is a most critical initial step. Developing sound guidelines and procedures can help alleviate the problem of receiving improper referral requests as well as save teacher and student time during evaluation. However, the construction of proper referral request forms which can easily identify movement problem areas is needed in order to help individuals with this process. Moreover, the special physical educator must educate all personnel who will be using the referral request procedure. Finally, the special physical educator who takes an active role in this process is working toward establishing proper student placement in physical education.

REFERENCES

Arnheim, D. D., & Sinclair, W. A. (1985). Physical education for special populations: A developmental, adapted, and remedial approach. Englewood Cliffs, NJ: Prentice-Hall, Inc.

Auxter, D., & Pyfer, J. (1985). Principles and methods of adaptedphysical education and recreation. St. Louis: C. V. Mosby.

French, R. W., & Jansma, P. (1982). Special physical education. Columbus, OH: Charles E. Merrill.

Lathen, L. (1983). Developing a comprehensive special education servicedelivery system. New York: University Press of America.

Morsink, C. V. (1984). Teaching special needs students in the regular classrooms. Boston: Little, Brown and Company.

Werder, J. & Kalakian, L. (1985). Assessment in adapted physical education. Minneapolis: Burgess Publishing.

Wessel, J. A. & Kelly, L. (1986). Achievement-based curriculum development in Physical Education. Philadelphia: Lea & Febiger.

Writing Task Force. (1986). Special physical education handbook. Albuquerque Public Schools, Albuquerque, NM.

REFERRAL FOR EVALUATION IN SPECIAL PHYSICAL EDUCATION

Student Name   Classroom Teacher
Birth Date   P. E. Teacher
Grade/Program Level   Parents' Name
School   Phone Number
Person Making Referral   Phone Number
Contact Person for Student Referral

PLEASE GIVE A BRIEF DESCRIPTION OF THE STUDENT IN THE FOLLOWING AREAS

1. Significant medical history which may cause limitations:

2. Vision or hearing deficits/concerns:

3. Movement limitations

4. Behavioral concerns:

Avoid making a referral if the student displays difficulties in the following areas:
irregular spacing in printing activities
doesn't color within spaces or lines
difficulties with writing skills

Referral Guidelines: After observing the student moving, the following reasons may be applicable
for referring a student fro a special physical education evaluation.
    Circle the areas where the child is displaying difficulty.

Fitness	Perceptual Motor
tires easily	can not properly identify body parts
unable to reach & stretch	unable to find one's space while moving
exhibits a limited range of movement	unable to judge the flight of an object
Motor Proficiency	misinterprets auditory directions
slow in starting, stopping etc.	unable to repeat movements that have
difficulty in performing such fundamental	demonstrated skills as run, jump skip, throw, catch

ASSESSMENT IS DIFFERENT FROM TESTING

Testing:

A data-gathering technique that uses a specific tool or procedure to make systematic observations (Seaman & DePauw, 1989).

Assessment:

An all-encompassing term used to make appropriate student placement and programming decisions. Ulrich (1985), defines assessment as the following: "The collection and interpretation of relevant student information to aid in making nondiscriminatory educational decisions. It should be a continuous process and involve a variety of formal and informal strategies. Various assessment techniques provide valuable information for individualizing the decision-making process."

Simply stated Assessment consists of:
1. Data Collection

2. Interpretation of the data to make the following decisions:
   a. proper placement
   b. present level of student performance
   c. program design (IEP)
   d. program implementation
   e. evaluate program effectiveness

3. This process should be ongoing and continuous

4. Involve a variety of techniques and strategies

NO SINGLE ASSESSMENT INSTRUMENT EXISTS

No one test exists to meet the unique needs of all persons who are handicapped. The person who is handicapped should never be made to conform to a particular test instrument. Rather, test selection should be based on critical tester judgement in the following areas:

A. Purpose of the Assessment

"Why am I testing?"

B. Characteristics of the Assessment Instrument:

"Is the test valid, reliable and administratively feasible?"

C. Appropriateness of the Assessment Instrument

"Will the test meet the unique needs of the particular student/group being tested?"

Eichstaedt & Kalakian (1987) have commented that there is no "cookbook" approach to evaluating persons with special needs. No single test can effectively measure all dimensions of a well rounded physical education program or provide the teacher with a complete profile of the person's movement abilities.

PURPOSE OF ASSESSMENT

A variety of purposes exist within the assessment process. Each purpose will considerably effect proper test instrument selection.

1. Placement
    a. Qualification for services should be based on appropriate referral, screening, and test procedures.
    b. Standardized (i.e. norm-referenced tests) assessment instruments are paramount in determining a student's present level of performance and to assure proper placement in the least restrictive environment.

2. Programming
    a. To individualize instruction (IEP) student needs and strengths must be properly determined.
    b. Student-centered program planning can only be implemented through sound assessment procedures (i.e. criterion-referenced tests).

3. Evaluate
    a. To evaluate and determine program effectiveness. Are group/ student needs being effectively met and progress is occurring (i.e. check lists)?

4. Motivation
    a. Testing can serve as added incentive for students to continue to participate and improve (i.e. charts/graphs).

5. Program Justification
    a. To demonstrate to parents, school board members, administrators and other professionals the importance of the program and contribution it is making towards the child's total educational development (i.e. charts/bar graphs).

CHARACTERISTICS OF ASSESSMENT INSTRUMENTS

Tests are used to make educational decisions, therefore it is paramount that professionals are careful in test selection.

Validity:
Test measures what it purports to measure.

A. Content Validity: The degree to which the test sample of items are representative of the domain or content (Safrit, 1990) (i.e. a test identified as measuring physical fitness should consist of a representative sample of fitness items).

B. Construct Validity: The degree to which a test measures an attribute or trait that cannot be directly measured (Safrit, 1986) (i.e. is the 50 yard dash a measure of a child's speed or reaction time?)

Reliability:
Consistency of results. Important to receive the same results under similar conditions.

Administrative Feasibility:
A. The time factor involved in test administration.
B. The test should be practical and useful for programming.
C. Monetary and personnel costs should be considered and when possible kept to a minimum.

Summary:
Obviously the test administrator must carefully weigh and balance all of these factors.

APPROPRIATENESS OF ASSESSMENT INSTRUMENT

The test selected must be appropriate for the particular age group or population (handicapping condition) being tested.

For example, is it appropriate to measure the cardiovascular endurance of children who are moderately mentally retarded by administering the one mile run/walk (AAHPERD) test?

The tester must realize that the following assumptions are made of many standardized tests.

a. The testee understands the concept of "doing your best". Are children who are handicapped always motivated to perform the items on a test to the best of their ability?

b. The testee is reinforced by the knowledge of results. Many students who are handicapped are not intrinsically motivated to perform to the best of their ability on the test.

c. For a test to be valid and reliable, the standardized directions must be specifically followed. Certain standardized test directions are too difficult for persons who are handicapped to follow and consequently effectively perform.

Summary: Most importantly, professionals in special physical education must keep abreast of various tests available in the profession and the different purposes they serve to meet the needs of varied populations. When in doubt the tester must use professional judgement.

ASSESSMENT INSTRUMENTS IN SPECIAL PHYSICAL EDUCATION

Wade and Davis (1982) have reported that although over 300 motor-based assessment instruments exist, most are not standardized. In fact, most are teacher made, leaving professionals with the dilemma of locating well designed standardized assessment instruments to meet instructional needs.

The following is a list of standardized assessment instruments used frequently to measure the physical ability of persons with disabilities. The title of the assessment instrument as well as an address is given. The assessment instruments are divided into the following categories: (a) physical fitness, (b) motor performance, (c) posture and, (d) sport skills.

PHYSICAL FITNESS

The first five assessment instruments can be obtained through the American Alliance for Health, Physical Education, Recreation, and Dance, 1900 Association Dr., Reston, VA 22091.

1. Physical Best (1989)
2. Health Related Physical Fitness (1980)
3. Youth Fitness Test (1976) (no longer in print)
4. Motor Fitness Test for Moderately Mentally Retarded (1975) (no longer in print)
5. Special Fitness Test for Mild Mentally Retarded (1976) (no longer in print)

Alabama Special Olympics Fitness Battery (1985). Roswal, G.M. Jacksonville State University, Dept. of Physical Education, Jacksonville, AL 36265.

Canada Standardized Test of Fitness (1981) Fitness and Amateur Sport, Ottawa, Canada KIAOX6

Fait Physical Fitness Test for Mildly and Moderately Mentally Retarded Students
A copy of the test is available in:
Dunn J.M. & Fait, H.F. (1989) Special Physical Education: Adapted, individualized, developmental, New York: Saunders College Pub.

Kansas Adapted/Special Physical Education Test Manual (Johnson & Lavay, 1988): Janet Wilson, Specialist in Physical Education, Kansas State

Department of Education, 120 East 10th St. Topeka, KS 66612.

National Children and Youth Fitness Study: Public Health Service, Office of Disease Prevention and Health Promotion, U.S. Dept. of Health and Human Services, (1985 & 1987)
Information regarding the study is available in:
Journal of Physical Education, Recreation and Dance (1985) January issue. (10-17 year olds).
Journal of Physical Education, Recreation and Dance (1987) Nov/Dec issue. (5-10 year olds).

Physical Fitness and Motor Skill Levels of Individuals with Mental Retardation: Mild, Moderate, and Down Syndrome ages 6-21 (1991). Eichstaedt, C.B, Wang, P.Y, Polacek, J.J., and Dohrmann, P.F. Illinois State University, Dept. HPERD, Normal, IL 61761.

Project TRANSITION Assessment System (1987). Jansma, McCubbin, Combs, Decker, & Ersing, The Ohio State University, Adapted Physical Activity, Columbus, OH 43210.

Project Unique Physical Fitness Testing of the Disabled (Winnick and Short, 1985) Human Kinetics, Champaign, IL 61820

MOTOR PERFORMANCE

Adapted Physical Education Assessment Scale Level-Elementary and Secondary (1981) Don Vance, Los Angeles Unified School District, 450 North Grand Ave. Box 3307, Los Angeles, CA 90051.

Basic Motor Ability Test: A copy of the test is available in the following textbook which is no longer available in print. Arnheim, D.D. and Sinclair, W.A. (1979) The Clumsy Child: A program of Motor Therapy, St. Louis: C.V. Mosby

Brigance Diagnostic Inventory of Early Development (Brigance 1978) Curriculum Associates, Inc., 5 Esquire Road, North Billerica, MA 01862.

Body Skills, Motor Development Curriculum, (Werder, J. & Bruininks, R. 1988). American Guidance Service, Circle Pine, MN 55014.

Bruininks-Oseretsky Test of Motor Proficiency, (Bruininks, R. 1978). American Guidance Service, Circle Pine, MN 55014.

Competency Testing for Adapted Physical Education Louisiana (1984 Revised) Louisiana Department of Education, P.O. Box 44064, Baton Rouge, LA 70804.

Cratty Six-Category Gross-Motor Test: A copy of the test is available in: Cratty, B.J. (1969). Perceptual-Motor Behavior and Educational Process. Springfield, IL Charles C. Thomas.

Data-based Gymnasium available in: Dunn, Moorehouse, & Fredericks, (1986). Physical education for the severely handicapped: A systematic approach to a data-based gymnasium. Austin, TX: PRO:ED.

Denver Developmental Screening Test (Frankenberg, W. and Dodds, J. (1967). Ladoca Project and Publishing Foundations Inc., East 51st Avenue and Lincoln Street, Denver, CO 80216.

Fundamental Movement Pattern Assessment Instrument: A copy of the test is available in: McClenaghan, B.A. and Gallahue, D.L. (1978) Fundamental Movement: A developmental and remedial approach. Philadelphia: W.B. Saunders.

Geddes Psychomotor Inventory: A copy of the test is available in: Geddes, D. (1981). Psychomotor individualized educational programs. Boston: Allyn and Bacon, Inc.

Hughes Basic Gross Motor Assessment (Hughes 1979). Office of Special Education, Denver Public Schools Denver, CO 80203.

I CAN Fundamental Skills Test (Wessel, 1976) PRO-ED Publishing Co., 5341 Industrial Oaks Blvd., Austin, TX 78735.

Ohio State University Scale of Intra Gross Motor Assessment. Loovis and Ersing (1989). College Town Press P.O. Box 669, Bloomington, IN 47402.

Project ACTIVE Motor Ability Test (Vodola, 1976) Project ACTIVE, Mr. Joe Karp, 13209 NE 175th, Woodenville, Washington 98072.

Test of Gross Motor Development (Ulrich 1985) PRO-ED Publishing Co., 5341 Industrial Oaks Blvd., Austin, TX 78735.

POSTURE

New York State Posture Rating Test, Revised (1976) Project ACTIVE, Mr. Joe Karp, 13209 NE 175th, Woodenville, Washington 98072

SPORTS SKILLS

Special Olympics Inc. Sport Skill Instructional Program Manuals (Special Olympics Inc.) 1350 New York Ave., Suite 500, Washington, DC, 20005.

SELECTED REFERENCES IN ASSESSMENT

The following is a brief list of textbooks/articles that will assist the practitioner in specifically addressing the issue of assessment and programming with special populations.

AAHPERD. (1975). Testing for impaired, disabled, and handicapped individuals. Reston, VA: AAHPERD Publications.

Folio, M.R. (1986). Physical education programming for exceptional learners. Rockville, M.D.: Aspen Pub.

Jansma, P. (Ed) (1989). The psychomotor domain and the seriously handicapped, (3rd ed.). Lanham, M.D.: University Press of America.

Kirkendall, D.R., Gruber, J.J. and Johnson R.E. (1987). Measurement and evaluation for physical educators. Champaign, IL: Human Kinetics Pub.

Miles, B. H., Nierengarden, M. E., & Nearing, R. J. (1988). A review of the eleven most often cited assessment instruments used in adapted physical education. Clinical Kinesiology, 42, 33-41.

Seaman, J. A. and DePauw, K.P. (1989). The new adapted physical education: A developmental approach. Palo Alto, CA: Mayfield

Safrit, M.J. (1990). Introduction to measurement in physical education and exercise science. St. Louis: Time Mirror Mosby.

Sherrill, C. (1986). Adapted physical education and recreation: A multidisciplinary Approach. Dubuque, IA: Wm C. Brown.

Werner, J.K. and Kalakian, L.H. (1985). Assessment in Adapted Physical education. Minneapolis, MN: Burgess Pub.

Wessel, J.A. & Kelly, L. (1986). Achievement based curriculum development in physical education. Philadelphia: Lea and Febiger.

Who is the Student with a Disability?

WHO IS THE STUDENT WITH A DISABILITY?

The student with a disability doesn't fit into a well-defined category. Emphasis must be placed on the individual and not the category.

Exceptionality: An individual who may deviate from the considered norm physically, mentally, socially and emotionally.

Impairment: The actual physical damage or disorder which can be identified.

Disability: The limitations, restrictions, or behavior patterns which may evolve from the impairment.

Handicap: The actual effect or reaction the individual has toward the disability causing functional limitations in lifestyle.

Beaver (1989) provides the following example:
Impairment: Paraplegia at T-3 (spinal cord lesion at the thoracic vertebra 3)

Disability: Manifests itself in the case of no useful balance when sitting & using the wheelchair for mobility. No innervation below the upper chest or middle back

Handicap: The actual negative impact or affect it has on the individual because of limited mobility when outside the wheelchair.

L'Abate and Curtis (1975) stated, "not every impairment results in a disability, and not every disability results in a handicap. The most significant aspect is the individual's own interpretation of his impairment and his ability to live with it" (p. 38).

A person in a wheelchair may be handicapped by steps, but not by a ramp.

What's in a Name (how you address a person can help to decrease the stigma) address the person as not "wheelchair bound" but rather as a person in a wheelchair or a person with a disability. Emphasize the person not the disability.

See: Beaver, D. (1989). What's in a word? Palaestra, 5 (2), 4.

CATEGORICAL AND NONCATEGORICAL APPROACH

Categorical Approach
Traditionally the individual with a disability has been categorized for a variety of reasons:

1. Too often programming exists based on specific physical, mental, social, or emotional conditions. This placement has become a programming convenience for the administrators.

2. The student may be labeled by the administration for funding purposes with the school receiving money and/or special services based on number of students identified as a certain disability.

3. Some background knowledge and information regarding various handicapping conditions can provide necessary information for programming. This information should be used as a simple guideline. For example:

   A. a student with epilepsy may have a seizure during class.
   B. certain exercises or activities such as rope climbing which involve toeing inward are contraindicated for the individual with spastic cerebral palsy.

Noncategorical Approach

It is a false assumption that all persons have identical needs, interests and abilities (Seaman & DePauw,1989). Uniqueness of each individual student must be recognized. How can this be accomplished?

1. Emphasis must be placed on ability rather than disability.

2. Design programs that meet individual needs, strengths, abilities, and interests of each student.

3. Deal with each individual as a whole person. Don't teach to just parts of the person.

4. Too often the individual with a handicap doesn't fit into one neat and well defined category.

Consider the following:

A teacher who makes little or no allowance for individual differences in the classroom is an individual who makes little or no difference in the lives of his students. (William A. Ward)

Unless the attitudes of physical educators change and become more favorable toward teaching handicap pupils, the chances are minimal that such pupils will successfully assimilate into regular classes" (Terry Rizzo).

Summary:
With low expectations too often comes low achievement.

THE STUDENT WITH A DISABILITY AS DEFINED BY LAW

The physical educator should become familiar with the following terms and definitions of "children with a disability" as stated in PL 101-476:

I. "Deaf" means a hearing impairment so severe that the child is hindered in processing linguistic information through hearing, with or without amplification, and educational performance is thus adversely affected.

II. "Deaf-blind" means concomitant hearing and visual impairments, the combination of which causes such severe communication and other developmental and educational problems that the child cannot be accommodated in special education programs solely for deaf or blind children.

III. "Hard of hearing" means a hearing impairment, whether permanent or fluctuating, that adversely affects a child's educational performance, but that is not included under the definition of "deaf" in this section.

IV. "Mentally retarded" means significantly subaverage general intellectual functioning that exists concurrently with deficits in adaptive behavior, is manifested during the developmental period, and adversely affects a child's educational performance.

V. "Multihandicapped" means concomitant impairments (e.g., mentally retarded-blind, mentally retarded-orthopedically impaired), the combination of which causes such severe educational problems that the child cannot be accommodated in special education programs designed solely for children with one of the impairments. The term does not include deaf-blind children.

VI. "Orthopedically impaired" means a severe orthopedic impairment that adversely affects a child's educational performance. The term includes impairments caused by congenital anomaly (e.g., clubfoot, absence of some member), impairments caused by disease (e.g., poliomyelitis, bone tuberculosis), and impairments from other causes (e.g., cerebral palsy, amputations, and fractures or burns that cause contractures).

VII. "Other health impaired" means limited strength, vitality, or alertness owing to chronic or acute health problems such as a heart condition, tuberculosis, rheumatic fever, nephritis, asthma, sickle cell anemia, hemophilia, epilepsy, lead poisoning, leukemia, or diabetes, which adversely affects a child's educational performance.

VIII. "Seriously emotionally disturbed" is defined as follows:
   A. The term means a condition exhibiting one or more of the following characteristics over a long period of time and to a marked degree, which adversely affects educational performance:
      1. An inability to learn that cannot be explained by intellectual, sensory, or health factors.
      2. An inability to build or maintain satisfactory interpersonal relationships with peers and teachers.
      3. Inappropriate types of behavior or feelings under normal circumstances.
      4. A general pervasive mood of unhappiness or depression.
      5. A tendency to develop physical symptoms or fears associated with personal or school problems.

   B. The term includes children who are schizophrenic or autistic. The term does not include children who are socially maladjusted, unless they are determined to be seriously emotionally disturbed.

IX. "Specific learning disability" means a disorder in one or more of the basic psychological processes involved in understanding or in using language, spoken or written, that may manifest itself in an imperfect ability to listen, think, speak, read, write, spell, or do mathematical calculations. The term includes such conditions as perceptual handicaps, brain injury, minimal brain dysfunction, dyslexia, and developmental aphasia. The term does not include children who have learning problems that are primarily the result of visual, hearing, or motor handicaps; of mental retardation; or of environmental, cultural, or economic disadvantage.

X. "Speech impaired" means a communication disorder such as stuttering, impaired articulation, a language impairment, or a voice impairment that adversely affects a child's educational performance.

XI. "Visually handicapped" means a visual impairment that, even with correction, adversely affects a child's educational performance. The term includes both partially seeing and blind children.

(Federal Register, 1977, p. 4247-4248)

THE LAW AND THE STUDENT WITH A DISABILITY

Individuals With Disabilities Education Act (1990)*

PL 101-476 (part B, permanent legislation)

1. Free and appropriate education with full service mandated to all individuals 3-21 years of age identified as special education students. For more information, see definition of special education in Individuals With Disabilities Education Act, PL 101-476 (p. 42480).
2. Educated in the least restrictive environment.
3. Parents and pupil (when appropriate) involved in decision making process regarding child's placement and programming (IEP process).
4. Personnel development of special education staff and support staff.
5. Federal Government provides funds to State Educational Agencies (SEA) & Locally Educational Agencies (LEA) to meet educational needs of students.
6. Physical education is specifically defined in the law and is identified as a direct service.

* Formerly PL 94-142 Education Handicapped Chidrens Act (1975).

P L 99-457, the Individuals With Disabilities Education Act Amendment of 1986 (part H)

Recognized the need to implement programs for at risk infants and toddlers from birth to five years and their families.

1. Preschool Grant Program: Free and appropriate education with full service mandated to all individuals 3-5 years of age identified as special education students by 1991. 3-5 years olds can receive services without being labelled.
    a. Individualized Family Service Plan (IFSP) similar to the IEP, but also includes multidisciplinary evaluation of family needs. Parental instruction is an allowable cost and home-based activity is encouraged.
2. Handicapped Infant Toddlers Program: Programs for children who are handicapped and at risk from birth to 3 years and their families. This program is voluntary and states may elect not to participate.

Excellent resources are:

Campbell, P. H. et al, (1988). Statewide intervention systems: An overview of the new federal program for infants and toddlers with handicaps. The Journal of Special Education. 22, 25-40.

Churton, M. W. (1988). Federal law and adapted physical education. Adapted Physical Activity Quarterly, 5, 278- 284.

ADJUSTING TO A DISABILITY

Whether an individual will adjust to a disability involves a complex interaction among the individual and:

(1) family

(2) school

(3) community

(4) peers

Each individual reacts differently to the condition ranging along a continuum from positive to negative. Stages of acceptance may depend greatly on the onset of the disability.

The individual may display any or all of the following defense mechanisms (Dunn & Fait, 1989):

Compensation - offsets a shortcoming

Identification - assumes memories of an admired individual or group

Repression - inhibits unpleasant memories

Sublimation - replaces an impulse that can not be satisfied with
    one that can

As a Teacher What Can Be Done?

The teacher can help a student adjust to the disability by considering:
Stress abilities.
Avoid comparisons.
Provide opportunities for experiences.
Be consistent in approach.
Provide for positive experiences & be positive in your own teaching.

During Teacher Instruction Consider the Following:

Relax.

Speak clearly and distinctly.

Be patient as it may take the individual extra time to complete a task.

Be firm and consistent, but positive in your teaching style and approach with each individual.

Don't feel sorry for the individual or allow him or her to manipulate you during instruction.

Most importantly, remember that although each person is unique, they are quite similar to all others.

To effectively design appropriate physical education programs for persons with a disability, various factors that contribute to adverse educational performance must be correctly identified. Only then can a plan be formulated and a movement program effectively implemented.

A child with a disability will usually be so in one of the following way(s):

Physically
Mentally
Socially
Emotionally

Various body systems and factors can affect the child's movement performance The instructor must realize that a variety of factors either individually or collectively can affect a person's ability to move.

For example:
1. Physical deviation (i.e. obesity, posture)
2. Neurological disorder (i.e. cerebral palsy, seizure)
3. Sensory system disorder (i.e. deaf, blind)
4. Social and emotional disorder (i.e. behavior disorder)
5. Developmentally delayed (i.e. physical fitness, motor)
6. Health impaired (i.e. diabetes, respiratory problem)

SENSORY SYSTEMS

Auxter & Pyfer (1989), discuss the importance of understanding the sensory systems in order to assist in providing programs of physical activity to persons who display sensory dysfunction and movement difficulties.

1. Vestibular System:

This mechanism is located in the inner ear and functions to help position the eyes in order to maintain balance.

2. Kinesthetic System:

This system functions to position the limbs in space to accurately plan movement.

3. Tactile System:

This system allows the body to learn where the body ends and space begins. The receptors in the skin receive information regarding the environment through touch.

4. Visual System:

This system allows the person to process information through sight. An important function is depth perception which is necessary in many movement activities.

5. Auditory System:

This system allows the person to process information through sounds. An important function in allowing the person to orient to sounds such as verbal commands.

SUMMARY:
All of these systems may work simultaneously and collectively to allow the person to negotiate and effectively move in the environment. Obviously, an impairment to any one of these senses causes movement difficulty.

Categorical Approach

MENTAL RETARDATION

Definition:

Significant subaverage general intellectual functioning, existing concurrently with deficits in adaptive behavior and manifested during the developmental period, which adversely affects a child's educational performance (AAMR, 1973).

Classification:

Consisting of 2.3-3.0% of the total population. For educational purposes persons with mental retardation are classified in general as follows:

Term	IQ	Grade Level	Skill Level
Educable or Mild	50-70	3rd-6th	Community independence partial to total support
Trainable or Moderate	49-30	1st-3rd	Learn self help, vocational skills, sheltered workshop group home
Severe	29-below	infant	Total care and Profound can not perform most self help skills with out supervision

Etiology:

Over 100 causes of mental retardation exist, some of which are not fully understood. Two broad categories are the following:
1. Organic: Brain damage, chromosomal abnormalities.

2. Familial Environmental: Adverse environmental conditions and lack of stimulation (i.e. poor nutrition, child abuse).

Developmental Considerations

Consider the following generalities:
1. This population is smaller in structure and lighter in weight than their nonhandicapped peers.
2. Consider the variety of health factors at birth and throughout life.
3. More severe the retardation the greater the deficit in motor ability.
4. Delay in maturation, developing at a slower rate than the normal child.
5. Reaction time is slower.
6. Limited in their mental ability especially in processing information.
7. Have the same developmental needs as all other persons.

Programming considerations:

In general, regarding the area of motor performance children with mental retardation may perform better in physical education than in other academic areas.
The EMR student may be 2 to 4 years behind their nonhandicapped peers while the TMR student may be 4-6 years behind in physical performance.

During instruction consider the following:
1. Select activities that are "age appropriate". For example do not play "duck duck goose" with a group of high school age individuals.
2. Keep directions simple using demonstration and physical guidance while verbal instruction is maintained at a minimum.
3. Because of low intellectual functioning directions and examples should be made clear with concrete, tangible examples provided.
4. Teach skills in a well planned sequential order. Use task analysis
5. Provide for positive experiences. These students have failed so often they may be reluctant to try new activities.

DOWN SYNDROME

Over 50% of the persons with moderate to severe mental retardation consists of individuals with Down syndrome (Cooke, 1984).

Etiology:

Chromosomal abnormality specifically associated with chromosome 21 in which there is an extra chromosome.

Translocation in which some cells have an extra chromosome.
 Mosaisism in which there is less one chromosome.

Unique characteristics to consider during program development are offered by Eichstaedt & Kalakian (1987):

1. Short and stocky tendency toward obesity: growth ceases at an earlier age, shorter for height, but same weight therefore obesity.
2. Upper respiratory infections: mouth too small for normal size tongue causing mouth breathing and problems with endurance activities.
3. Heart defects: circulatory system is less developed and arteries are thinner.
4. Poor muscle tone: 50 % are born floppy babies with a lack of support around the muscle and joint areas.
5. Generally slow delayed development with a lag in motor development and perception. Display balance difficulties.

Atlantoaxial instability is a condition which exists among 12-15% of individuals with Down Syndrome. This condition involves greater than normal mobility in the upper two vertebrae of the neck. This condition can cause serious injury to the person during certain physical activities. A more detailed description of this condition follows.

Excellent resources include:

Block, M. E. (1991). Motor development in children with Down syndrome: A review of the literature. Adapted Physical Activity Quarterly. 8,179-209.
Eichstaedt, C. B. & Lavay, B. (1992). Physical activty for persons with mental retardation: Infant to adult. Champaign, IL: Human Kinetics.

ATLANTOAXIAL INSTABILITY

1. What is it:

   Greater than normal mobility of the two upper vertebrae C1 and
   C2 (top of the neck).

2. What can happen:

   Exposes the individual to possible serious injury if forceful
   flexion of the neck occurs as vertebrae may shift and squeeze or
   sever the spinal cord.

3. Occurance:

   More than 50% individuals with moderate and severe mental retardation
   may have Down Syndrome and 12-15% of these individuals may
   have atlantoaxial instability.

4. Program Implications:
   Special Olympics restrict individuals with atlantoaxial instability
   from participating in the sporting events:
   A. gymnastics
   B. swimming - diving start, butterfly stroke,
   C. track
   D. soccer
   E. any warm-up exercise that would place pressure on the neck

5. Medical Examination:
   Individuals with Down syndrome should be examined with x-rays to
   detect this condition. Cost ranges from $75-$150.

The above information was taken from: Cooke, R.E. (1984). Atlanoaxial
instability in individuals with Down's Syndrome. <u>Adapted Physical Activity
Quarterly, 1</u>, 194-196.

Instruction of Team Sport Strategies for the Mild/Moderate Mentally
Handicapped

Reprinted with permission from: Lavay, B. (1985). Instruction of team sports strategies for
the Mild/Moderate Mentally Handicapped. Palaestra: The Forum of Sport and Physical
Education for the Disabled, 2 (1), 10-13.

Growth of Special Olympics programs and implementation of Public Law 94-142 (Education for All
Handicapped Children Act) have provided opportunities for the mildly and moderately mentally
handicapped to participate in various team sports. A great deal of information is available to the special
physical educator, therapeutic recreation specialist and special Olympics coach regarding modification
techniques and training principles of sport skill instruction for this population (Adams, Daniel, Mccubbin, &
Rullman, 1982; Bauer, 1981; Crowe, Auxter, & Pyfer, 1981; Fait & Dunn, 1984; Sherrill, 1982; Special
Olympics, 1979; Stein, 1972). However, there is only a limited amount of literature that systematically
explains teamwork concepts applicable to the mentally handicapped, such as player positioning, switching
from offense to defense and individual as well as team responsibilities while engaged in a particular sport.
Most of these concepts are abstract; however, a basic understanding is critical if the mentally handicapped
individual is to participate successfully in team sport.

The purpose of this article is to systematically present a number of strategies that practitioners
responsible for teaching team sport to the mentally handicapped can use. The following teaching
strategies will be discussed: fundamental skills, practice drills to simulate play, the playing area,
player positioning, defensive strategies, switching from offense to defense, and controlled play.
Many of the strategies discussed are taken from the author's experiences in teaching special
physical education to mildly and moderately mentally handicapped individuals.

Each sport is different, possessing its own set of unique rules and strategies. However, for
the purpose of this article, three sports (basketball, floor hockey, and soccer) have been chosen
for discussion because similar teaching strategies can be used with all of these sports.

Team sport participation challenges the mentally handicapped individual both physically and
intellectually. Certain individuals may never be developmentally ready to participate successfully
in team sport play. The instructor must determine when to begin instruction. Effective team play
among individuals will not occur immediately. Adult teacher aides, peer tutors or cross-age tutors
(Sherrill, 1982) or mentally handicapped individuals who are developmentally ready to begin team
sport instruction can serve as effective role models to students who may not be quite ready. Also,
the instructor must be prepared to exercise a great deal of patience, teaching teamwork concepts
in a systematic and sequential order. The instructor's initial considerations must always be in
meeting individual needs as well as program goals and objectives for each sport.

Fundamental Skills

Obviously the individual who is unable to dribble, pass, rebound, or shoot will have difficulty playing basketball. Therefore, initial instruction given to the mentally handicapped must emphasize the fundamental skills involved in each sport (Fait & Dunn, 1984). Successful performance of fundamental skills not only builds a strong sport skill foundation, but also indicates to the instructor those individuals who are ready to begin to participate in instructional strategy of sport.

Simple lead-up games can reinforce fundamental skill learning, while making instruction enjoyable and motivational to each individual. For example, circle games can be played with individuals taking turns standing in the middle while passing the ball to others. Other lead-up games which can be introduced during this time are dribbling and passing relays as well as dribbling around various cone formation (Dauer & Pangrazi, 1983). Additional lead-up games can be developed by the instructor to meet the needs of the particular group.

Social interaction and cooperation among individuals will not occur automatically. During the introduction of simple lead-up games the instructor must make a point of encouraging all individuals to work closely together toward the common goal of good play. The quality of play rather than the outcome or score must be stressed. Reinforcing social interaction during sport skill instruction is extremely important; for some mentally handicapped individuals playing simple lead-up games may be their first exposure to this concept.

Practice Drills to Simulate Play

Before beginning actual play, practice drills for the mentally handicapped should be designed to simulate game conditions. An excellent beginning instructional technique is to place two to four players around one goal or basket with the instructor encouraging participants to take turns passing to one another. For example, in floor hockey four players can stand a few feet outside the goal area with instructions to make three passes before a shot toward the goal can be taken. In basketball, two players spaced 5 to 10 feet apart can run the length of the court while passing the ball back and forth. Later, a third player can be added to this passing drill formation.

In both drills and any others the instructor may introduce to the players, they should be encouraged to move while passing and shooting to simulate game conditions. Emphasis by the instructor during this stage of play should be to correctly demonstrate fundamental skills to all players. The addition of defensive players at this stage of instruction would only add confusion and is, therefore, omitted.

When players are ready, more sophisticated drills may be introduced into practice sessions. The instructor must carefully design each drill to fit individual and team needs. The following is an example of a practice drill designed to encourage players to move toward the puck to receive a pass during floor hockey play. Two lines are formed, one at the center circle and one on the wing. The first player in the center circle line dribbles around a set of cones and then passes the puck to a player on the wing who is moving to receive the pass and take a shot toward the goal. Players involved would then move to the next line, repeating the drill from a different position. This particular drill can be easily incorporated into basketball and soccer instruction.

The Playing Area

The playing court or field with numerous boundary lines and areas can be quite confusing to the mentally handicapped individual. The instructor can reduce this problem by arranging cones or flags on the field or court to make boundary areas as visible and tangible to all players as possible. Startzell (1981) suggested that the instructor walk the playing area with all participants before actual play begins, explaining various boundary lines and areas. For example, the instructor may point to and explain the location of the goal area in a soccer game or the positioning of each player while shooting a foul shot during a basketball game.

Player Positioning

An extremely difficult concept to teach the mentally handicapped is player positioning and area responsibility in relation to the ball or puck. When play begins, individuals will want to converge immediately on the ball or puck. Initially, cones can be used to mark each player's position. Players can also be made aware of area responsibilities by having the instructor physically guide them to their position on the court or field.

An effective strategy used to discourage players from converging on the ball during play is to have them freeze their movement upon hearing a whistle or a clap of the hands from the instructor. Players are then guided back to their designated positions. This practice may need to be repeated numerous times until all individuals become aware of their positions and area responsibilities. Once made aware, players must be constantly reminded by the instructor to watch the ball or puck and be ready to receive a pass while playing their assigned positions.

Whether to teach a player a variety of positions should be determined by the skill level of each individual and the skills involved in playing each particular position. For example, in floor hockey a player who learns the strategies involved in playing right forward may be able to switch easily to left forward as the skills are quite similar. However, switching a player from right forward to goalie requires learning some entirely different skills.

Although each individual should be afforded opportunities to play as many different positions as possible, rotation among various positions may initially confuse the mentally handicapped. The individual should feel comfortable and gain confidence playing one position before instruction at a new position begins. To assure smoother play during games, the instructor may need to assign skilled players to the more difficult positions. For example, if only one or two individuals on a basketball team are capable of controlling the ball while dribbling, then the instructor should designate these players as guards, with responsibility for dribbling the ball up the floor to set up offensive play.

Defensive Strategies

The addition of defensive players will dramatically change the complexity of a game. Initially, defensive fundamental instruction to each individual should consist of assuming proper stance, practicing footwork, maintaining balance and staying with an assigned opponent. Proper defensive movement can be taught by having each player assume the proper position and mirror the instructor who slides from side to side as well as back and forth. More complex defensive strategies can be introduced through simple two-on-two and three-on-three keep-away or chase games. Players are scattered around a small area of the gymnasium or playing field and the offensive team passes the ball or puck among themselves while trying to keep it away from the defensive team. After a few minutes the two teams can switch from offense to defense (Special Olympics, 1979).

Another activity which can be used to teach defensive strategies is to have two players pair off at a goal or basket. The offensive player attempts to dribble past the defensive player who moves into proper position to stop the offensive player. The defensive player must be encouraged to slide both feet and move the body into proper position without fouling. To aid players in distinguishing between offensive and defensive play, different colored jerseys should be worn. The freeze technique, with the instructor physically guiding defensive players back to their assigned players, may aid defensive players from converging on the ball. Later, simple zone defenses can be introduced with each player responsible for an assigned area.

Switching from Offense to Defense

Introducing full field or court play in which players must distinguish between the offensive and defensive goal or basket may prove quite confusing to the mentally handicapped. To help players make this transition, offensive and defensive goals or baskets can be painted different colors with each team wearing the same colored jersey as the goal or basket towards which they are shooting. In a soccer game the team wearing red jerseys would shoot at the goal painted red and during half time would not switch goals but rather remain with the same goal throughout the game.

Perhaps the most difficult and abstract concept for the mentally handicapped individual to understand and perform is continuous adjustments that must be made when switching back and forth between offense and defense during a game. To help alleviate confusion, before actual play begins the instructor can bring the players onto the field or court and have them practice as a team switching back and forth between offense and defense.

A rule used by the Illinois Trainable Mentally Handicapped Athletic Association in basketball to aid in a smoother transition during play is to prohibit fastbreaking after steals, rebounds or made baskets (Constitution and Bylaws, 1979). The offensive team must wait for all players on the opposing team to be in their defensive positions before advancing the ball up the court. This not only makes for a smoother transition during play but allows players time to make adjustments from offense to defense. Players should be instructed that after a steal, rebound or made basket they are to pass the ball to a designated player who is responsible for dribbling the ball up the floor. This particular player is instructed not to advance the ball up the court until all teammates are in their proper offensive positions.

Controlled Play

Individual and team play must always be performed under control (Levine & Langness, 1983). The instructor should discourage over-aggressive play that leads to fouling, for example, disallowing full court pressure by the defensive team. Whether to play the game at a walk, jog, or full run will be determined by the fitness and skill levels of players involved. Therefore, it is important that the instructor incorporate drills during practice sessions that raise the fitness and skill level of the players involved. Raising the players' skill and fitness levels also helps to control play. Teamwork among individuals must always be encouraged with the instructor realizing that social praise in the form of a smile, handshake or positive statement can be quite motivational. Such positive reinforcement helps enhance performance levels of the mentally handicapped during play.

Conclusion

Instruction in sport modification techniques and training principles to assure proper team play is simply not enough. The special physical educator, therapeutic recreation specialist and Special Olympics coach must accept the challenge of teaching abstract teamwork concepts to all individuals in a systematic manner in order to enhance team play. The instructor can meet this challenge by utilizing proper instruction, imaginative practice sessions and positive encouragement of each player to develop successful proper team play among individuals. The mentally handicapped individual deserves to enjoy the same physical, social and psychological benefits which can be derived from team sport participation as others do.

References

Adams, R. C., Daniel, A. D., McCubbin, J. A., & Rullman, L. (1982). Games, sports, and exercise for the physically handicapped (3rd ed.). Philadelphia: Lea & Febiger.

Bauer, D. (1981). Aerobic fitness for the moderately mentally retarded. Practical Pointers, 5 (5), 1-31.

Constitution and Bylaws of the Illinois Trainable Mentally Handicapped Athletic Association. (1979). Available from Barry Lavay, CSULB, Dept. of HPER, 1250 Bellflower Blvd., Long Beach, CA, 90808.

Crowe, W. C., Auxter, D., & Pyfer, J. (1981). Principles and methods of adapted physical education and recreation (4th ed.). St. Louis: C. V. Mosby Co.

Dauer, V. P., & Pangrazi, R. P. (1983). Dynamic physical education for elementary school children. Minneapolis: Burgess Publishing Company.

Fait, H. F., & Dunn, J. M. (1984). Special physical education: adapted, individualized, developmental. (5th ed.). Philadelphia: W. B. Saunders.

Levine, H. G., & Langness, L. L. (1983). context, ability, and performance: Comparison of competitive athletics among mildly mentally retarded and non-retarded adults. American Journal of Mental Deficiency, 87, 528-538.

Sherrill, C. (1982). Adapted physical education: A multidisciplinary approach (2nd ed.). Dubuque, IA: Wm. C. Brown.

Special Olympics, Inc. (1979). Special Olympics basketball sports skills instructional program. Special Olympics, Inc. 1350 New York Ave., N. W. Suite 500, Washington, D. C. 20005.

Startzell, S. (1981). Soccer Teamwork: A sport for all. Journal of Physical Education, Recreation, and Dance, 52 (5), 55-56.

Stein, J. U. (1972). Special Olympics instructional manual. Washington, D. C.: American Association for Health, Physical Education and Recreation and the Joseph P. Kennedy, Jr. Foundation.

SEVERELY & PROFOUNDLY RETARDED

Until recently little attention has been given to this particular population. These people remained in institutional care receiving very little programming. However, with the move toward deinstitutionalization, more and more of these individuals in the 1980's began being taught in the educational environment.

To date, little research has been conducted regarding the physical education programming needs of persons with severe/profound mental retardation. Dunn & Fait (1989), offer the following suggestions:

1. The range of activities in physical education programming will be limited due to this population's low mental and physical ability. In general, making them usually totally dependent.

2. Sensory motor experiences provide activities which increase awareness of stimuli and improve manipulative activity. Activities which develop all senses help to raise the individual's personal level of sensory awareness.

3. Play with brightly colored toys can increase rudimentary skills of reaching, grasping, holding, and releasing.

4. Sand, water, and clay play can increase the use of arms, hands, and finger movements.

5. Always include functional skill activities that promote basic movements of daily living. For example, lifting the feet over various objects or up-steps. Rudimentary and fundamental motor patterns can be enhanced through various obstacle courses.

6. Behavior modification techniques may be needed to elicit the desirable response. Effective teaching strategies include positive reinforcement and modeling.

7. Task analysis procedures designed to meet the needs of each student and the particular skill may need to be employed.

Jansma (1988) has identified 12 pedagogical models in Special Physical Education specific to this population. A brief description of a some of these models follows:

1. Functional Skills Model: what skills will this individual need to function in society?
2. Task Analysis Model: Sequencing skill from rudimentary to advanced.
3. I CAN Model (Wessel et al 1976): A curriculum and teaching model that can be adopted to the SPH
4. Data-based Gymnasium Model (Dunn et al 1987): Emphasizes physical skill development in a behavioral framework.
5. Project Transition Model (Jansma,1987): Emphasizes physical fitness and hygiene training for adults with mental retardation.

Excellent resources follow:

Dunn, J.M., Moorehouse J.W., & Fredericks, H.D. (1986). Physical education for the severely handicapped: A systematic approach to data-based gymnasium. Austin, TX: PRO-ED.

Jansma, P. (1988). Teacher training in adapted physical education for the severely & profoundly handicapped student, In Sherrill, C. (ED). Leadership training in adapted physical education. Champaign, IL: Human Kinetics.

Jansma, P. (Ed.), (1989). The psychomotor domain and the seriously handicapped. Washington, D.C.: University Press of America.

BEHAVIOR DISORDERED

Definition
No universally accepted definition exists among experts. Persons with a behavior disorder are a very heterogenous group displaying a wide range of behaviors from hyperactive to withdrawn. Most authorities agree that it is necessary to rely upon the individual assessment of each person's behavior in order to design appropriate instruction.

1. Inability to learn which can not be explained by intellectual,
    sensory, or health factors.
2. Inability to maintain satisfactory interpersonal relationships
    with family, peers, and/or teacher.
3. Inappropriate behavior under normal circumstances. It is
    important to realize that all children display inappropriate
    behavior on occasion. The key is if chronic inappropriate behavior
    persists over time.

Etiology
2% of all children and youth are identified as behaviorally disordered. Caused by such factors as:
1. Hereditary
2. Organic
3. Functional causes

Characteristics
Because persons with a behavior disorder are such a heterogenous group, each child may exhibit one or more of the following characteristics as discussed by (French & Jansma, 1982 ; Moran & Kalakian,1977):
1. A wide range (high-low) of motor ability and fitness functions.
2. Specific behavioral disturbances such as nonattending,
    aggression, withdrawal, hyperactive, short attention span,
    distractable behavior.
3. Rigid in expectations becoming frustrated easily.
4. Lack of motivation and poor work habits.
5. Deficient social skills and inability to conform to group goals.
6. Challenges authority and sensitive to touch.

Programming Considerations:

The physical education setting can be quite different from other educational environments. Movement is encouraged in a constantly changing environment. Physical education classes are usually large with an insufficient teacher/student ratio.

1. Provide for positive experiences that will motivate the student.
2. Classes must be conducted in a structured and controlled manner. Structure the teaching environment, as too much freedom can be contraindicated to this child (i.e. see grading procedure on next page).
3. Have a positive systematic plan of behavior management. Design appropriate rules.
4. Individual and small group activities may need to be introduced first before large group activities become part of the program.
5. Teach students to perform skills under control. Initially do not place these students in highly competitive activities.
6. Teaching these students can be emotionally draining. Therefore, the teacher must "act, not react" to situation that arise!

Two articles which outline a number of behavior management principles follows:

Lavay, B. (1985). Help, class out of control! Kansas Association for Health Physical Education, Recreation and Dance, 53 (2), 29-31.
French, R., Lavay, B. & Henderson, (1985). Take a lap. Physical Educator. 42, 180-185.

Excellent resources are:

French, R., & Lavay, B. (1990). Behavior management skills for physical educators and recreators. Kearney , NE: Educational Systems Associations Inc.
Hellison, D.R. (1985). Goals and strategies for teaching physical education. Champaign, IL: Human Kinetics Pub.

Grading Procedures and Point System for Physical Education Class

Students will earn points toward their grade in physical education class each week in the following manner:

2 points for dressing properly for physical education class.
2 points for performing all the required exercises in the 10-minute warm-up period.
2 points for cooperating and participating in the actual lesson of the day.
2 points skill evaluation (performance improvement and periodic skill tests).
2 points for cooperation and participating in the relaxation exercises at the end of each class.
A student can earn a total of 10 points each class meeting. The following is the grading system:

GRADING SYSTEM - 5 DAYS   GRADING SYSTEM - 3 DAYS

Grade	Points		Grade	Points
A	50-45		A	30-27
B	44-40		B	26-24
C	39-35		C	23-21
D	35-30		D	20-18
F	30- below		F	18-Below

DISMISSAL FROM PHYSICAL EDUCATION CLASS

A student not cooperating in physical education class will be given one warning. On a student's second warning, he will be given a one minute time out. On a student's third warning, he will be sent back to class. The following are the gymnasium rules to follow in class:

1. Take care of all equipment like it is your own.
2. Listen to the teacher during instruction.
3. Follow and participate in all directions given by the teacher.
4. Treat your classmates as you wish to be treated.

Help! Class Out of Control

Reprinted with permission from: Lavay, B. (1985). Help, class out of control! <u>Kansas
Association for Health Physical Education, Recreation and Dance, 53</u> (2), 29-31.

For the past 15 years lack of student discipline and the decline of student interest have been
cited by the annual Gallup surveys as two of the major problems in the public schools. (Elam,
1983). Most physical educators would agree that for learning to occur specific steps to remediate
behavior problems and promote student interest must be available.

No easy solutions to either problem exists. In recent years a variety of behavior management
strategies and programs have been successfully incorporated into classroom settings (Gardner,
1978). Physical educators, however, have been reluctant to accept these procedures as a
solution to the problem (Loovis, 1980; Presbie & Brown, 1977; Siedentop, 1983).

<u>Justification of Behavior Management</u>

A lack of proper training in behavior management procedures is one reason often cited for
physical educator's reluctance to incorporate these strategies with student instruction. Dunn and
French (1982, p. 43), stated:

"Physical educators are seldom taught how to competently manage the behavior problems
with which they are frequently confronted. The emphasis in their training is primarily on
educational and psychological principles without sufficient attention to the pracitical use of the
behavior management principles in the physical education setting."

This lack of training may be caused by physical educator's misconceptions about the use of
behavior management systems with their teaching. Such misconceptions include the following:
(a) a misinterpretation of behavior management terminology among professionals; (b) the attitude
that these techniques are dehumanizing; (c) the belief that the application of reinforcement is
merely bribery which in turn leads to the assumption that once the behavior is reinforced, the
student will perform the desired behavior only for the reward; and (d) the assumption that the
administration of reinforcers will become financially too expensive for the teacher's budget. To
give the physical educator a clearer picture of how behavior management has been effectively
incorporated into the physical education program each of these misconceptions deserves special
attention.

A lack of the proper understanding of terms such as behavior management, behavior modification, and operant conditioning has led to terminology being used interchangeably, causing confusion among practitioners and professionals alike. These terms are defined as follows:

"Behavior management encompasses all of the strategies that the physical educator utilizes to develop effective and appropriate student behavior...Presently, the most effective behavior management strategy used in the school setting is behavior modification. The purpose of this specific strategy is to elicit a behavior...Respondent and operant conditioning are two basic forms of behavior modification...Operant conditioning involves the use of consequences to increase the probability that a behavior will be strengthened, maintained, or weakened." (Dunn & French, 1982, p. 45).

Many physical educators believe that behavior management programs are dehumanizing and mechanistic, associating these practices with the laboratory research conducted by animal psychologists. However, few physical educators would disagree that an organized and well-taught physical education program is a basic educational need of all children. Therefore, the profession must continuously explore effective teaching strategies to assure that the learning of each student does occur. Behavior management involves exact systematic observation and measurement (Wehman, 1977). When these principles are systematically applied in apositive manner, they allow the physical educator to more effectively communicate student needs to other teachers, administrators, and parents.

The application of reinforcers to students during instruction doesn't have to mean bribery. A definite difference does exist between bribery and reinforcement. Bribery being defined as the illegal use of rewards.or gifts to corrupt the conduct of an individual while reinforcement is designed to change a behavior in such a manner that the student will improve (Kazdin, 1980). When properly administered, reinforcers are an accepted part of everyday life. In fact, how many teachers would continue to work and stay on the job if they were not paid?

Many physical educators fear that once the reinforcement is administered, the individual will only perform the desired behavior for that reward or the desired behavior change will last only for the duration of the particular program. The termination of a reinforcement program does not necessarily mean extinction of the new behavior:

"Changing an individual's behavior sometimes produces noticeable changes of how others in the person's environment respond to him. Even when extrinsic reinforcers are withdrawn, the reactions of others to the person whose behavior was changed may maintain the recently acquired behavior." (Kazdin, 1980, p. 58).

Finally, for reinforcers to be effectively applied, they need not be expensive. Rewarding students with extrinsic reinforcers such as edibles, toys, and money can reach high costs to the teacher's budget. However, the use of tangible reinforcers is not the only means of student reinforcement available to the physical educator. The physical educator setting usually contains readily available reinforcers in the form of equipment and games; such reinforcers add no extra cost to the budget (Allen & Iwata, 1980; McKenzie, 1979).

For instance, the Premack principle is a management system that can be used to reinforce student behavior or performance. This principle is defined simply as a more preferred behavior or activity the student enjoys is received contingent when the student's perform a less preferred behavior (Jansma, 1978). For example, the teacher might state at the beginning of the class, "All students who participate in and successfully complete the warm-up exercise program [the less preferred behavior] at the beginning of class may play 5 minutes on the scooter boards [the more preferred behavior] at the end of class."

Program Application

The following are a few of the teaching strategies that physical educators can use to effectively incorporate behavior management strategies into their classes. These techniques are merely suggestions; the teacher must consider student needs as well as program goals and objectives.

1.   With proper planning, behavior problems can be prevented before they begin. Before students enter the class the teacher should structure the gymnasium to alleviate behavior problems from occuring. For example, carpet squares, lilly pads, or hula hoops can be given to each student and used as their personal space while involved in movement activities. It is also important to give each student his or her own piece of equipment during an activity to keep the students busy and most likely out of trouble.

2.   In any management system the teacher must first identify the particular student behavior to be increased, maintained, or alleviated. This is defined as the target behavior, and this particular behavior must always be observable and measureable (White & Haring, 1980). The student may possess a number of behavior problems; however, at first the teacher should attend to one behavior at a time, choosing the most obvious one.

3.   Implementing a new management system into the program may not work immediately.

The teacher must be patient. At first certain students will want to test the new system and the teacher's consistency.

4.   Develop a plan that is consistent and direct. For example, allow only those students who meet the specific criterion of performing all warm-up exercises to be reinforced with five minutes of play on a minitrampoline at the end of class.

5.   Make class rules simple and clear so students know what is expected of them. Posting rules in the locker room or gymnasium will help to serve as a reminder to students.

6.   Evaluate the management program periodically to determine if the target behavior is being correctly identified and progress is being made. The "A-B-C Analysis" [antecedent - behavior - consequence] is one method that can be used (French & Jansma, 1978). For example, the teacher says, "Line up for attendance [antecedent] the first student to be in his or her designated area and quiet [behavior] will be chosen to lead warm-up exercises" [consequence].

7.   Individualize the behavior management systems to meet the specific needs of the class and each student. The teacher can not assume that one particular management system or reinforcer will work effectively with all students. Reinforcer preference can be determined by observing the student during activity, talking with the student's classroom teacher or parents, who usually know the student best; or by simply asking the student.

8.   Proper timing of certain strategies such as the application of the reinforcer is extremely important. For example, a student may need to be reinforced immediately upon performing the new target behavior. Later, an interval schedule of reinforcers can be introduced with the student earning one point toward a reinforcer for every two minutes the student is on task in a ten minute soccer lesson. When possible, the behavior management program should be explained to the student.

9.   Incorporate the behavior management system in a positive manner; students should never be made to run laps or exercises as a punishment in order to decrease inappropriate behavior. For example, having students earn points toward a reinforcer rather than taking points away will enable the students to feel responsible for their actions.

10.   Involve students in their own behavior management programs by allowing them to

select class rules or determine the particular reinforcers to be used. Students who have input into the system will feel more responsible for and compliant with the management program being used.

In physical education, alternative teaching strategies are needed with students who are undisciplined and seem disinterested. In the past many physical educators have been reluctant to accept behavior management as a justifiable teaching strategy. However, controlling student discipline and promoting interest in physical education, exists to physical educators able to systematically incorporate behavior management programs in their teaching. In short, behavior management is simply good teaching!

References

1. Allen, L. A., & Iwata, B. A. (1980). Reinforcing exercise maintainance: Using existing high-rate activities. Behavior Modification, 4, 337-354.

2. Dunn, J. M., & French, R. W. (1982). Operant conditioning: A tool for special physical educators in the 1980's. Exceptional Education Quarterly, 3, 42-53.

3. Elam, S. M. (1983). The Gallup education surveys: Impressions of a poll watcher. Phi Delta Kappan, 65, 26-32.

4. French, R., & Jansma, P. (July, 1978). Behavior Management. Unpublished Manuscript, University of Utah.

5. Gardner, W. I. (1978). Children with learning and behavioral problems: A behavior management approach. Boston: Allyn & Bacon.

6. Jansma, P. (1978). Operant conditioning principles applied to disturbed male adolescents by a physical educator. American Corrective Therapy Journal, 32, 71-78.

7. Kazdin, A. E. (1980). Behavior modification in applied settings. Homewood, IL: The Dorsey Press.

8. Loovis, M. E. (1980). Behavior modification: Its application in physical education/motor development with children of special needs. American Corrective Therapy Journal, 34, 19-24.

9. McKenzie, T. L. (1979). Token economy research: A review for the physical educator. Motor Skills: Theory into Practice, 3, 102-114.

10. Presbie, R. J., & Brown, P. L. (1977). Physical education: The behavior modification approach. Washington, DC: National Education Association.

11. Siedentop, D. (1983). Developing teaching skills in physical education. Palo Alto, CA: Mayfield.

12. Wehman, P. (1977). Helping the mentally retarded acquire play skills: A behavioral approach. Springfield, IL: Charles C. Thomas.

13. White O. R., & Haring, N. G. (1980). Exceptional teaching. Columbus, OH: Charles E. Merrill.

Take A Lap

Reprinted with permission from: French, R., Lavay, B., & Henderson, H. (1985). Take a lap. Physical Educator, 42, 180-185.

In nature there are neither rewards
nor punishments, there are consequences.

Robert G. Ingersoll
"Some Reasons Why," 1896

Poor sportsmanship, inattention, bullying, fighting, swearing, not dressing out or properly, talking out, and arguing with others are typical forms of inappropriate behaviors that can be observed in physical education classes. A widely used technique by physical educators is punishing a student who displays one of these inappropriate behaviors by requiring the student to "take a lap" or perform numerous exercises such as situps or pushups. Not only do physical educators use physical activity as punishment to decrease inappropriate behavior, but they also use it in an attempt to increase performance. For example, "go-homers" or "get out" swims can elicit good initial efforts, however, the best performers leave class early while the below average performers are "punished" by continuing to swim, run, shoot foul shots, etc.

Is punishment in the form of physical activity appropriate to use in physical education? Initially the teacher may be able to justify this form of punishment because of its immediate results. However, the long term ramifications of punishment must be carefully considered. Our goal as physical educators is to create positive attitudes in our students toward physical activity and sport and ultimately to instill in them a desire to pursue a physically active lifestyle.

Having students exercise or run laps because they are exhibiting inappropriate behaviors may initially make them behave, however, we may be turning students off to physical activity. Punishment needs to be administered and used only as a last resort after all preventative and positive approaches have been exhausted (Gallahue, 1978). The purpose of this paper is to present preventative and alternative positive strategies which can be used to alleviate inappropriate behaviors in the physical education setting.

If the proper preventative and positive measures are applied appropriately and consistently and still do not work, then mild forms of punishment such as time out, response cost, or mild verbal reprimands may be used.

Preventative Techniques

Most inappropriate behaviors can be prevented by having the physical educator initiate preventative classroom management techniques to decrease the probability that inappropriate behavior will occur. Some preventative techniques are:

1). Withitness - This is a trait of teachers who know what is going on in the class at all times (Kounin, 1970). If the students know the teacher is "tuned in" and knows what is going on they will be less likely to misbehave.

2). Movement Management - This is the movement ability of the teacher to structure the activities in the class so they move smoothly from one activity to the next while maintaining momentum (Kounin, 1970).

3). Class Structure - The teacher must structure the class in such a way that: a) all students are participating the maximum amount possible in all activities, b) all students know they are going to be held accountable for performing the skills, and c) all students are paying attention.

4). Teacher Enthusiasm - The teacher must be enthusiastic about what is being taught. Enthusiasm is contagious, so is boredom.

5). Teacher Competence - The students will respect, listen and want to learn from a teacher they feel is competent and knowledgeable of the skills being taught.

6). Self-Sufficiency - The teacher needs to solve problems in the class without the help of an outside authority. If the student is sent to the principal's office each time he/she misbehaves then what the teacher is saying to the student and the principal is "I cannot handle this student."

7). Control of the Physical Environment - Extreme temperatures, improper lighting, lack of ventilation, strong odors, excessive or lack of equipment, inappropriate space, etc., can all create behavior problems. Most of these can be controlled by the teacher.

8). Interest Boosting - If the teacher takes a special interest in a student who may be a potential behavior problem, the student will probably be more willing to cooperate with the teacher.

9). Teacher Proximity - The teacher is a source of protection, strength, and identification. The proximity of the teacher may help control the student's tendency to be disruptive.

10). Classroom Rules - Rules must be established early in the school year. Class rules can be posted in the lockerroom. Once the student knows what behaviors are not acceptable and the consequences of those behaviors the probability of misbehaviors will decrease.

11). Signal Interference - The teacher must possess a number of clearly identifiable positive attention signals such as the time out sign for "get quiet." These signals will only be effective if they are administered consistently and with consequences.

12). Create a Learning Environment - Of utmost importance is the teacher's ability to generate a challenge and interest in every student and to provide motivating and instructionally sound activities.

Positive Techniques

If preventive classroom management techniques are unsuccessful, there are numerous positive techniques that can be initiated to remediate problems: Six of the positive techniques for reducing inappropriate behavior are Modeling, Premack Principle, Group Contingencies, Contracting, Antiseptic Bounce, and Direct Discussion.

1. Modeling: Basically involves imitation learning. A teacher or peer demonstrates a behavior or skill with the expectation that the other student(s) will copy it. For modeling to work effectively, it is crucial that the student is capable of imitating the behavior being modeled. For instance, the teacher can serve as a model by dressing in proper attire and actively participating in class activities. Another example is the teacher who praises a student (model) for standing in line quietly. The other students, then, hopefully, will model the behavior of the student who was praised. In this instance, the teacher has recognized and made a positive statement toward the well-behaved student rather than raising his or her voice to reprimand the noisy student(s), a positive vs. a negative approach.

2. Premack Principle: This principle is, "Do what I want you to do then you can do what you want to do." An example would be for the teacher to tell a student or the entire class that if they pay attention to class instructions and participate in the planned lesson for 30 minutes, they then can play Battleball (or another well-liked activity) for the last 10 minutes of the class.

3. Group Contingencies: Is the presentation of a highly desired reinforcer to a group of students as a unit based on following an appropriate set of rules (Vogler & French, 1983). This procedure may be more effective with other students who seek and desire peer approval rather than teacher approval. Group contingencies can be categorized based on the application of the reinforcement to the entire group or to an individual student as follows: (Smith, 1981):

a. Dependent Group Contingency: A target individual must earn the desired reinforcer for the entire group. To assure that undue peer pressure is not placed on the target individual the instructor must be certain the individual is capable of earning the reinforcement.

b. Independent Group Contingency: A group goal is stated, and the students work individually to earn the desired reinforcer. This strategy eliminates the competitiveness of other group contingencies.

c. Interdependent Group Contingency: Receiving the desired reinforcer is dependent on the behavior of the entire group. This is the most commonly used and the most effective group contingency method. If one student or group of students constantly ruins the chances of the entire group to earn the desired reinforcer, an individual behavior management procedure may need to be implemented. Two examples of group contingency games are the Flip Chart Game and the Good Behavior Game. In the Flip Chart Game (Sulzbacher & Houser, 1968), a scoreboard, or a flip chart numbered from 10 to 0 is placed in the gymnasium with the first card showing being a 10. It is explained to students that the last 10 minutes of the class period will be provided for students to engage in physical education activities they enjoy, however, each time the class or an individual does not follow the class rules outlined previously, the chart will be flipped and the entire group will lose one minute of their reward time. In the Good Behavior Game (Vogler & French, 1983) the instructor places the students in various squads and explains they will earn 10 minutes of free time as a group to engage in physical education activities they enjoy by following class rules outlined previously. For example, each squad begins with 10 points and is awarded 10 minutes of free time if a total of eight points or more are retained by the end of class period. All groups are capable of winning and are not necessarily competing against one another.

4. Contracting: A contract is a written agreement between a teacher and student regarding behavioral or performance improvement. Whenever possible, the student should be allowed to have input into the specific terms of the contract such as the rewards to be earned. The specific guidelines for developing and implementing a contract are (Homme, Csany, Gonzales, & Rech, 1970):

a. Read and explain the conditions of the contract aloud to the student and receive verbal affirmation or a signature.

b. Insure that the contract is fair and suitable to all persons.

c. Design the contract in a positive manner, stressing accomplishments.

d. Design the initial contract in small approximations which will lead to the student meeting the target behavior. This allows for frequent rewards.

e.   Consider reinforcer preference by providing a reward that is highly prized by the student and that is not easily obtained outside the conditions of the contract.

f.   Give reward immediately following adequate compliance with the contract.

g.   Provide a bonus clause to reinforce outstanding and persistent appropriate behavior or performance.

h.   Enforce the contract consistently and systematically.

i.   Renegotiate if the initial contract is ineffective.

j.   Include the dates that the agreement begins and ends.

k.   Insure that the contract is signed by all persons concerned and that each person receives a copy.

l.   Begin the contract as soon as possible after the signing.

5.   Antiseptic Bounce: This technique is used when a student is misbehaving in class and the teacher asks that student to leave the class to go on an errand or leave the group to join another-perhaps to be a leader. Examples of this technique are:

a.   If Jane is teasing Mary, the teacher may ask Jane to go to the office and get the basketball nets or some other item the teacher may need; the mission should be purposeful.

b.   If Jack and Paul are disagreeing about how to perform a drill, the teacher may ask Jack to help Billy put up the soccer nets. The student will be removed from a disruptive situation and provided an opportunity to do something constructive.

6.   Direct Discussion: When a student is misbehaving the teacher may either pull the student aside immediately or tell the student to stay a few minutes after class to talk. The teacher then presents the situation to the student in such a way as to show him why the particular behavior was not conductive to the learning environment. This can be very effective if handled properly.

Punishment

Punishment is the presentation of an unpleasant consequence of a behavior in order to reduce the probability of future occurrence of that behavior. Five basic types of punishment are: a) time out, b) response cost, c) physical activity, d) psychological abuse, and e) physical harm or corporal punishment. As used in a physical education setting, time out and response cost are mild forms of punishment. Moderate forms of punishment are physical activity and psychological abuse. The use of physical harm, or actually hitting the student, is considered the most severe form of punishment.

Punishment is the most frequently used behavior modification technique because it works quickly to decrease inappropriate behavior. However, the use of any type of punishment, mild to severe, has the potential and often an actual effect on the emotional health of both the student being punished and the other students who observe the punishment.

The use of punishment may create a variety of emotional reactions from the student(s), such as fear, anxiety, anger, depression, hostility, and lowered self-esteem. These emotions may cause the student to withdraw or become aggressive. The student may passively withdraw by not paying attention or not participating in class activities. The student could also actively withdraw by not coming to physical education class or by skipping school. The student's hostility may be exhibited in aggressive acts such as making negative verbal remarks to or about the teacher. The student may also model teacher aggression by being aggressive to other students when they do something he/she does not like. Overall punishment negatively effects the student's ability to concentrate on positive and meaningful educational activities.

In addition to the emotional effects, there are other drawbacks in the use of punishment to decrease inappropriate behaviors. Punishment tends to suppress the inappropriate behavior instead on extinguishing it. Frequently, the behavior will recur in the absence of the punisher. Also, when punished behaviors do recur, they usually do so at a higher rate (Sulzer-Azaroff & Mayer, 1977).

If preventative and positive management techniques have been applied appropriately but still do not seem to be decreasing the behavior, mild forms of punishment may need to be resorted to. Such mild forms include time out and response cost.

1.   Time out - The removal of a student from a reinforcing environment contingent upon the emittance of inappropriate behavior in an attempt to decrease that behavior. Time out procedures can take various forms and strategies. Contingent observation, the mildest form, combines modeling and time out procedures. This is an effective technique in physical education because although the student is removed from the group, he/she remains close by to observe peers demonstrating appropriate behavior. If the student enjoys physical activity he/she will desire to reenter and participate. The physical educator may need to arrange with the classroom teacher that students who remain disruptive during the contingent observation period be sent back to the classroom. For example, the following time out procedure can be used:

A student not cooperating in physical education class will be given one warning. On a student's second warning, there will be a two-or-three-minute time out. On the third warning, the student will be sent back to class.

If time out is not working to manage the behavior, it may not be the appropriate procedure or perhaps the location of the time out may be reinforcing to the student if he/she is allowed to talk to other students or play with playground equipment. It is important that the location be isolated from other students such as a painted circle on the playground or a bench. The time out procedure will not be effective with students who do not enjoy physical education class because it will give them the opportunity to escape from an environment they dislike. In such cases, other strategies are needed.

2.   Response Cost - The withdrawal of a certain amount of an extrinsic reinforcer contingent upon the occurrence of an undesired behavior in an attempt to decrease the occurrence of that behavior in the future (Walker & Shea, 1984). This technique is used in everyday situations. For example, police officers use response cost in order to reduce speeding behaviors by giving a speeding ticket which has a fine attached to it. They are taking away a positive reinforcer (money) contingent upon the undesirable behavior (speeding). Teachers use response cost in the classroom when they lower students grades for not dressing out, not participating, disrupting class, etc. Another example might be if the last five minutes of class were going to be devoted to playing scooterboard activities, a student who misbehaves might lose the right to play on the scooterboard.

The three other types of punishment which are more severe include physical activity, psychological abuse, and physical harm. These three types should only be used as a very last resort to control behavior.

1.   Physical Activity - Is often used as a punisher for inappropriate behavior. For example if a student is displaying poor sportsmanship the teacher may instruct him/her to "Take a Lap." This technique has many repercussions for the student who is punished. The student learns to dislike physical activity which may generalize to dislike of the teacher and/or physical education. In addition, the negative effects of punishment as discussed earlier may apply with the use of this technique.

2.   Psychological Abuse - Refers to those situations in which the teacher verbally abuses the student for inappropriate behavior. This can be done in private or even worse, in front of the student's peers. Both have humiliating effects on the student and almost

always result in some emotional trauma for the student.

3.   Physical Harm or Corporal Punishment - Is the most severe form of punishment. This technique is not recommended for use in the educational environment because of the extreme negative consequences that can occur.

In summary, due to the potential negative side effects of punishment, other preventive and positive approaches to behavior management need to be explored so the teacher does not resort to the punishment in desperation. It was the intent of this paper to provide the physical educator with alternatives to the use of physical activity as a punisher, since our goal is not to turn students off to physical activity but to turn them on to its many positive benefits.The potential negative side effects of punishment make exploring other preventive and positive approaches to behavior management more desirable. Teachers should not have to resort to punishment in desperation but rather should enter class with a positive systematic plan of behavior management. Providing alternatives to the use of punishment will enable physical educators to turn students on to the many positive benefits of physical education rather than turn them off.

References

Gallahue, D. (1978). Punishment and control-Part I: Negative results. Physical Educator, 35, 58-59.

Homme, L., Csany, A., Gonnzales, M., & Rech, J. (1970). How to use contingency contracting in the classroom. Champaign, IL: Human Kinetics Pub. Co.

Kounin, J. (1970). The Kounin Model: Withitness, alerting and group management. Discipline and group management in classrooms. New York: Holt, Rinehart and Winston.

Smith, D. D. (1981). Teaching the learning disabled. Englewood Cliffs: Prentice-Hall.

Sulzbacher, S. I., & Houser, J. E. (1968). A tactic to eliminate disruptive behaviors in the classroom: Group contingent consequences. American Journal of Mental Deficiency, 73, 88-90.

Sulzer-Azaroff, B., & Mayer, G. R. (1977). Applying behavior analysis procedures with children and youth. New York: Holt, Rinehart & Winston.

Vogler, W., & French, R. (1983). The effects of a group contingency strategy on behaviorally disordered students in physical education. Research Quarterly for Exercise and Sport, 54, 273-277.

Walker, J., & Shea, T. (1984). Behavior management. St. Louis: Times Mirror/Mosby

LEARNING DISABLED

A specific definition is difficult to determine as this group of individuals do not learn for a variety of reasons. One commonality among this population is that an educationally significant discrepancy between their estimated intellectual potential and actual academic achievement exists. The definition does not include children who have learning problems that are the result of vision, hearing, motor, or mental retardation; or of environmental, cultural, or economic disadvantage.

Etiology
Incident rates vary because of differences in definition and diagnostic procedures. The most common theory is that a neurological impairment exists.

Characteristics
Persons with a learning disability are a heterogeneous group and may exhibit one or more of these characteristics as outlined by Milne, Haubenstricker, & Seefelt (1991):
1. May exhibit a developmental delay lagging behind their age qroup peers in certain fundamental movements.
2. Inconsistency in performance often vacilating when performing certain skills.
3. Perseveration is the continious performance of a task when the circumstance no longer requires it.
4. Mirroring: copies movements and can not exhibit independent movements from verbal cues.
5. Asymmetry: of body parts in activities that require bilateral use of limbs. Body limbs stablized in a rigid fashion.
6. Falling after performance: may exhibit a loss of balance after performing a movement.
7. Extraneous movements: do not perform skills in a smooth and efficient manner. For example, flailing the arms while running.
8. Inability to control force: exhibits too much force during skills requiring control.
9. Inappropriate motor planning. Many times the appropriate motor response is dependent on sensory input with past experiences.

Specific Programming Considerations:
Persons with a learning disability are a heterogeneous group and consequently programming may need to be on an individual basis.

1. A number of students may be under medication to control attention span deficits and behavior problems. This medication can have an adverse effect on motor performance (French & Jansma, 1992).

2. Programming may be necessary on a long term basis. Consider early childhood and parent intervention with quality movement instruction.

3. Initially structure the environment designing the program to be teacher directed. Eliminate all irrelevant stimuli and have the child focus in on only the most important teaching cues. For example, be sure the child is making eye contact with the teacher and listening to instructions.

4. Make directions clear and concise. Have the student repeat the instructions you have provided before starting the particular activity.

5. Use behavior management systems such as tangible feedback and positive reinforcement. Display attention span deficit disorders.

6. Each class period should consist of strategies for teaching students to move under control and with proper force. For example, impulse control games and relaxation techniques can be utilized. See relaxation techniques outlined on page 92

7. Attention span may be short. Therefore, plan for a number of activities spending a shorter amount of time on each than you would with other children of the same age (Sherill & Pyfer, 1985).

8. Initially, the program should be designed to promote sensory input functioning before concentrating on perceptual motor

integration or output behavior (Sherrill & Pyfer, 1985).

9. Provide for a positive program. These children have failed so
often their movement confidence may be low.

10. The learning disabled are a very heterogenous group. Therefore
the program should be individualized to meet student movement
needs.

Excellent resources include:

Haubensticker, J.L. (1982). Motor Development in Children with LD.
JOPERD, 53(5), 41-42.
Milne, C. D., Haubenstricker, J.L., & Seefelt, V. D. (1991). Remedial motor
education: Some practical suggestions. Strategies. 4(4), 15-18.
Sherrill, C. & Pyfer, J.L. (1985). Learning disabled students in
physical education. Adapted Physical Activity Quarterly, 2, 283-291.

INCORPORATING RELAXATION TECHNIQUES
IN PHYSICAL EDUCATION CLASS

Advantages of Teaching Relaxation Techniques
1. Aids students in conserving energy and moving in a smooth, coordinated manner while performing various motor skills and activities.
2. Helps calm hyperactive students and enables them to focus on the skill at hand.
3. Teaches the student a socially appropriate way to control his/her emotions when upset, or how to handle a stressful situation.

Teaching Tips
1. These techniques may be used when students become too excited during a game, or incorporated into the last few minutes of physical education class to calm a student before returning to class. The classroom teacher will thank you!
2. Setting should be as quiet as possible.
3. Lights dimmed, if possible, to reduce stimuli.
4. Dress should be comfortable, wearing loose-fitting clothing.
5. Positioning may be lying in a supine manner or sitting cross-legged.
6. Soft music may enhance the students' mood to relax.
7. The instructor's voice should be soothing, slow, and comforting.

Various Activities
1. Breathing techniques: Teach students to take slow, deep breaths, inhaling through nose and exhaling through the mouth while maintaining a rhythm.
2. Tension-relaxation techniques: Teach students to tense and relax various muscle groups, starting from the head and moving to the feet.
3. Impulse control games: Teach students to move their body parts as slowly as possible. Examples: walking on the moon, moving in a sea of jello, being a slowly melting ice cream cone.
4. Fantasy trips: Have the students imagine pleasant scenes such as walking in a forest, sitting by a campfire or watching a sunset.

VISUALLY IMPAIRED & BLIND

PL 101-476 defines visual impairment as a condition that even with correction, adversely affects a child's educational performance. The term includes partially seeing and blind.

Differences between the partially sighted and the blind exist. The educational definition of the two follows:

Blind: Those who are so severely visually impaired they exhibit a complete loss of sight.

Partially Sighted (functional): Visual acuity better than 20/200, but not greater than 20/70 in the better eye (unable to read a newspaper) (Seaman & DePauw, 1989).

Classification (Seaman & DePauw, 1989):

Level	Description
Legal blindness 20/200	The ability to see at 20 feet with the better eye what the normal eye can see at 200 feet.
Travel vision 10/200.	The ability to see at 5 to 10 feet what the the normal eye can see at 200.
Motion perception 5/200	The ability to see at 3 to 5 feet what the normal eye can see at 200 feet. This ability is limited almost entirely to motion.
Light Perception 3/200	The ability to distinguish a strong light at less than a distance of 3 feet from the eye what the normal eye would see at 200 feet. Motion of the hand at 3 feet would be undetected.
Total blindness	The inability to recognize or respond to a strong light shone directly into the eyes.

Age of Onset:
The age of onset at which the visual impairment occurs is also an important consideration. Blindisms which are extrationary movements such as rocking are the result of the individual's need to receive sensory stimulation through movement.

Developmental Considerations:
1. Vision affects movement: Delayed development may be due to lack of mobility and exploring the individual's environment which is due to lack of or poor vision.
2. These individuals in general display difficulties in spatial perception, laterality, and body image.
3. Parental attitudes of these individuals may be one of overprotection.
4. The classification system and the severity of sight loss is an important teaching consideration.
5. Severity of the visual impairment: The more severe the visual impairment the lower the fitness level displayed by the individual (Winnick, 1985).

Programming Considerations:
1. Proper mobility training with this population is extremely important. Consider sound awareness, location, & environment (Eichstaedt & Kalakian, 1987).
2. Physical fitness training is important because everyday transport and mobility is much more difficult.
3. Provide feedback regarding maintaince of proper posture and walking gait as these individuals in general display poor posture, because they have no visual model.
4. Utilize a buddy system with a visual partner assisting the visual impaired individual during activities.
5. Make all verbal instructions clear and complete. Also use physical guidance, however, don't over-assist. Do not shout during instruction.
6. Through out activity provide points of reference verbally or through sound. For example, "take 5 steps forward and then turn left."
7. Provide large tangible markings for boundaries. For example, follow a railing during a run on a track.
8. Clear all unnecessary equipment during and after class.

9. These persons can participate in the majority of physical activities offered. At times some slight modifications may be necessary.

Excellent resources include:

Buell, C. (1975). <u>Physical education for blind children</u>. Springfield, IL: Charles C. Thomas.

Winnick, J.P. (1985). The performance of visually impaired youngsters in physical education activities: Implications for mainstreaming. <u>Adapted Physical Activity Quarterly</u>, <u>2</u>, 292-299.

HEARING IMPAIRED & DEAF

It is important to realize that a difference between the deaf and the hearing impaired exist. P.L. 101-476 defines the difference between the two as follows:

"Deaf" means a hearing impairment which is so severe that the child is impaired in processing linguistic information through hearing, with or without amplification, which adversely affects educational performance...

 "Hard of hearing" means a hearing impairment whether permanent or fluctuating, which adversely affects a child's educational performance but which is not included under the definition of deaf.

Classification
The hearing losses used in the classification system from Eichstaedt & Kalakian (1987) follows:

Normal	-10-26 dB	
Slight	27-40 dB	difficulty hearing distance speech
Mild	41-55 dB	favorable sitting, can understand conversational speech 3-5 ft away
Moderate	56-70 dB	can understand loud conversations, needs hearing aid
Severe	71-89 dB	may hear loud voices 1 foot away and identifies environmental sounds
Profound	90 dB & >	relies on vision rather than hearing

Etiology:
Genetics accounts for 50 % of the causes. Other causes include accidents and illness.

Onset of Hearing Loss

The age the individual acquires the hearing loss is another important consideration. If the deafness occurs at birth or the first few years of life there will be little opportunity for language development. Too often the hearing impaired are delayed in educational achievement which is due to lack of incidental learning and not necessarily intellectual functioning.

Developmental Considerations
1. Youngsters with a hearing impairment etiology other than vestibular dysfunction do not differ significantly from age group peers in balance activities (Schmidt, 1985).

2. The research has not clearly identified if a difference exists in the motor ability and characteristics between the hearing impaired and their age group peers.

3. The intensity or classification of the hearing loss is an important teacher consideration.

Summary: It is important for the teacher to take into consideration all of the following factors: (a) degree of loss, (b) age of onset, (c) type of impairment, & (d) etiology (Eichstaedt & Kalakian,1987).

Program Considerations

1. Effective communication between the teacher, hearing impaired youngster and classmates is most important. Make sure the hearing impaired youngster can see you when providing instruction. During instruction always face the student.
2. Utilize total communication skills. For example, demonstrate skills and use vision while keeping verbalization to a minimum. However, too much stimuli or physical assistance may be distracting.
3. Learn a few basic signs to begin communication as well as utilizing hand signals for fostering attention. Eichstaedt & Kalakian (1987) provide the reader with approximately 50 signs which can assist in physical education programming.

4. Incorporate effective visual aids, charts, pictures and label equipment.
5. Because of deficits in communication skills these individuals tend to socially withdraw and isolate themselves from the group. Encourage student interaction through activities, games, and sports.
6. Incorporate a buddy system in which a hearing partner assists the hearing impaired individual with instruction of the activity.
7. Allow the individual time to initially watch others before beginning the activity. Modeling appropriate movements is important for these individuals.
8. It is a misconception that all individuals with a hearing impairment have balance problems. Only those with equilibrium damage will display deficits in this area. A variety of static and dynamic balance activities should be offered. However, balance activities involving heights and spinning may be contraindicated.
9. Effective teacher demonstration is important, however, keep in mind too much can detract from the students creativity (Schmidt, 1985).

These program considerations were adopted from the following references and are excellent resources:

Kraft, R.E. (1981). Movement experiences for children with auditory handicaps. Physical Educator, 38, 35-38.

Schmidt, S. (1985). Hearing impaired students in physical education. Adapted Physical Activity Quarterly, 2, 300-306.

Stewart, K.A. (1984). The hearing impaired student in physical education. Palaestra, 1, 35-37.

POSTURAL DEVIATIONS

The individual should display and maintain proper body mechanics throughout all movements. Body segments should support each other in proper vertical alignment directly over the base of support.

In the past (1920s to 1950s) a major emphasis in special physical education had been corrective exercise programs to remediate postural deviations. Currently, programs are emphasizing skill, game, and sport progressions. However, exercise programs to counterbalance and remediate postural deviations should remain an integral part of all physical activity programs.

Two major types of postural deviations exist (Dunn & Fait, 1989):

1. Structural: Bony tissue or structure of the body is affected to the point that the deviation is only correctable through surgery. This may result from a congenital abnormality, trauma, or a functional deviation that was ignored over a period of time.

2. Functional: The deviation is in the muscle or connective tissue causing an imbalance. The bony tissue is not affected. When soft tissue alone is involved the condition can be corrected through a therapeutic exercise program.

Evaluation:
To determine if the deviation is functional or structural have the individual assume hang with both arms from a bar. If the deviation is functional the problem will straighten out.

One quick screening method is to have the child assume the "Adam's position" in which the child bends over as if he or she was touching their toes. The instructor can then examine the child's curvature of the spine.

All students' posture should be routinely evaluated. An excellent assessment device is the New York State Posture Test, Project ACTIVE revised.

Classification:

Scoliosis: A rotolateral curvature of the spine with as many as 20%
of the school age population displaying this problem. A single
curve (C shape) or a double curve (S shape) may exist.

Lordosis (hollow back): Results in an increase in the lumbar curve
creating a strain on the abdomen. There is a forward or
downward tilt of the pelvis. This condition is normal among
preschool and young elementary school-aged children.

Kyphosis (hunchback): Abnormal increase in the amount of curvature
to the spine or thoracic region which causes round shoulders and
a forward head tilt.

Winged Scapula: Occurs when both shoulder blades are further away
from the spinal column than normal. Slow developing or weak
muscles cause this condition. This condition is normal among
preschool and elementary school-aged children.

Contraindicated Exercises

Be aware of exercises that may be harmful to the individual's condition. The
exercise program should be designed so as to remediate the specific postural
deviation exhibited in the individual.

Programming Considerations:

Two excellent books which contain remedial exercise programs for various
postural deviations are:

Adams, R.D., & McCubbin, J. (1990). Games, sports, and exercises for the
physically handicapped (5th ed). Philadelphia: Lea & Febiger.

Crowe, W.C., Auxter, D., & Pyfer, J. (1981). Principle and methods of
adapted physical education and recreation. St. Louis: C.V. Mosby.

OVERWEIGHT & OBESITY

French & Jansma (1992), have stated that a person is:

Overweight: 10 to 20% over expected weight for height and body frame.

Obese: Men 20% over expected weight for height and body frame, women 30% over expected weight for height and body frame.

The physical educator should be more concerned with measuring the individual's percent body fat rather than using reference tables based on height, weight and body frame measurements (males 10-15%, females 15-20%).

Etiology:

Many factors are interrelated to the cause of this problem:
(a.) Genetics (b.) Sedentary lifestyle (c.) Overeating & (d.) Psychological

Obesity Tendencies:

A child without an obese parent has only a 10% chance of being obese. One obese parent increases the chances for that child by 40% and with two obese parents the risk doubles (Sherrill, 1986).

The Vicious Cycle of Obesity:

A. Child is overweight or obese.
B. Poor self-image and body is perceived as undesirable.
C. Not accepted by peers and socially isolates from others.
D. Lack of activity refusing to be seen or participate in public.
E. Continued cycle of overweight and obesity.

The following is an excellent school weight management program: Physical Management- Adapted Physical Education for Overweight Students. Ellen Solberg, Project Director, PO Box 891, Billings, Montana, 59103.

Exercise and Weight Control

Common misconceptions regarding exercise and weight control are:
1. Overeating is the major cause of an individual becoming overweight. NO! Research indicates that inactivity is the leading cause and often an overweight person may consume less calories than an active person.
2. Exercise requires little calorie expenditure, therefore increasing physical activity will rarely change a person's weight. NO! In fact, energy cost is proportional to body weight. If two people are performing the same bout of exercise, the overweight person will burn more calories than the person of less weight.
3. An increase in physical activity will cause in increase in appetite. NO! Vigorous physical activity actually decreases the appetite and when possible should be planned close to meal time.
4. You can spot reduce and lose weight in certain areas. NO! In fact, you draw from total fat stores not just a particular area. What often happens initially when dieting is a loss of water weight. Special diets can be dangerous because you don't receive the essential nutrients needed for every day activity.

The Facts Are:
1. Maintaining a desired body weight is rather simple, a balance must exist between the number of calories taken into the body (eaten) and the number of calories burned (exercise).
2. Two alternatives (diet & exercise) exist and should be sensibly combined. In fact, the U.S. Health Department recommends never losing more than 2 lbs. per week. Does this mean starving to death and running a marathon each day? No, rather a sensible approach must be taken by combining the two over an extended period of time. The key is "lifestyle change and commitment."
3. To lose one pound of weight, 3,500 calories must be burned. At first this may seem like a monumental task, however, reducing calorie intake by 250 calories (not eating a donut or drinking a milkshake) per day and burning 250 calories (running 3 miles or slow swimming for an hour) per day will lead to the reduction of 500 calories per day. Continuing this program for a week (7 x 500 = 3500) would lead to the reduction of 1 lb. Maintain this program and in 10 weeks you have lost 10 lbs!

Programming:

French & Jansma (1992), offer the following suggestions for designing a program:

1. Work in a transdisciplinary approach, no one professional can develop the program alone. Family support is paramount (outside of school). Involvement from the physician, school nurse, counselor, classroom teacher, and friends is paramount.
2. Develop a management program system that meets the needs of the particular student. Research indicates a contract approach which combines activity with proper eating habits is a most effective approach. Do not weigh the child every day.
3. Programs should be aerobic in nature; progress slowly with exercise monitored carefully. Walking programs are excellent.
4. Utilize frequent rest periods or areas to rest during activities, always encouraging involvement.
5. Program for fundamental skill development, because of excess weight, these individuals may have a fear of falling and develop incorrect patterns to compensate for these movements. If they can not perform these skills, they will never be accepted by peers and asked to participate.
6. Individual self competition in which the student competes against a previous standard is better than team competition. Again, encourage involvement and not so much winning.

Contraindicated Activities

1. Inner thighs may be constantly rubbing against one another during exercise and cause chaffing. The student should be made aware of this problem and how to effectively manage the problem.
2. Activities requiring body support such as gymnastics may be extremely difficult.
3. Avoid activities involving quick movements that require sudden stopping or changing of direction. These activities can cause damage to joints, ankles, or knees.
4. Be aware of the psychological ramifications of the program and how the child feels. For example, during participation allow the student to wear a warm-up suit.

CEREBRAL PALSY

Cerebral palsy is defined as damage to the brain's motor center causing movement dysfunction. It is characterized by paralysis, weakness, uncoordination, and a retention of the primitive reflexes. Cerebral palsy is not contagious or progressive. However, it is not curable because any brain cell damage is irreversible. In summary damage occurs to the CNS causing muscular weakness and dysfunction.

Etiology
90% of the cases occur before and during birth and are a result of oxygen deprivation, poisoning, cerebral bleeding, or direct trauma to the brain.

Classification Systems (3 types of systems exist, Eichstaedt & Kalakian, 1987).
Physiological Classification: (observed clinically to the reflex pattern of the child)
1. Spastic (66%): Significant increase in muscle tone (hypertonus) characterized by exaggerated stretch reflexes making free movement quite difficult.
   Stretch reflex: When the prime movers are activated to perform a movement the antagonistic muscles do not relax. These muscles resist stretching and recoil making voluntary movements difficult. This often limits range of motion, making movement stiff & rigid.

2. Athetoid (20-30%): Continuous overflow and purposeless involuntary movement of the involved part of the body. Little muscle tone (hypotonus) is displayed. These persons move in a slow and wormlike motion. Lack of head control causing visual tracking difficulty.

3. Ataxia (8%): Display disorders of balance and kinesthetic sense limiting spatial awareness. Movement appears as if the person is in a drunken state.

4. Rigid (4%): Constant muscle tension in both the agonist and antagonist muscle groups causes diminished movement (tends to freeze movement). This type is associated with severe retardation and brain damage.

Topographical Involvement: (clinical classification regarding involved body parts). Movement difficulties to parts of the body such as paraplegia, hemiplegia, triplegia, quadriplegia and diplegia.

Broad categories of mild to severe describe the degree of motor involvement to each area or limb.
Mild: can walk adequately, needing no particular care.
Moderate: difficulty with speech and movements such as locomotion.
Severe: limited to a wheelchair, nonambulatory.

Program Considerations

1. Do not expect high quality and efficient movement (French & Jansma, 1992). These individuals should never be rushed into exercise and physical activity programs. Teach movement control.
2. Incorporate relaxation training into the overall program (see pg. 92). Relaxation and rest periods should be incorporated during and after program activities with certain classifications such as athetoid & ataxia.
3. Movement efficiency will deteriorate with fatigue. Therefore, physical fitness training is important because muscular inefficiency makes everyday movement and functional skills difficult to conduct. Fatigue and improper handling will lead to more movement difficulties.
4. Structure the environment to minimize excitement and external stimuli. If the individual becomes too excited, movement will become inhibited and deteriorate.
5. Handling students, allowing them proper support and physical assistance during exercises and activities is extremely important. The individual should be made to feel safe and comfortable, and not fearful of falling during performance.
6. Do not startle the person when approaching the individual to provide physical assistance. Avoid loud sudden noises if possible during activities.
7. Lack of head control may cause difficulty in vision and the abiilty to track objects.
8. Be aware that the retention of primitive reflexes may remain with many of these individuals throughout life; therefore, they must learn to cope with this inconvenience (Sherrill, 1986).
9. Swimming is an excellent activity because the buoyancy of the

water allows the individual to move in a medium that is virtually impossible on land. The water in the pool should be warm (85) as muscles will tighten up if the water is too cold.

10. Incorporate a team approach by working closely when possible with the physical therapist and other professionals.

11. Be aware of exercises and activities that are contraindicated. For example, individuals with athetoid and ataxia should perform holding positions and exercises while individuals displaying spasticity and rigidity should perform slow range of motion and relaxation exercises (French & Jansma, 1982).

12. It is extremely important to properly warm-up before performing any activity.

13. These individuals should be afforded the opportunity to participate in sport. Information is available through the United States Cerebral Palsy Athletic Association (USCPAA).

14. The physical educator should work closely with the individual to determine what sports the person can successfully participate in and enjoy. For example see the article by Sherrill, C. & Rainbolt, W.J. (1986). Sociological perspectives of cerebral palsy sports. Palaestra, 24, 21-26, 50.

An excellent resource is:
Jones, J. A. (1988). (Ed). Training guide to cerebral palsy sports. Champaign, IL: Human Kinetics.

SEIZURE DISORDERS

One of the least understood disabilities and is commonly referred to as convulsive disorder or epilepsy. With proper supervision this individual can participate in most physical activities.

Definition: Neurological condition triggered by an irregular series of excessive electrochemical brain waves. During a convulsion the body or parts of the body react to the brain wave irregularly by tensing or contracting involuntarily (French & Jansma, 1992).

Types - A variety of conditions exist; however, the two most common are:

1. Grand Mal: most common & severe resulting in a spastic jerking phase. Dramatic manifestation, resulting in falling to the ground. 10% of all seizures are this type.
2. Petit Mal: short seizure (1-30 secs.) characterized by a daze appearance with no falling.

French & Jansma (1992) caution physical educators to be aware of the condition and consider the following during instruction:

1. Physical fatigue and intense concentration can trigger the disorder. Be aware of certain clues, such as lack of sleep.
2. Because of the stigma attached to seizure disorders, many individuals and families will attempt to conceal this condition.
3. There is a possibility of injury from falling during a Grand Mal seizure.
4. Some seizure disorder individuals may be taking heavy doses of anticonvulsant drugs which tend to affect muscle coordination and consequently, participation in movement activity.

Instructional Strategies:

French & Jansma (1992) offer the following adminstrative procedures for handling a Grand Mal seizure:

1. Remain calm: allow the seizure to run its course as it can not be stopped. Do not restrain the individual.
2. Assist the pupil who is collapsing to the ground, lowering the body gradually to a cushioned soft spot if possible. Do not allow the head to bang.
3. Be sure to clear all obstacles and equipment in the general area in order to prevent injuries while the body is thrashing.
4. If it is common for the student to fall during the seizure a helmet may need to be worn.
5. Loosen any tight fitting clothing on the individual and turn the individual to their side. Keep them comfortable through out the course of the seizure.
6. Observe the pupil throughout the seizure, and allow the rest of the class to continue the particular activity they were engaged in.
7. After the seizure the individual will be exhausted so allow time for rest.
8. Above all, keep your poise as an instructor during the course of the seizure. Report the seizure to the school nurse.

Preventative Techniques:

1. Be aware of all students in your classes who have had seizures in the past. The degree of the seizure will vary from time to time, among each particular student, some will have their seizures under control and others will not.
2. Always be aware of and have these students easily identifiable and in your vision during activity.
3. Intense (cardiovascular) activity should be monitored very carefully and a program should be designed which adheres to a gradual progression.
4. Any activity that would be considered dangerous if a seizure occurs could be considered contraindicated (such as climbing activities). During swimming activities the individual should have a buddy. Also, diving and underwater swimming is not recommended (French & Jansma, 1992).

DIABETES

Definition:
An abnormal metabolic condition in which the body is unable to properly utilize sugar, either because there is an insufficient amount of insulin or because the body can not adequately use the insulin produced (French & Jansma, 1992). In summary, it is the inability of the body to metabolize or utilize foods properly for energy.

Etiology:
Although the specific cause of diabetes is unknown at present, proper diet, weight control, and exercise are major components of properly managing diabetes. Excess weight will cause a strain on the heart, circulatory system, pancreas, and liver.

Two types exist (Eichstaedt & Kalakian, 1987):

Type I or Juvenile Diabetes: occurs in 10 to 20% of the diabetics diagnosed before the age of 18. This individual can not produce insulin and is usually slender.

Type II or mature Onset Diabetes: the blood glucose level will increase after eating, but the body can not use the glucose for energy. This person retains some ability to produce natural insulin, but exhibits excess body fat.

Common symptoms: It is important to determine from the school nurse which children are identified as diabetic. However, some children may be unaware that they have diabetes. Common symptoms include excess thirst & hunger, frequent urination, loss of weight, fatigue, & a slow healing of cuts and bruises.

Program Considerations:

The majority of students with this condition can actively engage in physical education with supervision. French & Jansma (1992) offer the following teaching considerations:

1. Determine physical activity tolerance levels by discussing this matter with the student, nurse, parents, and/or physician. The student should be made aware of their own warning signs.
2. Avoid self-imposed circulatory restrictions such as wearing tight fitting clothing during activity.
3. Be aware that a hard bout of exercise with little food intake can cause "insulin shock." Coordinate food and insulin intake with your physical activity program. Food or insulin may need to be adjusted especially when the student is going to increase their activity level.
4. Moderate progression is important in an exercise program. When possible keep the program consistent and systematic from day to day .
5. The student's metabolic rate can be influenced by psychological stress. Therefore proper exercise can have a relaxing therapeutic effect on the body's system. However, extreme competition can also influence metabolic rate.
6. Because of restricted blood flow attention must be given to skin care especially regarding proper foot care. This can become a problem during extreme exercise or if cuts or bruises occur and remain unattended.

Excellent resources are:
Engerbretson, D. (1977). The diabetic in physical education. Journal of Physical Education and Recreation, 48, 18-21.

Rush, G. S. & Rush, T. L. (1988). Understanding diabetes and exercise. Physical Educator, 45, 124-128.

Winnick, J.P. (1970). Planning physical activity for the diabetic. The Physical Educator, 27, 15-16.

ASTHMA

A chronic lung disorder causing a swelling of the mucus membrane lining of the bronchial tubes and excessive secretion of mucus. This condition causes excessive coughing, wheezing, breathlessness, and a constriction in the chest (Dunn & Fait, 1989). There is a narrowing of the air tubes in the lungs which consequently restricts breathing.

Etiology

Asthma is a most prevalent childhood disease. Sherrill (1986) reports that over 6 million American youngsters under the age of 15 years suffer from this condition. Extrinsic asthma is caused by an irritability of the bronchi to different types of substances such as animal fur, cold air, dust, pollens, cigarette smoke, etc. Intrinsic asthma which is less prevalent and is exercise induced.

Developmental Considerations

1. Asthma attacks can vary greatly in severity and duration among individuals. According to Dunn & Fait (1989), these attacks progress through three stages:
    (a) a hacking nonproductive cough is the first warning,
    (b) breathlessness (dypsnea) consisting of a wheezing of air in and out of constricted bronchial tubes and accumulated mucus, and
    (c) severe bronchial obstruction which places the individual in an emergency state.

2. Exercise-induced Asthma (EIA) refers to asthma attacks which are induced by exercise usually after 6-8 minutes of exercise. Sherrill (1986), states the newly accepted principle is intermittent exercise consisting of no more than 5 minutes of vigorous activity followed by 5 minutes of rest, etc. This should include an adequate warm up and cool down period.

3. Treatment to prevent or stop an attack may include avoidance of irritants, medication, and relaxation (French and Jansma, 1992).

4. Two techniques useful in removing excess mucus consist of drinking room temperature liquids and assuming certain postural positions for drainage of various portions of the lungs.

An excellent resource is:

Rimmer, J. H . (1989). A vigorous physical education program for children with exercise induced asthma. Journal of Physical Education, Recreation & Dance, 60 (6),91-95 .

Program Considerations:

1. Be aware that some parents and physicians will be over
   protective and may wish to have the child with asthma
   avoid all physical activity.
2. According to the American Academy of Pediatrics children with
   asthma should be encouraged to participate in physical education
   especially activities which are aerobic in nature. These
   children can derive the same benefits as all other children.
3. Intense aerobic activity should be closely monitored and
   progressive in nature. Students who possess exercise-
   induced asthma should be placed on an intermittent schedule of
   exercise. Exercise progress must be carefully monitored.
4. Certain medications the child is taking may cause possible
   side effects on the individual's movement performance and behavior.
5. Provide games which assists the student's expiration and
   clears mucus from the passages of the lungs. Include activities such as
   laughing marathons, balloon and ping pong relays (Sherrill, 1986).
6. Many children with asthma will breathe incorrectly, in a rapid & insufficient
   manner. Breathing must be taught to be relaxed & not forced (Eichstaedt &
   Kalakian, 1987). See page 92.
7. A change in the physical education environment can have an
   adverse effect on the child with asthma. For example, activities
   held outdoors under extreme weather changes may prove
   difficult for these students to adjust to and handle.
8. Stress may not only cause an attack but can help to extend its
   course. During an attack help the child to remain calm while
   finding an area where the child can be alone and avoid embarrassment.
9. Allow the student to frequently drink fluids during activities.
   Cold drinks, however, are contraindicated because they can cause
   a spasm to the bronchial tubes.
10. Swimming is an excellent activity for these individuals because
    of the environment in terms of humidity and temperature.
11. The student may not know or want to understand the nature and or
    limitations associated with their condition. It is important to educate
    the child with asthma about their condition.

MUSCULAR DYSTROPHY

Definition:
This condition is characterized by degeneration and atrophy of the muscle tissue in the body. It is a muscle disorder which weakens muscle groups (usually on both sides of the body). The muscular systems progressively deteriorates and there is no known treatment to reverse this condition.

Etiology:
The cause is unknown, however, researchers believe a defective gene is linked to the condition.

Four forms of muscular dystrophy affect school-aged children with Duchenne's Muscular Dystrophy being the most common (Eichstaedt and Kalakian, 1987).

Program Considerations:
Physical activity should be selected carefully, with consideration given to the following:

1. Periodic rest breaks and rest areas should be utilized. The physical educator should know the child's work tolerance and not exercise the child past undue fatigue.
2. The area where the activity is taking place should never be damp, as this can lead to respiratory infection. Avoid damp lockerrooms and swimming areas.
3. Stretching and range of motion exercises should be part of the program to not only prevent atrophy but to help reduce muscle contractures and tight muscles.
4. Be aware of stages of muscle degeneration the individual is going through especially regarding ambulation. Although this can not be controlled or stopped, developing an exercise program will help maintain endurance and strength in the functional muscle which will arrest deterioration of the diseased muscle tissue (Croce, 1987).
5. These children may demonstrate emotionally immaturity due to over protective parents.
6. Design activities for social interaction to help the child develop emotionally. Therefore, it is important to teach leisure skills which can be played with peers, especially for children in the later stages

who are nonambulatory.

7. During the early stages of the condition, the individual may be misunderstood and teased by peers. This person may be viewed by peers as weak (Eichstaedt & Kalakian, 1987).

8. In the later stages of the condition use correct techniques to lift, and position children. Work with other professionals such as the OT and PT who have expertise in these areas.

9. Be aware that this individual may eventually need to leave your class. Death occurs usually from respiratory failure and deterioration of the heart in Duchenne Muscular Dystrophy by the age of 20.

An excellent resource is:

Croce, R.V. (1987). Exercise and physical activity in managing progressive muscular dystrophy: A review for practitioners. Palestra: The Forum of Sport, Physical Education, and Recreation for the Disabled; 3(3), 9-15.

THE ORTHOPEDICALLY IMPAIRED

Sherrill (1986) has identified a variety of different types of orthopedic conditions. Examples include persons who use a prostheses, wear braces, ambulate with crutches or a cane, and maneuver in a wheelchair. This population can be further divided into ambulatory and nonambulatory, congenital (birth), acquired (disease), temporary or permanent, and degree of severity.

Examples of congenital impairments include club foot, cleft palate and/or lip, spina bifida, congenital dislocation of the hip (CDH), amputee. Acquired can include such disease or trauma to the body as cancer, poliomyelitis, growth disorders (i.e. Perthes Disease, Osgood-Schlatter disease, amputee). Many orthopedic impairments are not handicaps in the sense that movement is restricted. These persons learn to compensate and adapt to the inconvenience.

Regardless of the type of program offered whether it is therapeutic, competitive, and/or leisure the goal of the program is to afford the individual with a orthopedic impairment the opportunity to find personal achievement in selected activities (Adams & McCubbin, 1990).

Program Considerations:

In general it must be remembered that with this population many different types of orthopedic conditions exist within a wide range of abilities. Programs must always be developed with the individual in mind.

The following general programming considerations and the role of the physical educator were taken from Winnick & Short (1985):

1. The foundation of the program should be based on the direction, recommendations, and records of a qualified physician.
2. Plan well rounded programs with activities that would be typically included in the scope of physical education programming including physical fitness. Do not plan for only specific exercises.
3. It may be necessary to include related services (i.e. physical therapy) to enhance programming. These professional must work closely together to coordinate efforts to meet the student's unique needs.

4. Plan programs for both affected & nonaffected parts of the body. It is important to consult with the student's physician. Care must always be taken not to place undue stress or muscular imbalance on the unaffected body part. Consider balance in program design.

5. Assist the individual in the use supportive devices (ie. canes, braces) that are appropriate for physical education. However it is important to remember that is not the sole responsibility of the physical educator to train the student to use these devices in activities of daily living (ADL).

6. When possible consult with the student regarding the type of activities he or she would like to participate in as well as the frequency, duration, and intensity level of training.

7. It is most important for the physical education specialist to develop the individual's skill, attitude, and habits so they can be generalized and practiced in current and adult leisure time activities.

8. Consider physical activity in the mainstream as well as alternative placements depending on the orthopedic condition. Segregated Sport opportunities that are available include: National Wheelchair Athletic Association (NWAA), National Wheelchair Basketball Athletic Association (NWBAA), National Handicapped Sports and Recreation Association (NHSRA), & United States Amputee Athletic Association (USAAA).

Excellent resources include:

Adams, R.D., & McCubbin, J. (1990). Games, sports, and exercises for the physically handicapped (5th ed). Philadelphia: Lea & Febiger.

Winnick, J. & Short, F. (1985), Physical Fitness Testing of the Disabled: Project Unique, Champaign, Ill: Human Kinetics.

Journals such as Palaestra and Sports n Spoke provide excellent information regarding physical activity programming for persons with orthopedic impairments.

Developmental/Individualized Instructional Approach

DEVELOPMENTAL/INDIVIDUALIZED INSTRUCTIONAL APPROACH

Philosophy

This approach is based on the strong conviction that physical activity is beneficial and should be provided for each individual and not just the gifted few. Each person is unique and should be afforded the opportunity to reach their full potential.

Systematic Program

Although the developmental/individualized approach is a systematic program of instruction it is not a set technique or teaching package following predetermined activities. Rather, it is individualized and designed to meet the needs of each person in order to make learning more effective. This requires a great deal of flexibility with the instructor offering a wide range of instructional strategies and program activities. Therefore, program prescription must be tailored to meet the unique needs of each person.

More specifically, only when the instructor has interpreted each individual's strengths and needs (present level of performance) can a program be effectively developed. This process will not be easy, especially when one considers the heterogeneity of persons with disabilities. A variety of programs such as I CAN and Project ACTIVE following this diagnostic prescriptive teaching format. More information on these programs are located on pages 172-173.

The following is a diagnostic prescriptive teaching format modified from Achievement Based Curriculum (Wessel & Kelly 1986):

1. Plan
2. Test
3. Assess
4. Prescribe
5. Teach
6. Evaluate

Summary: the ultimate goal of the program is for each student to reach their full potential.

PRESCRIPTIVE TEACHING FORMAT

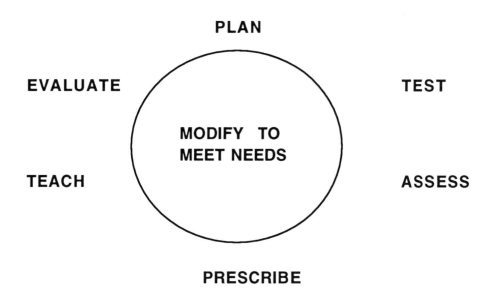

EFFECTIVE INSTRUCTION MUST BE BASED ON A SYSTEMATIC
PROGRAM OF INSTRUCTION, DESIGNED TO ALLOW EACH
STUDENT TO REACH THEIR FULL POTENTIAL.

Modified from: Wessel, J. & Kelly, L. (1986). Acheivement-based curriculum
development in physical edcuation. Philadelphia: Lea & Febiger.

MOVEMENT AND CURRICULUM GUIDE SUGGESTIONS

The curriculum should be student centered meeting the individual needs of each student taught. A sound physical education program should offer a wide variety of activities in the following areas:

Fundamental Movements

Physical and Motor Fitness

Lead-up Games and Activities

Sports Activities: individual, dual, team and leisure activities

Aquatics & Dance

Fundamental Movements

1. Locomotor Movements

walk

run

jump

hop

slide

gallop

leap

skip

2. Nonlocomotor Movements

stretch

bend

turn

twist

swing

push

pull

3. Stability Movements

static balance

dynamic balance

4. Object Control

overhand throw

catch

trap

strike

dribble

volley

kick

Physical Fitness

1. Health Related Fitness
   muscular strength
   muscular endurance
   flexibility
   cardiovascular endurance
   percent body fat

2. Motor Fitness
   coordination
   agility
   speed
   power

Leadup Games and Activities

   movement exploration
   rhythmic activities
   relaxation activities
   obstacle courses
   station drills
   balloon activities
   beanbag activities
   cageball activities
   hoop activities
   tire activities
   rope activities
   scooterboard activities
   parachute activities
   climbing activities
   stunts and tumbling
   low organized nontraditional games
   table games

Sports Activities: individual, dual, team and leisure time activities

1. INDIVIDUAL	2. DUAL	3. TEAM
Air riflery	Badminton	Flag Football
Archery	Racquetball	Soccer
Aquatics	Tennis	Basketball
Boating	Paddle tennis	Floor Hockey
Canoeing	Table Tennis	Volleyball
Sailing	Fencing	Wrestling
Bowling	Shuffleboard	Track & Field
Horseshoes	Frisbee	Softball
Put Put golf		Lacrosse
Rollerskating		Ice Skating
		Cross Country Skiing
		Downhill Skiing
		Hiking & Camping
		Fishing
		Horseback riding
		Dance (various types)
		Gymnastics
		Boxing
		Weightlifting
		Running
		Cycling

HEALTH/RELATED FITNESS COMPONENTS AND MODIFICATIONS

CARDIORESPIRATORY ENDURANCE
Ability to perform numerous repetitions of stress requiring the use of the circulatory and respiratory system. Muscular endurance specific to the heart, lungs, and vascular system. Considered the best single measure of fitness. For example, running tests of various distances and time.

MUSCULAR STRENGTH
Ability of the body to exert force. It is usually one maximum effort. For example, number of pullups which can be completed.

MUSCULAR ENDURANCE
Ability to perform work repeatedly against a moderate resistance. For example, number of bent knee situps completed in 60 seconds.

FLEXIBILITY
Ability of the joints to move through their full range of motion. It is joint specific. For example, sit and reach test.

PERCENT BODY FAT
An individual's degree of body fat as demonstrated by skinfold thickness. Measurements may be taken at such sites as the tricep, subscapula, & calf.

TEST MODIFICATIONS TO MEET INDIVIDUAL NEEDS

Professionals who administer fitness tests to children with special needs are faced with a number of critical issues. Too often, these problems do not allow special needs children to receive proper fitness testing. The Kansas Adapted/Special Physical Education Test Manual(KA/SPET) was developed in an effort to effectively address the unique needs of children with various resulting disabilities (Johnson & Lavay, 1988). The physical fitness components selected are similar to previous health related physical fitness components (HRPFT) such as "Physical Best". The primary difference is the adaptations and rationale used to modify the HRPFT items selected in order to allow all students to be tested. A more detailed description of each test item including adaptations and rationale are discussed in the following references:

Johnson, R. E. & Lavay, B. (1988). Kansas adapted/special physical education test manual. Kansas State Department of Education, 120 East 10th Street. Topeka, KS 66612.

Johnson, R. E. & Lavay, B. (1989) Fitness testing for children with special needs: An alternative approach. Journal of Physical Education Recreation and Dance, 60 (6), 50-53.

Shepard, R. J. (1990). Fitness in special populations. Champaign, IL: Human Kinetics.

IEP DEVELOPMENT

According to French & Jansma (1992):
A physical educator should be specifically aware of the following factors regarding the written IEP:

1. Physical education is a direct service and must be included by law.

2. A student only needs a written IEP in the curricular area of physical education when that student has unique special educational needs in the physical domain.

3. The physical educator should have direct input into the formulation of the student IEP in the physical domain.

4. The IEP is not a legally binding contract. The teacher is not legally held accountable if program goals are not met by the projected dates.

5. The actual physical format of the IEP is left to Local Educational Agency (LEA).

6. The teacher's involvement and input in the IEP should be sought before actual program implementation. The student should never be merely dumped into a class before an individualized program based on the student's unique needs has been prepared.

WRITING THE IEP (Individualized Education Program)

PL 94-142 states that the IEP contain the following information:
1. Statement of the student's present level of educational performance.
2. Statement of annual goals, including short-term objectives which are written in behavioral terms.
3. Statement of the specific educational and related services to be provided to the student and the extent to which the student will be able to participate in regular educational programs.
4. Projected dates for initiation of services and anticipated duration of services as well as strategies/materials necessary to achieve these goals.
5. Appropriate objective criteria, evaluation procedures, and schedules for determining at least on an annual basis whether the objectives are actually being achieved.
6. Evaluation on an annual basis to determine that instructional objectives are being achieved.

Present Level of Performance

This should be based on the individual assessment of the student with data gathered by direct measurement and observation. The data must then be interpreted to determine the student's present level of performance. This should be a clearly written statement of the student's strengths and needs. The statement should never be based on one single test score. For example:

John's fundamental motor ability as measured by the Test of Gross Motor Development (TGMD) is at age group except in the areas of throwing and catching. His overall physical fitness level as measured by the Health Related Fitness Test is below the 25% in cardiovascular endurance, abdominal strength, and upper body strength. The students flexibility is at the 45%. The student's posture is normal.

Summary
The IEP should serve as a blueprint to the student's educational services and assist the teacher in maintaining a focus on the necessary objectives to meet individual student needs. (Seaman & DePauw, 1989).

Annual Goals (long term objectives)

These are written statements of student learning outcomes during the academic school year. They should be broad in scope but specific enough so as to communicate what the student is to learn. For example, it is too broad a statement to state, "to improve in physical fitness." Rather state: "The student will improve in physical fitness by scoring above the 25% on the majority of Health Related Fitness test items".

Annual goals should be based on the student's present level of performance which is determined by the testing and assessment of the individual. For example, an annual goal in physical fitness would be stated with students who had individual needs in this area.

Choose annual goals:
1. From the various areas listed in the definition of physical education in PL 101-476. These include such areas as physical fitness, fundamental movements, games, and sports.
2. Annual goals should be taken from the three educational learning domains:
    1. Physical: movement skills
    2. Cognitive: intellectual
    3. Affective: social skills

PL 94-142 only specifically addresses the physical domain in the definition of physical education. However, these other educational domains should be included in the written IEP if they meet the individual needs of the student. For example, the student that demonstrates outstanding physical and motor skills, but can not cooperate with the teacher and/or classmates, may need instruction on goals in the affective domain, more specifically in social skills.

Sherrill (1986), offers excellent information regarding prioritizing goals. See Long Range Goals of Adapted Physical Education (GAPES), pp. 192-194.

Short Term Objectives (behavioral objectives)

These are statements which describe how annual goals and short term objectives will be effectively met. The short term objectives must be written in behavioral terms being observable and measurable.

The behavioral objective consists of the following 3 parts:

1. Performance/Behavior: the student is doing something observable. Choose action verbs to write this part of the objective such as run, jump, swim.

2. Condition: is described with limited specifications. Under what conditions did the student run? On a track.

3. Criteria: the behavior must meet certain standards such as a time limit or percentage of trials. 9 out of 10 trials or under 10 minutes.

The following is an incorrectly written short term objective: to improve in sit-up ability.

Rather state: The student will demonstrate 25 sit-ups with knees bent and arms folded on the chest in one minute.

Performance: the student demonstrating 25 sit-ups.
Condition: knees bent and arms across the chest.
Criteria: in one minute.

For more examples of behavioral objectives refer to:

Seaman, J. & DePauw, K. (1989). The New Adapted Physical Education. Palo Alto, CA: Mayfield Publishing, pg. 285.
Werder J., and Kalakian L. (1985). Assessment in Adapted Physical Education. Minneapolis: Burgess., Appendix B.

Short term objectives should be stated in sequence to meet individual needs. For example:

Annual Goal: The student will improve in the area of striking by successfully making contact with a thrown object 80% of the time.

Short Term Objectives
1. The student will strike a stationary 8" nerf ball off a batting tee with his hand 8 out of 10 times.
2. The student will strike a stationary 8" nerf ball off a batting tee with a wiffle ball bat 8 out of 10 times.
3. The student will strike a slowly moving 8" nerf ball from a swinging rope with a wiffle ball bat 8 out of 10 times.
4. The student will strike a ball thrown slowly from a pitcher's hand with a wiffle ball bat 8 out of 10 times.

Cognitive and Affective Behavioral Objectives

Public Law 94-142 requires that goals and objectives be written for the child only in the physical domain. However, the following are examples of behavioral objectives in the cognitive and affective domain.

Cognitive Domain
1. John will be able to successfully answer 80% of the questions on a soccer skills test.
2. When provided instruction Sharon will assume all the playing positions during a softball game with 100% accuracy.
3. Charlie will be able to explain to his classmates two different defensive aligments used in a basketball game.

Affective Domain
1. Steve will listen and follow teacher directions (policy statements) in class 100% of the time.
2. Penny will cooperate with others in the class by taking turns and sharing equipment during 9 out of the 10 class meetings.
3. Gary will respect the physical education equipment by using it properly and safely during each class meeting.

Timelines for Meeting Objectives (Achievement date)

Meeting proper timelines can be very difficult to determine. One strategy is for the teacher to locate test score norms and examine the particular student's raw scores. The instructor would then move up the table of test scores norms to the next realistic set of scores to project a written achievement date.

Another method is to calculate the ratio between the student's present level of motor performance and the student's chronological age (CA).

By law the teacher is not negligent if the student's projected achievement date is not successfully met.

Strategies/Materials to Achieve Goals:

Certain strategies or specific materials may be needed to achieve the behavioral objective.
For example, in order to successfully measure the students sit-up performance a mat and stopwatch is needed.

Summary

Overall the IEP and more specifically the student's present level of performance, annual goals, and behavioral objectives are important because it will serve as a blueprint to that student's educational services in physical education for the entire school year (Seaman & DePauw, 1989).

Individualized Educational Program of Physical Education

Name_____ Age_____ HT___ Wt___ Placement_____
Exceptionality (major health problems)_____
Present level of physical performance (based on assessment)

_____
_____
_____

1. Annual Goal

Short Term Objectives	Projected date	Materials
1.		
2.		
3.		

2. Annual Goal

Short Term Objectives	Projected date	Materials
1.		
2.		
3.		

3. Annual Goal

Short Term Objectives	Projected date	Materials
1.		
2.		
3.		

Modfied from: Eichstaedt, C. & Lavay, B. (1992). Physical activity for persons with mental retardation: Infant to adult. Champaign IL: Human Kinetics.

IEP ASSIGNMENT #1

Name: Charlie M.   School/placement: 3rd grade
CA: 9 yrs.   Exceptionality: LD
Sex: Male   HT: 53" (15%) WT: 98 (85%)

Charlie's physical fitness score as measured by the AAHPERD Health/Related Fitness Test revealed that he was below the 25% in cardiovascular endurance and abdominal strength, flexibility was measured at the 45%, and body composition was measured at 50%.

Charlie can perform locomotor skills such as running, jumping, galloping, and sliding at age group norms as determined by the Test of Gross Motor Development (Ulrich, 1985). However object control skills such as throwing, catching, and striking are very difficult for him to perform and he is 2-3 years below age group norms in these areas of fundamental movement. His skills in the area of balance were tested at age group norms.

Charlie gets along well socially with the other students in his class and is very willing to try new activities and games. During testing he expressed an interest in soccer which he watches played on TV with his father.

His teacher noted a short attention span when he is at his desk working and he displays difficulty following and performing simple directions.

Assignment:
With this information write an appropriate IEP in physical education for Charlie. To date he has not received any type of structured physical education program.

TASK ANALYSIS

This procedure is used to make a task easier for the individual to learn. The task is broken down into component parts or steps. The task must always be designed to fit the needs of the individual being taught. The unique needs of the individual must be considered first when analyzing a particular task. The task analysis consists of the performance objective (target behavior) and the steps necessary to accomplish the particular behavior.

The target behavior or performance objectives must be written in behavioral terms and consist of the following:

(a) performance/behavior, (b) conditions, and (c) criteria

The following is an example of a performance objective:

The child will perform a horizontal striking pattern while successfully contacting a nerf ball with an implement off a batting tee, 9 out of 10 times:

1. performance/behavior: horizontal striking pattern
2. conditions: plastic wiffle ball bat using 2-3 inch nerf ball positioned on a batting tee
3. criteria: successfully perform the activity 9 out of 10 times (90%)

STEPS (task analysis of the performance objectives):

1. Introduction of the implement which will be used to perform the striking pattern.
2. Holding the implement properly (dominant hand on top).
3. Visually attend to the object which will be used to perform the striking pattern (brightly colored objects may draw the child's attention).
4. Proper position in regards to the batting tee and implement (may use foot prints).
5. Bring the implement back only slightly from the batting tee and strike the object in a horizontal plane. (Various' size objects and implements may be used in accordance to the child's skill level.)
6. Bring the implement further back from the batting tee and strike the object in a horizontal plane.

7. Bring the implement back to shoulder height with both elbows flexed and strike the object squarly in a horizontal plane.
8. Develop proper follow-through upon contact of the object.
9. Increase the velocity of the swing of the implement (increase in velocity should not sacrifice overall control of the striking pattern).
10. Strike the object in various directions (left-right).
11. Strike the object in various speeds (hard-soft).

In order for certain individuals to meet a particular task, it may need to be further broken down into smaller steps. Dunn, Moorehouse & Fredericks (1986), refer to this procedure as branching. For example, moving from step 7 to 8 may be too difficult, consequently step 7 is further broken down.

7.0 Bring the implement back to shoulder height with both elbows flexed and strike the object in a horizontal plane.
7.1 Properly grip the implement and bring it back to shoulder height with both elbows flexed.
7.2 Stand with feet shoulder width apart and knees comfortably flexed.
7.3 Turn the body slightly to the side.
7.4 Turn the head and eyes toward the object on the batting tee.
7.5 Position the weight on the back foot.
7.6 Begin the horizontal swing with a lateral step forward of the front foot.
7.7 Begin to extend the arms forward toward the object on the tee.
7.8 Rotate the hips in the direction of the object.
7.9 Shift weight to the front foot upon making contact of the object.

Modfied from: Eichstaedt, C. & Lavay, B. (1992). <u>Physical activity for persons with mental retardation: Infant to adult</u>. Champaign IL: Human Kinetics.

Difficulty Performing or Meeting the Target Behavior

If an individual is demonstrating difficulty performing the target behavior the instructor should consider the following:

1. Inability to interpret stimuli
   a. Failure to determine speed or direction of ball.

2. Inappropriate past experiences or proper instruction
   a. Not developmentally ready to perform the skill.
   b. The individual may not have prior experience or instruction in striking a ball.
   c. Does not use appropriate feedback from previous experience

3. Lack of physical strength to perform task
   a. Use of a lighter bat

4. Lack of Motivation
   a. Child doesn't care about hitting the ball, may need to be reinforced through various methods.

For additional information the reader is referred to the following resources:

Auxter D., & Pyfer, J. (1989). Principles and Methods of Adapted Physical Education and Recreation. St. Louis: C.V. Mosby.
Dunn, J.M., Moorehouse, M.W., Fredericks, H.D. (1986). Physical education for the severely handicapped: A systematic approach to data-based gymnasium. Austin, TX: Pro Ed.
Wickstrom, R., (1983). Fundamental Motor Patterns. Philadelphia: Lea & Febiger.

Combining Students of Different Abilities in Games and Sport

Reprinted with permission from: Arbogast, G. & Lavay, B. (1987). Combining students of different abilities in games and sport . Physical Educator, 44, 255-260.

One of the most difficult and frustrating situations facing the physical education teacher is not being able to successfully combine students possessing different ability levels in games and sports. The advent of coeductional activities and mainstreaming handicapped with nonhandicapped students have made this endeavor of combining students of different ability an even more difficult accomplishment. The teacher rather than become frustrated, must accept the challenge of meeting the individual needs of all students. Thus, the purpose of this paper is to discuss various instructional strategies teachers can use to ensure that learning is occurring among all students.

The teacher must realize that the structure of the game or sport is not sacred and can be changed to account for unique student learning outcomes (Marlowe, 1979; Martens, Rivkin, & Bump, 1984; Morris, 1980; Morris & Stiehl, 1985). Certain games and sport will more easily meet student needs without many changes being made while others will require a variety of changes. The following strategies are merely suggestions, each teacher must consider the variety of environmental situations they may encounter, as well as student differences unique to their own individual program.

The critical first step in combining students of different ability levels is to examine the particular game or sport the students will be participating in. When analyzing a game or sport the teacher should have the following instructional concerns:

1. What movement and fitness demands are required to successfully perform this particular game or sport?

2. What is the purpose and skill complexity of the game or sport?

3. What are the environmental considerations of the game or sport?

4. What are the cognitive and social considerations of the game or sport?

Movement and Fitness Demands

Initial consideration must be given to the fundamental movement and fitness demands involved in the particular game or sport. In general, the developmental sequence of all individuals is similar, however, the rate and extent of the movement will vary (Gallahue, 1982). This is known as the developmental approach and successful application of this approach suggests individualized instruction (French & Jansma, 1982; Nichols, 1986; Winnick, 1978). Therefore, the teacher's understanding of each student's present level of physical performance is paramount if individual needs are to be met during games and sports instruction.

For the developmental approach to be successful, each student's movement must be placed along a continuum from simple to complex with game and sport skills contingent on sound fitness levels and fundamental movement patterns (Gallahue, 1982; Morris, 1980; Seaman & DePauw, 1982). The ability levels of each student in physical education class will vary along this developmental continuum and as a student grows older, fitness and movement discrepancies may become even more apparent. Therefore, modifications will be needed that accommodate the different developmental levels of each student. The following are examples of how the physical educator can effectively apply this developmental instructional approach: In a game of tag, students who display superior strength and speed can be made to hop while slower students are allowed to run to designated areas made available to take a needed rest. Another example using this approach could include the implementation of scooter boards in floor hockey to neutralize the superior strength and speed of certain students, making the game even more challenging and consequently fun for all students.

Purpose and Skill Complexity

Too often, it is assumed that students understand the purpose of the skills that are required by a game or sport. How many times has a skill been demonstrated by the teacher with the assumption that the students have understood the skill. Then, within a few short moments of practice or game play, the teacher realizes the students were focusing attention on skill mechanics to the point they had a difficult time understanding the objective of the activity. Stallings (1982) suggested that learners must first and foremost understand the purpose of the skill(s) that comprise the game. For example, students should be asked to focus their attention on the purpose of "setting the volleyball" during a demonstration of this skill. Only when skill or activity objectives are clearly understood by the learner, can students make the necessary mechanical or technique adjustments required to improve skills and play the game. The teacher must direct the learners' attention to the objective of the skill. Once this is clearly understood, movement techniques and game strategies can be improved through appropriate demonstrations and corrective feedback.

Skill complexity will vary with each game or sport. The teacher must realize that some activities are comprised of skills that are extremely complex while some skills even within the same activity or sport may have low complexity (i.e., advancing a soccer ball in opponent's defensive zone is more complex than executing a direct free kick). It is important to remember that complexity may also be relative to the information processing capabilities of each student. That is, the same skill may vary in complexity among students. This may be possible because of experience or lack of experience with the skill, or because of limited perceptual and decision making capabilities of various students. The key concept for the instructor to understand is how to reduce skill complexity when necessary so that students of different ability levels can successfully participate in the same activity. However, a brief understanding of skill complexity by the teacher is necessary.

Magill (1985), defined skill complexity by the number of component parts that make up a task or activity and the information processing demands of the task or activity. he continued, "a highly complex task would have many components and require much attention (information processing) throughout" (p. 378).

For beginning learners, students with limited prior movement experiences, or students that are developmentally delayed, skill complexity should be matched to the student's ability level so success can be achieved. Altering the skill complexity is not difficult and it does not disrupt the "flow " of any game or sport characterized by variability in student readiness and capability. For example, some students may be ready to move into position and kick a larger, stationary ball. Therefore, to assure the success of all players in a game of kickball the ball can either be pitched at various speeds or placed on home plate. The same analogy can be made for playing a game of soccer where the information processing demands are great, thereby increasing skill complexity. Here, students are required to attend to a teammate's or opponent's position to the ball, what to do when they get the ball, and not to mention implementing simple team strategies. Can skill complexity be reduced to accommodate all students? Once basic skills are somewhat mastered, the teacher can organize "lead-up" games to reduce task complexity. A simple lead-up game which involves shooting, passing and trapping would be circle soccer. Once success in this activity is achieved, more complex lead-up games such as line soccer can be initiated. These lead-up games assist in reducing attention and decision making demands. In summary, a game or sport should be designed not to frustrate the low achiever or bore the highly skilled performer.

Environmental considerations

Equipment and facilities to various degrees affect how students learn movement skills and ultimately games and sport. Equipment and facilities may need to be modified or completely changed if optimal learning is to be achieved by students of varying ability levels. Students' safety is a foremost consideration and any equipment or facility adjustment must always be a teacher concern.

The acquisition of skills by all learners can be facilitated by using equipment that is appropriate in size and weight. Siedentop, Herkowitz, and Rink (1984) suggested that the learning of motor skills by children could be facilitated with lighter weight equipment. The National Recreation and Parks Association (1976) suggested to the Consumer Product Safety Commission that equipment should be provided which children can change in order to accommodate their own unique growth and development level. Examples might include using a balance beam that could be adjusted to varying heights and widths; or a suspended ball that could be adjusted to different heights for striking. Use of equipment that is lighter than regulation equipment may enable some students to develop more appropriate mechanics where strength may be a factor in successful skill performance. Lighter, more resilient objects (foam balls, yarn balls) may also eliminate some students' fear of being hit and injured by an object while catching or striking. A student can therefore practice or play a game with greater confidence and enjoyment.

For some students, size and contrast of equipment may be as important as weight in facilitating the acquisition of skills. When catching, kicking and striking, implements larger than regulation size can be used to facilitate learning for those students experiencing difficulty in acquiring such skills. The teacher should realize that as long as the larger balls are not characterized by less resiliency and significantly greater weight or size, they will remain appropriate for the student to effectively handle (Morris & Stiehl, 1985). Although it may be true that larger objects can be more easily seen and traced by learners, any object regardless of size should contrast significantly with the external environment (Isaacs, 1980). Students are more successful in catching, kicking and striking objects when they clearly stand out. The intensity of visual stimuli should be kept to a maximum when students are acquiring skills.

As students learn skills that require them to propel objects either with a hand or an implement the teacher may consider using not only lighter equipment, but smaller equipment. Students must be able to effectively throw and strike equipment such as balls, bats, and hula hoops.

Just as equipment characteristics are important considerations leading to the successful acquisition of game skills, facility characteristics must also be considered. Facility modifications can enhance game play. Modifying a facility may include decreasing the size of a game field or court to reduce the physical intensity or demands for less able students. Another consideration is making height and width adjustments in goals and nets to accommodate diverse ability and skill levels. Decisions to modify a game facility should be based on the rationale that the teacher is responsible for providing a physical environment in which all students can experience success.

Cognitive and Social Considerations

A neglected teacher consideration in games or sports is often the cognitive and social aspects. For some students, certain rules and strategies may prove to be quite complex and abstract. Initially, the teacher should make rules and strategies simple, clear, and concise. Certain modifications will allow rules to be more concrete and easier for students to understand. For example, obscure boundaries can be highlighted with flags or cones. Dauer and Pangrazi (1986) felt that games that are spontaneous in nature and demand little concentration are often the most popular among students. Initially, too many rules may have a negative effect and hinder participation. Lead-up games may be one method for gradually introducing rules and strategies to the participants.

Proper social interaction among students during games and sport will not occur automatically (Marlow, 1979; Orlick, 1982). Merely placing students together in a game or sport does not assure social interaction, cooperative play, or even the development of a positive attitude toward peers (Santomier & Kopczuk, 1981). The teacher can begin to foster positive social experiences by avoiding and/ or changing elimination type games such as musical hoops, dodgeball, and tag games. For example, a person who would be eliminated from a traditional game of dodgeball would merely change teams with the person who hits them with a sponge ball. Too often the student who should benefit most from the additional practice is the first to be eliminated. The teacher should always consider providing positive feedback to those students who socially interact with others during play. A peer tutor/ student helper program (DePaepe, 1984) can be utilized in a game or sport setting with a student of superior ability playing alongside a student with lesser ability. Nontraditional games which are designed to meet instructional objectives (Fluegelman, 1976) can also be introduced with players encouraged to cooperate in order to reach a common goal. An example would be the "lap game" in which each student sits on another person's lap while forming a circle. During games and sport the teacher should encourage the quality of play rather than the outcome or score. Another strategy suggested by Seland (1981) is that competition and cooperation among students be minimized by having players periodically change teams. Finally, when poor sportsmanship occurs during a game or sport the teacher should lead the group through a discussion, exploring the reasons why this action is considered inappropriate.

Putting it all Together

Listed is a brief description of a game called, "softball, volleyball, and basketball (SVB)." This game example is used to demonstrate to the reader how the four major considerations discussed in this paper can be properly implemented.

The physical set-up of the game is a traditional softball diamond in the gymnasium. The batter strikes a ball into the field by using a volleyball serve. The fielders must pass the ball to a teammate of the opposite sex before it is thrown to the catcher located at home plate who must make a successful basket before the runner circles the bases and returns home. If the batter/ runner scores before the basket is made by the catcher a point is awarded. However, a basket made before the runner scores is an out. The number of outs is determined by the instructor or class. All players must run/ walk in place until the batter makes contact and the play ends. After each batter, the fielders rotate positions to assure that there is a new catcher each time and that one particular student does not dominate the game.

A. Movement and fitness demands:
1. Students of low physical ability may walk in place when they become fatigued.
2. Lighter balls can assure that less physically fit students meet with success when throwing the ball.
3. More relay passes before throwing to home plate can be initiated when the batter/ runner is significantly slower than other.

B. Skill Complexity
1. The ball can be hit off a batting tee.
2. Strike a larger ball to decrease skill complexity while using a smaller ball to increase skill complexity.
3. The teacher can provide a cue to the initial fielder as to the most appropriate teammate to pass, assuring a good relay to the catcher. The catcher with low shooting skills may only be required to hit the basket rim to make an out.

C. Environmental Considerations
1. The distance between bases can be modified commensurate with the age group or ability level of the students.
2. Various size balls can be made available.
3. To assure better contrast for striking and fielding, brightly colored balls should be used as well as having the gymnasium well lighted.

D. Social Considerations

1. The initial fielder must pass the ball to a fielder of the opposite sex.
2. After each play all fielders rotate a position.
3. When changing from offense to defense each player must shake hands with a player from the other team.

Summary

In order to effectively combine students of different ability levels in the same game or sport, the teacher must consider the following: The teacher must carefully analyze the movement and fitness demands the activity requires for each student. This is described as the developmental approach to instruction. Also, the overall purpose of the game or sport including skill complexity must be considered. Skill complexity as well as the student's prior experiences may necessitate practice modifications and the use of the lead-up game teaching approach. These considerations may aid in simplifying the information processing demands placed on the student. Another important teacher consideration is how equipment and facilities to various degrees will affect the student's learning of movement skills. If optimal learning with students of various ability levels is to occur, equipment and facilities may need to be modified or completely changed. A final and often neglected teacher consideration is the cognitive and social aspects of the game or sport. Rules and strategies of each game must be made simple, clear, and concise if they are to be understood by all involved. Furthermore, social interaction among students will not occur automatically. The instructor must actively work with students to enhance this process.

Combining students of different ability levels in the same game at the same time will never be easy. However, the instructor that considers the student, the skill, the equipment and environment during planning is taking a positive step toward enhancing successful participation, enjoyment, and learning of all games and sport.

References

Dauer, V. P., & Pangrazi, R. P. (1986). Dynamic physical education for elementary school children. Minneapolis, MN: Burgess Publishing.

DePaepe, J. L. (1984). Mainstreaming malpractice. Physical Educator, 41, 51-56.

Gallahue, D. L. (1982). Understanding motor development in children. New York: John Wiley & Sons.

French, R., & Jansma, P. (1982). Special physical education. Columbus: Merrill Publishing.

Isaacs, L. D. (1980). Catching performance: Implications for the practitioner. Journal of Physical Education & Recreation. 51 (8), 56-58.

Fluegelman, a. (ed.) (1976). The new games book: Play hard, play fair, nobody hurt. Garden City, NY: Dolphin Books.

Magill, R. A. (1985). Motor learning: Concepts & applications. Dubuque, IA: Wm. C. Brown.

Marlowe, M. (1979). The game analysis intervention: A procedure to increase the peer acceptance and social adjustment of a retarded child. <u>The Education & Training of the Mentally Retarded</u>, <u>14</u>, 262-268.

Martens, R., Rivkin, F., & Bump, L. A. (1984). A field study of traditional and nontraditional children's baseball. <u>Research Quarterly for Exercise and Sport</u>, <u>55</u>, 351-355.

Morris, G. S. D. (1980). <u>How to change the games people play</u>. Minneapolis: Burgess Pub.

Morris, G. S., & Stiehl, J. (1985). <u>Physical education: From intent to action</u>. Columbus: Merrill Publishing.

National Recreation & Parks Association. (1976). Proposed safety standard for public playground equipment. Developed for the consumer product safety commission. Arlington, VA: National Recreation & Park Association.

Nichols, B. (1986). <u>Moving and learning: The elementary school physical education experience</u>. St. Louis: C. V. Mosby.

Orlick, T. (1982). <u>The second cooperative sports and games book</u>. New York: Pantheon Books.

Santomier, J., & Kopczuk, W. (1981). Facilitation of interactions between retarded and nonretarded students in a physical education setting. <u>Education and Training of the Mentally Retarded</u>, <u>16</u>, 20-23.

Seland, S. J. (1981). Cooperative games promote positive student interactions. <u>Teaching Exceptional Children</u>, <u>13</u>, 76-79.

Seaman, J. A., & DePauw, K. P. (1982). <u>The new adapted physical education: The developmental approach</u>. Palo Alto, CA: Mayfield Publishing.

Siedentop, D., Herkowitz, J., & Rink, J. (1984). <u>Elementary physical education methods</u>. Englewood Cliffs, NJ: Prentice-Hall.

Stallings, L. (1982). <u>Motor learning: From theory to practice</u>. St. Louis: C. V. Mosby Co.

Winnick, J. P. (1978). Techniques for integration. <u>Journal of Physical Education and Recreation</u>. <u>49</u> (6), 22.

The Mainstreaming Process

THE MAINSTREAMING PROCESS

SUCCESSFUL MAINSTREAMING OF THE STUDENT WITH A DISABILITY INTO REGULAR PHYSICAL EDUCATION WILL NOT OCCUR AUTOMATICALLY.

MAINSTREAMING IS A COMPLEX CONCEPT. IT IS NOT SIMPLY
A QUESTION OF EITHER INTEGRATING OR SEGREGATING A PUPIL WiTH A
HANDICAPPING CONDITION FROM NONHANDICAPPED PUPILS.
French & Jansma, 1982

THE HANDICAPPED STUDENT SHOULD NOT BE INCLUDED BUT INTEGRATED. Winnick, 1978

BY THE VERY NATURE OF THEIR PROGRAM PHYSICAL EDUCATION TEACHERS ARE CONSTANTLY REMINDED THAT TEACHING CHILDREN WITH HANDICAPS IN A MAINSTREAMING PROGRAM CAN BE FRUSTRATING AND DISAPPOINTING. THE TIME HAS COME TO MEET THE CHALLENGE. Mizen & Linton, 1983

ATTITUDES TOWARD MAINSTREAMING

Too often the handicapped are more handicapped by attitudes and misbeliefs than they are by their own condition. (Stewart, 1980).

 We must recognize that helping teachers to deal with the uniqueness of children is basically an attitudinal problem. (Martinez, 1982).

Access is not just wide doors and ramped stairways or elevators; . . . it is feeling that you belong and not that your presence is simply being tolerated. (Price, 1986).

Unfortunately, whereas one can quite easily pass a law requiring that all doors in public buildings will be at least 750 mm wide, it is another thing altogether to attempt to legislate for a change of attitude. (Price, 1986).

A teacher who makes little or no allowance for individual differences in the classroom is an individual who makes little or no difference in the lives of his students. (William A. Ward)

SUMMARY: Unless the attitudes of physical educators change and become more favorable toward teaching handicap pupils, the chances are minimal that such pupils will successfully assimilate into regular classes. (Rizzo, 1984).

Is Mainstreaming in Physical Education, Recreation and Dance Working?

This article is reprinted with permission from the **JOPERD** (Journal of Physical Education, Recreation & Dance), September, 1987, page 14. **JOPERD** is a publication of the American Alliance for Health, Physical Education, Recreation and Dance, 1900 Association Drive, Reston, VA 22091-1599.

A variety of issues and problems exist which make it difficult to assess if mainstreaming in physical education, recreation, and dance is effective.

First, mainstreaming remains one of the most misunderstood and abused concepts in our profession. In many settings the mainstreaming environment has become a dumping ground for handicapped students. Not all handicapped students should be automatically mainstreamed into regular physical education, recreation, and dance. The intent of PL 94-142 is to place each handicapped student in the least restrictive environment- an environment in which each individual can reach their own optimum potential. This environment must be individualized, dynamic and able to change in order to meet each student's present level of performance in the psychomotor, affective and cognitive learning domains.

A second issue which makes this question difficult to answer is little data-based research in physical education, recreation, and dance exists (Dunn & Craft, 1985; Watkinson & Titus, 1985). More mainstreaming research has been conducted with the handicapped student in the classroom setting. To date, however, conflicting findings make it difficult to draw conclusions (Hallahan & Kauffman, 1982). In fact, the authors caution that in the past before the practice of placing handicapped students in special education classes, these students were either mainstreamed or did not attend school. Because they failed in regular classes, special education classes were established. Unless special provisions are made we may be placing these students back in a situation we already know they can not handle. Obviously, more research is desperately needed before this issue can be resolved.

A third consideration is each setting (i.e. school, recreation program) will possess its own unique set of circumstances. In a recent article by Lavay & DePaepe in the September, 1987 issue of JOPERD, the authors discuss a number of preplanning factors which facilitators of mainstreaming must consider if this strategy is to be effective. The roles and attitudes of all professionals involved is most important. Recent research indicates a positive attitude of the regular physical education teacher toward the handicapped students(s) being mainstreamed may be the most critical factor towards success. Other preplanning factors include: (a) the program schedule and facilities; (b) the profile of the class where the student will be mainstreamed; (c) and a factor too often overlooked; the actual student to be mainstreamed.

Another critical factor is research indicates that many professionals (i.e., regular physical educators) assigned to provide physical activity to the handicapped in a mainstreamed setting do not feel adequately prepared. Effective inservice and preservice education in this area is needed.

University HPERD departments must make a commitment to develop programs which prepare their students to graduate with the necessary competencies to teach all children including the handicapped.

With so many critical factors and problems associated with mainstreaming, professionals must ask the question is it worth it? While more empirical research is needed, the literature indicates with proper program planning the advantages of mainstreaming can far outweigh the disadvantages. Major benefits can be derived for both the handicapped and nonhandicapped, making the additional effort by all professionals involved worth it. The nonhandicapped student can be an effective role model toward the handicapped student by displaying appropriate motor and social behaviors. With proper modifications, various activities and games can help the handicapped learn to socially interact with the nonhandicapped, allowing these individuals to adjust to real life situations which adheres to the principle of normalization. Many (not all) handicapped students may be motivated to perform better in the presence of nonhandicapped peers. Perhaps most importantly, the nonhandicapped student, by working closely with the handicapped student, will learn to appreciate and respect persons who are handicapped allowing them to reach their optimum potential.

References

Dunn, J. M. & Craft, D. H. (1985). Mainstreaming theory into practice. Adapted Physical Activity Quarterly, 2, 272-276.

Hallahan, D. P., & Kauffman, J. M. (1982). Exceptional children: Introduction to special education. Englewood Cliffs, NJ: Prentice Hall.

Lavay, B., & DePaepe, J. (1987). The harbinger helper: Why mainstreaming doesn't always work. JOPERD, 58 (7), 98-103.

Watkinson, E. J., & Titus, J. A. (1985). Integrating the mentally handicapped in physical activity: A review and discussion. Canadian Journal for Exceptional Children, 2, 48-53.

THE LEAST RESTRICTIVE ENVIRONMENT IS NOT ALWAYS MAINSTREAMING!

Mainstreaming:

The integration of the student with a disability with the nondisabled student into the regular educational setting.

Not every student will be successfully mainstreamed into the regular educational setting. The nature of the student's disability may be such that he or she is unable to properly function in a mainstreamed setting. Placement must be based on the student's need.

French & Jansma (1992) stated, "Mainstreaming is a complex concept. It is not simply a question of either integrating or segregating the pupil with a handicapping condition from nonhandicapped pupils. Unfortunately this is how the term is too often defined and used" (p.6).

The Least Restrictive Environment:

The placement of the student is based on individual need determined by the individual's educational program (I.E.P.). The student's present level of functioning must always be considered. The least restrictive environment is further discussed on pages 146-147.

PHYSICAL EDUCATION AND THE LEAST RESTRICTIVE ENVIRONMENT PLACEMENT ALTERNATIVES

A number of placement alternatives in the physical education program must be made available to the student with a disability based upon an individual motor assessment, programming, facilities, and the normalization process. The following are examples of various placement alternatives:

1. Placement in a full-time, self-contained special physical education setting taught by a special physical educator.

2. A combination approach moving from a special physical education setting to a regular physical education setting, depending on the student's needs and the particular programs available.

3. A team approach between the special physical education instructor and the regular physical education instructor.

4. Placement in regular physical education with special assistance or consultant services from the special physical educator.

5. Placement in full-time regular physical education with no assistance.

See the least restrictive environment in physical education flow chart, located on the next page, which is modfied from: Eichstaedt, C. & Lavay, B. (1992). Physical activity for persons with mental retardation: Infant to adult. Champaign IL: Human Kinetics. This flow chart provides a continuum of services for the student to move along as individual needs and situations arise.

LEAST RESTRICTIVE ENVIRONMENT FLOW CHART

```
                    ┌─────────────────────┐
                    │ Placement based:    │
                    │ Student need        │
                    │ Assessment          │
                    │ Programming         │
                    │ Facilities          │
                    └──────────┬──────────┘
          ┌────────────────────┼────────────────────┐
┌─────────┴──────┐   ┌─────────┴──────┐   ┌──────────┴─────┐
│ Full-time      │   │ Combination    │   │ Team Teaching  │
│ Placement      │   │ of Services    │   │ Between SPE    │
│ in SPE         │   │ SPE & RPE      │   │ & RPE          │
│                │   │                │   │ SPE Consult    │
└────────────────┘   └────────────────┘   └────────────────┘
                                           ┌────────────────┐
                                           │ Full-time      │
                                           │ Placement in   │
                                           │ RPE            │
                                           └────────────────┘
```

The least restictive enviroment is a philosophy where the educational direct and related services of all children with disabilities are effectively met. Children with disabilities have a wide range of abilities varying in intensity and duration. These continuum of services must be flexible so as to change to meet the students needs. The law states that to the maximum extent possible and when appropriate each child with a disability must be educated with their nondisabled peers. The least restictive enviroment for each child will vary and is not always mainstreaming.

Modfied from: Eichstaedt, C. & Lavay, B. (1992). Physical activity for persons with mental retardation: Infant to adult. Champaign IL: Human Kinetics.

FACTORS TO CONSIDER TO ASSURE PROPER PHYSICAL EDUCATION PLACEMENT

(Each program will have a unique set of circumstances)

A. Special Physical Education Program: well rounded program
B. Referral System: proper system to receive appropriate testing requests
C. Assessment: in order to properly determine student performance
D. Student Profile: present level of functioning in motor, cognitive, social, and behavior skills

Summary:
These are general considerations.

Factors Specific to Mainstreaming
A. Special Physical Educator's knowledge and attitude
B. Regular Physical Educator's knowledge and attitude: perhaps the single most important factor
C. Regular Physical Education Curriculum/Program: well rounded program
D. Scheduling
E. Facilities
F. Profile of the Students in the Regular Physical Education Class
G. Availability of other personnel: teacher aides, peer tutors
H. Administration/Special Education Classroom Teacher: educated in this area
I. Student Mainstreamed: too often overlooked and not asked an opinion
J. The importance of the "normalization process"

All of these factors must be carefully weighed and considered. For example physical development at the expense of social development?

Summary:
Too often mainstreaming fails because these factors are not carefully considered and planned. Mainstreaming should never be dictated by negative teacher attitudes, financial, facility and administrative restrictions.

STUDENT MAINSTREAMING PROFILE

*To be answered by the special physical education instructor or classroom teacher and to be given to the regular PE teacher.

Student: Name:

Grade Level:

Age:

School:

Contact Teacher:

Health factor considerations (vision, hearing, medication and/or other health impairments):

Briefly describe the student's present level of functioning (if available attach all student motor assessment and IEP information):

    1. fundamental movement ability

    2. physical fitness

    3. cognitive ability

    4. social and self-management skills

    5. behavior

List any teaching styles and behavior management techniques which may work effectively with this student:

Briefly list the desired student outcome(s) from the mainstreaming experience:

Student's class schedule and most appropriate period(s) for mainstreaming to occur (reasons why):

Reprinted with permission from: Lavay, B. & DePaepe, J. (1987). The harbinger helper : Why mainstreaming in physical education doesn't always work: Journal of Physical Education, Recreation, and Dance, 58(7), 98-103.

TEACHER MAINSTREAMING PROFILE

*To be answered by the regular physical education teacher

Name of Student to be Mainstreamed:
Regular Physical Education Teacher:
Teacher Schedule:

1. Briefly list the general physical education expectations of your
   students in the following areas.
   A. Motor Ability (fundamental movements, physical fitness,
      sports-related skills):
   B. Social Skills (ability to interact):
   C. Behavior (class rules):
   D. Cognitive Ability (understanding game rules):

2. What type of support do you feel is needed to effectively
   facilitate the mainstreaming process with this student?
   A. Facilities and equipment:
   B. Personnel:
      Consultation from specialist:
      Team teaching with specialist:
      Paraprofessional or aide:
      Peer Tutor:

3. What period of the day or particular class do you feel would be
   most appropriate for the student to be mainstreamed ?
   (state any particular reasons).

The Harbinger Helper: Why Mainstreaming in Physical Education Doesn't Always Work

This article is reprinted with permission from the **JOPERD** (Journal of Physical Education, Recreation & Dance), July, 1987, pages 98-103. **JOPERD** is a publication of the American Alliance for Health, Physical Education, Recreation and Dance, 1900 Association Drive, Reston, VA 22091-1599.

Successful mainstreaming of disabled students into regular physical education will not occur automatically. Mainstreaming is a complex concept and not simply administered through the integration or segregation of disabled students (Dunn & Craft, 1985 ; French & Jansma, 1982). The disabled student who is involved in the mainstreaming process must be successfully integrated rather than merely included into physical education (Winnick, 1978). In an investigation conducted by Bishop (1986), the perceptions of 134 Nebraskan elementary and secondary physical educators toward mainstreaming were examined. Nearly 40 percent of the respondents believed that the integration of nondisabled students with disabled students in regular physical education was ineffective.

Too often mainstreaming is unsuccessful because of the inadequate planning of all professionals who should be involved. Teaching children in a mainstreamed physical education program requires a great deal of planning, cooperation and communication. To guarantee mainstreaming success, the special education teacher must act as a program manager setting the stage long before the handicapped student enters physical education. The purpose of this paper is to discuss the variety of planning factors illustrated as the harbinger approach which must first be considered before the student can actually enter a mainstreamed physical education class. In effect the harbinger technique is used as a prelude to a course of action that sets the stage and ensures appropriate placement and programming for all children.

Topics critical to special education and specific to physical education mainstreaming are:
* the mainstreaming concept;
* the role of the special and regular education classroom teacher, special physical educator and regular physical educator, both separately and together;
* the program's schedule and facilities;
* the profile of the class into which the student will be mainstreamed; and
* a factor frequently overlooked- the student to be mainstreamed.

The reader must remember that each school and physical education class will have its own unique set of circumstances which must be carefully considered and therefore, these guidelines should serve only as suggestions.

The mainstreaming concept

Although Public Law 94-142 (the Education for All Handicapped Children's Act of 1975) has been in existence for the past 10 years, the term least restrictive environment remains a subject of considerable misunderstanding. To alleviate some of the mystery and ambiguity surrounding the least restrictive environment concept, it is imperative to recognize what the term implies. According to this law, the least restrictive environment means that individuals exhibiting disabilities between the ages of three and 21 are entitled to participate within a regular educational setting to the maximum extent relative to their concomitant abilities. In physical education this does not mean that all students attending public school facilities will be automatically mainstreamed by being placed in a regular physical education program. Rather, a disabled child should be placed in an environment (class) that promotes successful motor development. If the progress of the disabled child or the progress of the class is negatively affected because of the placement, an alternative must be made available. The degree to which this is accomplished will depend upon several factors. Mainstreaming must be treated as an individualized process- considered as only one alternative in the myriad of least restrictive placements and used only when conditions are appropriate. Careless or thoughtless mainstreaming has been termed mainstreaming malpractice and serves no purpose within the educational system (DePaepe, 1984).

Special physical education teacher

The special physical education teacher, or in some cases the special educator, must play a most critical role in the successful integration of disabled students into regular physical education. Proper psychomotor assessment of students to be mainstreamed is paramount. Without it, systematic individualized programming essential to the success of mainstreaming is lost. Student strengths and needs must be determined first before a decision can be made regarding placement in the least restrictive environment. After the psychomotor results are determined, cognitive and affective information collected by the special educator need to be considered. The child who lacks specific physical skills but possesses good intellectual ability and strong social skills must be examined very carefully before mainstreaming is considered. Physical education's primary concern is psychomotor development. Without a proper special physical education assessment, the special educator as program manager will be unaware of the student's present level of functioning and unable to convey a realistic profile of the student to the regular physical education teacher.

Another critical factor is that a special physical education program will provide a number of activities that enhance a student's developmental needs and allows for a smooth transition from special to regular physical education. The special physical educator or classroom special educator that overprotects the child in the self-contained setting is doing that student a great disservice in mainstreaming preparation.

Regular physical education teacher

Perhaps no other factor is more critical to the success of mainstreaming than the attitude of the regular physical education teacher (Aloia, Knutson, Minner, & VonSeggern, 1980; Minner & Knutson, 1982; Mizen & Linton, 1983; and Rizzo, 1984). If this teacher demonstrates a favorable attitude toward disabled students being mainstreamed, the other students of the class will be more accepting. Rizzo (1984) stated that "unless the attitudes of physical educators change and become more favorable toward teaching handicapped pupils, the chances are minimal that such pupils will successfully assimilate into regular classes" (p. 271).

The teaching style and physical education program of the teacher is also a critical factor which merits consideration. The program should be student centered and developmental, structured to meet the individual needs of all students. A traditional program with a teacher who is extremely rigid in student expectations and unprepared or unwilling to change to meet individual needs is perhaps not the best placement alternative for disabled students. In many school systems this traditional approach may be the only mainstreaming placement alternative available. When this occurs the special physical educator and special educator need to work closely with the regular physical education teacher to assure that proper mainstreaming for each particular student is successful. For example, the special physical educator must become part of the transdisciplinary team and aid in the writing of the student's individualized educational program (IEP).

Special and regular physical education working effectively together

Physical education teachers receiving their teacher training prior to the enactment of Public Law 94-142 more than likely are not prepared adequately to meet the needs of disabled students in regular classes. Many teachers who learn that a disabled student will enter their gymnasium become anxious and frustrated. Frequently, the unknown can cause more of a strain on the teacher than the disabled student being mainstreamed. Indiscriminate placement of students into the regular program without formal consultation with the regular physical education teacher will usually result in an unsuccessful mainstreaming attempt. The special physical educator as well as the special education classroom teacher must make every effort to prepare the regular physical educator for the student being mainstreamed.

One effective strategy practiced by the authors for preparing the regular teacher for mainstreaming is the "Student Profile for Physical Education Mainstreaming Consideration" form. The form, although brief, gives the regular teacher preplacement information regarding the student to be mainstreamed. The form lists information such as:
* present level of performance
* medical considerations
* past teaching styles or management techniques that have been effective
* desired mainstreaming outcomes
* the most appropriate period(s) for the student to be mainstreamed

The regular physical education teacher may see as many as 200 students a day. For this reason the form can help save time and transform the mainstreaming endeavor into a successful experience.

In addition, the special physical educator can team teach with the regular teacher or offer after school inservice training sessions (Jansma & Schulz, 1982). Other alternatives are the use of a paraprofessional (teacher aides) or the development of a peer-tutor program (DePaepe, 1985 ; Sherrill, 1986). This program can use school-aged peers as well as older students or senior citizens.

Program scheduling and facilities

Often the class schedule becomes the major obstacle to successful mainstreaming. For example, the ideal physical education class period for a certain student to be mainstreamed may meet third period -however that period might be the only time remedial reading is offered during the school day. To alleviate this problem, all educators involved, including the special education classroom teacher(s), regular and special physical educators, and therapists must work together to determine a schedule which best fits the student's needs. Guidelines for promoting better communication among allied professionals are suggested by Lavay and French (1985). Physical educators must have a thorough understanding of their own job role as well as the job responsibilities of the teacher or therapist with whom interaction is necessary.

Facilities can also become a deterrent to successful mainstreaming. Placing three mentally retarded youngsters in a class of 31 students in half a gymnasium is not in the best interest of all and can only help to compound negative feelings toward mainstreaming. If this situation does exist, team teaching between the regular and special physical educator can be a viable alternative.

The Regular Physical Education Class Profile for Mainstreaming can also be an effective alternative for overcoming existing scheduling and facility conflicts. The profile allows the regular physical educator to briefly discuss his or her program, the type of support needed, and the most advantageous period(s) for mainstreaming to occur. Perhaps most important is that the profile allows the regular physical educator input into the mainstreaming process.

The mainstreamed class

Still another important consideration is the profile of the students within the mainstreamed class. For example, it is not advisable to mainstream two behaviorally disordered students into the most misbehaved class a regular teacher has. Therefore, the maturity level of the class must be strongly considered if mainstreaming is to be successful. It has been the authors' experience when teaching on the secondary level that an elective rather than a required class may be more advantageous to effective mainstreaming. Students in the elective class have chosen to be there and enjoy physical activity. In many schools, however, elective classes in physical education are nonexistent. Moreover, it cannot be assumed that all the students in the class will automatically accept the disabled youngster. The class must be prepared for the arrival of this special student. Mizen and Linton (1983), offer the following excellent suggestions for preparing the environment in which individual student differences are respected:

* do not ignore differences; encourage students to ask questions
* simulate disabling conditions in order that the nondisabled can learn to understand the experiences of their disabled peers
* discuss why people may ridicule or tease another person
* invite a disabled adult to visit and talk with the class

The student to be mainstreamed

Oddly enough, the student to be mainstreamed is often overlooked and the last to be informed regarding placement into a regular physical education setting (Tymitz-Wolf, 1984). The student's feelings toward being mainstreamed must be considered. For some students this can certainly be a stressful and frightening situation. The disabled student who possesses a positive attitude and willingness to participate in physical activity can overcome many adversities which may arise during the entire mainstreaming process. Educators must consider if the child performs differently in a one-on-one, small group or large class setting. For example, this can be determined by observing how the child reacts and performs in such settings as recess. The teacher can determine if the child plays with others or engages in only isolated play. The student, when mainstreamed, may be reluctant to participate in a large group or in front of nondisabled peers, feeling more protected in the small group setting of a special class. Physical education is unique from other academic areas in that students must perform and compete in an open setting for all to see. For example, it can be devastating for a disabled child to perform in front of their peers in a movement-oriented activity. A teacher must be aware of the anxiety the disabled student may feel when he or she is first mainstreamed. Every student must be carefully prepared for the move into a mainstreamed setting and never carelessly dumped into the gymnasium.

Weigh all factors before mainstreaming

Mainstreaming is important; however, too much emphasis has been placed on the concept and not enough on the process. Statements made in the literature suggest physical education as the most obvious and appropriate arena to host initial student mainstreaming attempts. Nothing may be further from the truth. As stated, for mainstreaming to be effective several factors need to be addressed when considering the individual. An assessment of the individual's abilities is paramount before a decision can be justly administered. The considerations for appropriate placement in physical education may outweigh the considerations in any other discipline. In any other subject students must demonstrate a minimal competency level or be given individual work commensurate with their ability. They also must demonstrate appropriate affective behavior. Affective and cognitive abilities are equally important criteria in physical education, but with the addition of the psychomotor considerations. Motor ability, motor fitness, physical fitness, physical size and perceptual-motor development are all additional factors which complicate the placement decision in physical education.

When mainstreaming fails educators must ask themselves why. If all factors are considered and each signifies possible successful integration, there are still no guarantees. The harbinger approach will help to increase the chances for success. When it has been determined that placement integration is appropriate, a plan must be developed. This placement information maps out a new area in preparation for those who will eventually pass through. This planning prepares the disabled student, the class, and the teacher for what each can expect and what each must do to make the mainstreaming passage a safe, successful, and enjoyable journey.

References

Aloia, G., Knutson, R., Minner, S. J., & Von Seggern, M. (1980). Physical education teachers' initial perceptions of handicapped children. Mental Retardation, 18, 85-87.

Bishop, P. (1986). Physical educators' perceptions of mainstreaming effects. Nebraska Journal for Health, Physical Education, Recreation & Dance, 17 (1), 6-8, 32.

DePaepe, J. L. (1984). Mainstreaming malpractice. Physical Educator, 41, 51-56.

DePaepe, J. L. (1985). The influence of three least restrictive environments on the content Motor-ALT and performance of moderately mentally retarded students. The Journal of Teaching inPhysical Education, 4, 34-41.

Dunn, J. M., & Craft, D. H. (1985). Mainstreaming theory and practice. Adapted Physical Activity Quarterly. 2, 273-276.

French, R. W., & Jansma, P. (1982). Special Physical Education. Columbus: Charles E. Merrill.

Jansma, P., & Schulz, B. (1982). Validation and use of a mainstreaming attitude inventory with physical educators. American Corrective Therapy Journal, 36, 150-157.

Lavay, B., & French, R. (1985). The special physical educator: Meeting educational goals through a transdisciplinary approach. American Corrective Therapy Journal, 39, 77-81.

Minner, S. H., & Knutson, R. (1982). Mainstreaming handicapped students into physical education: Initial considerations and needs. Physical Educator, 39, 13-15.

Mizen, D. W., & Linton, N. (1983). Guess who's coming to PE: Six steps to more effective mainstreaming. Journal of Physical Education, Recreation and Dance, 54 (8), 63-65.

Rizzo, T. L. (1984). Attitudes of physical educators toward teaching handicapped pupils. Adapted Physical Activity Quarterly, 1, 267-274.

Sherrill, C. (1986). Adapted physical education and recreation. Dubuque, IA: Wm. C. Brown.

Tymitz-Wolf, B. (1984). An analysis of EMR children's worries about mainstreaming. Education and Training of the Mentally Retarded, 19, 157-168.

Winnick, J. P. (1978). Techniques for integration. Journal of Physical Education and Recreation, 49, 22.

ADVANTAGES AND DISADVANTAGES OF MAINSTREAMING

Advantages

1. In general, the motor performance of the student with a disability is more "normal" than not and the student may perform better in the physical education environment than in other academic areas. In this setting the physical educator is able to teach the student through demonstration and physical guidance.

2. Both the student with a disability and the nondisabled student can benefit from the mainstreamed setting. The nondisabled student can be an effective role model to the student with a disability by demonstrating appropriate motor, cognitive, and social behavior. In addition, the nondisabled student learns to respect rather than pity the student with a disability.

3. Normalization process: through activities and games the student with a disability learns to socially interact with other students and is made to adjust to real life settings rather than remain in a sheltered environment. Merely placing this student with the nondisabled student in a mainstreamed setting doesn't assure for social interaction.

4. The student with a disability may be motivated to perform better in the presence of nondisabled peers.

5. Integrating various students may save time, personnel, facilities, equipment and consequently reduce the school budget.

Disadvantages

1. Extra facilities, special equipment, and planning time may be needed when integrating the student with a disability into the regular physical education setting.

2. The regular physical education instructor may be unaware of certain teaching strategies or behavior management techniques to use with the student with a disability. Consequently the teacher may resent having student with a disability participating in class and this negative attitude may carry over to all students participating.

3. Grouping students of different ability levels may be difficult during games and sports.

4. This student may withdraw in a large group and be reluctant to participate in a mainstreamed setting. The student may feel more protected in the small group setting.

TEACHING SUGGESTIONS FOR MAINSTREAMING

Unfortunately for many students with a disability mainstreaming has become a series of miserable and embarrassing failures such as being picked last or dropping a fly ball in front of peers. In general, the instructor must emphasize success and a positive experience by organizing the environment and instructional strategies that are responsive to each individual's needs. More specific strategies follow:

1. Assess the individual needs of the student. Activity selection should be based on student strengths, needs, developmental ages, chronological age, and interests.

2. If possible obtain some background information regarding the particular student mainstreamed into class. This information will be very valuable in programming and understanding the student.

3. Initially provide for positive experiences by reinforcing student strengths. Once confidence is gained the instructor can provide more challenging activities. The student with a disability is similar to all students and must be challenged and made to understand that it is acceptable to sometimes fail.

4. Instruct the student with a disability through demonstration and physical guidance while keeping verbal directions to a minimum. In general most student with a disability learn best by instruction which is made tangible and concrete.

5. Task analysis should be used when teaching skills and activities, progressing slowly in a well planned sequential order.

6. Transfer of learning may be difficult for the student with a disability, skills once developed must be applied in a variety of situations and environments.

7. The attention span of the student with a disability may be short, therefore provide for a variety of stimulating activities to

maintain interest.

8. When a student fails it may be because the teacher is not using the most effective method of instruction. Not all students learn best by one particular teaching method. Instruction should be student centered and not dictated by a certain curriculum or teacher centered.

9. Keep students active by shortening lines, providing each student with equipment or using teaching stations. Teaching stations allow students to perform activities according to ability level while providing a variety of tasks or activities.

10. Utilize "PEER TUTORS or the BUDDY SYSTEM" by having mature and skilled students instruct student with a disability.

11. Be familiar with various behavior management techniques in order to manage behavior as well as motivate student learning.

12. As a teacher, do not internalize student inappropriate behavior, lack of progress or failure. During class be patient and have a positive attitude.

13. Avoid embarrassing circumstances such as playing elimination games or having students pick teams.

14. Do not ignore or avoid a student's disability but rather allow other students to question and discuss this topic in an educational manner.

STRATEGIES FOR MODIFYING GAMES AND SPORT

A student with a disability has usually developed the modification techniques needed to successfully participate in the activity. Students may resent activities being modified to the point they are unrecognizable. However, some slight modifications may be needed to assure student success. Modfied from: Eichstaedt, C. & Lavay, B. (1992). Physical activity for persons with mental retardation: Infant to adult. Champaign IL: Human Kinetics.

Environment
- a. lower the net in a volleyball game or the basket in a basketball game
- b. reduce the size of the playing field
- c. make boundaries more tangible (ie. use cones, flags)

Equipment
- a. use large brightly colored nerf balls
- b. use a batting tee rather than a pitcher
- c. use lighter and larger equipment

Time of Play
- a. use frequent rest periods
- b. reduce the number of minutes played in a period

Feedback
- a. insert buzzers or bells on goals to reinforce the concept of scoring
- b. reinforce children who display teamwork during play

Playing Positions
- a. rotate positions giving each child an opportunity to learn various skills

Movement
- a. have objects (i.e. ball) move slowly
- b. reduce the size of the playing area
- c. increase or dercrease the number of children participating

Insure Success:
- a. avoid elimination games
- b. stress self-competition rather than team competition

MAINSTREAMING INTO ACTION

The following is a brief description of a physical education program in a large urban high school. The physical education department consisted of eight regular full time physical education teachers and an itinerant special physical education teacher who taught at the school for one period a day. The staff members followed a department curriculum and taught a different activity in a different teaching station, changing activities approximately every four weeks. To facilitate the mainstreaming process the special physical education program was developed to be similar to the regular physical education program.

The following are examples of successful mainstreaming practices:

Team Teaching

1. Student with disabilities were brought into the regular physical education class which offered a variety of activities such as aerobic dance, soccer, volleyball, archery, and ping pong. Each student with a disability was assigned a peer tutor or "buddy" from the regular class to serve as an assistant. The regular physical education teacher and the special physical education teacher shared teaching responsibilities.

2. The regular and special physical education classes were combined and then placed into squads of equal ability with approximately 10 to 12 students per a squad. Two squads would play soccer with the regular physical education teacher while the third squad would participate in such nontraditional activities as crab soccer and scooterboard hockey. The squads would rotate among the two activities each day.

Reverse Mainstreaming

1. Students in the regular physical education class were selected by
   their teacher to to be a peer tutor and help an assigned special
   education student enrolled in the self contained special physical
   education class. During this class the peer tutors received a
   grade toward their regular physical education class. At the
   beginning of class the regular education students were briefed by
   the special physical education instructor regarding the lesson to
   be taught for that particular period. The classes were always
   followed by a discussion between the peer tutors and the special
   physical education instructor. The following page shows an example of the
   peer tutor grading system.

Modfied from: Eichstaedt, C. & Lavay, B. (1992). Physical activity for persons
with mental retardation: Infant to adult. Champaign IL: Human Kinetics.

PEER TUTOR GRADING SYSTEM

Student Name: **Class Period:**

Date: **Regular PE Class:**

Each student will be graded and receive a maximum of 4 points in each of the following areas:

1. Ability to assist peer: 1 2 3 4

2. Skills practice: 1 2 3 4

2. Class participation: 1 2 3 4

3. Cooperation with others: 1 2 3 4

5. Enthusiasm: 1 2 3 4

TOTAL GRADE: (A) 15-13   (B) 12-10   (C) 9-7

Comments:

Modfied from: Eichstaedt, C. & Lavay, B. (1992). <u>Physical activity for persons with mental retardation: Infant to adult</u>. Champaign IL: Human Kinetics.

PEER TUTOR PAPER

The assignment is to write a paper about your experiences in the Thursday Special Physical Education class. The paper should be a page and a half or more in length. The assignment will be worth extra points toward your grade in your regular physical education class. The following is a list of ideas which may help with the assignment:

1. Compare how you felt before starting the class to how you feel now in class.
2. Have your feelings toward the other students changed since starting the class and what are they?
3. What have you learned since participating in this class?
4. What have you enjoyed most about the class?
5. What changes would you make to improve the class?

Remember the important thing is to have fun and write what you feel!

The following are examples of responses by two student peer tutors enrolled in the program:

Peer Tutor 1

" I know some of us sort of dreaded going at first. All of our feelings about the class has changed to the better. I now understand how they must feel around other students who think of them as being so different. I'm glad I can be friends with them and help them learn".

Peer Tutor 2

"I have also learned that these students are really special and all they need is someone to encourage them. They need someone to tell them they are doing good and help them to keep trying. I think that maybe some of their problems are not that they are that slow, but that they don't have much self-confidence. If they have someone to help them develop this, I think that they will be able to do considerably better in everything".

MODIFYING GAMES TO MEET INDIVIDUAL NEEDS

List 3 ways to change the environment to meet all student's needs

List 3 ways to change equipment to meet all student's needs

List 3 ways to change the fitness demands of a game to meet all student's needs

List 3 ways to change the rules of a game to meet all student's needs

List 3 ways to assure that the children on both teams socially interract and get along

List 3 ways to change traditional elimination games

List ways to make the following skills less complex

A. striking a ball in a softball game

B. playing a game of volleyball

C. playing a game of soccer

A Bibliography of Mainstreaming in Physical Education

Reprinted with permission from: DePaepe, J. & Lavay, B. (1985). A bibliography of mainstreaming in physical education. Physical Educator, 42, 41-43.

"By the very nature of their program physical education teachers are constantly reminded that teaching children with handicaps in a mainstreaming program can be frustrating and disappointing. The time has come to meet the challenge." (Mizen & Linton, 1983, p. 63.)

The following bibliography has been compiled by the authors to enable physical educators to gain greater insight into the mainstreaming process in order to meet the challenge of effectively integrating the exceptional student into the regular physical education setting. The citations are not exhaustive, but each has been reviewed by the authors and considered appropriate and relevant.

All references cited in the bibliography met the following criteria:

1. Each reference specifically pertains to mainstreaming in physical education being categorized into one of three groups: research, overview, and practical application.

2. All references have been verified by the writers of the bibliography through examination of the original book, journal article, unpublished paper, dissertation or dissertation abstract to the spring of 1984.

Research

Aloia, G., Knutson, R., Minner, S. J., & Von Seggern, M. (1980). Physical education teachers' initial perceptions of handicapped children. Mental Retardation, 18, 85-87.

Aufderheide, S., Knowles, C., & McKenzie, T. (1981). Individualized teaching strategies and learning time: Implications for mainstreaming. The Physical Educator, 38, 20-26.

Aufderheide, S. K., McKenzie, T. L., & Knowles, C. J. (1982). Effect of individualized instruction on handicapped and nonhandicapped students in elementary physical education classes. Journal ofTeaching in Physical Education, 1, 51-57.

Aufsessor, P. M. (1982). Comparison of the attitudes of physical education, recreation and special education majors toward the disabled. American Corrective Therapy Journal, 36, 35-41.

Beuter, A. C. (1983). Effects of mainstreaming on motor performances of intellectually normal and trainable mentally retarded students. American Corrective Therapy Journal, 37, 48-52.

Beuter, A. (1984). Ethobehavioral analysis of the social behaviors of trainable mentally retarded andintellectually normal children in an integrated educational setting. American Corrective Therapy Journal, 38, 11-13.

Brunt, D., & Broadhead, G. D. (1983). The use of discriminant analysis in the assessment of deaf children for physical education. American Corrective Therapy Journal, 37, 43-47.

Burnes, A. J., & Hassol, L. (1966). A pilot study in evaluating camping experiences for the mentally retarded. Mental Retardation, 4, 15-17.

Gauthier, R. A. (1980). A descriptive-analytic study of teacher-student interaction in mainstreamed physical education classes. (Doctoral dissertation, Purdue University, 1980). Dissertation Abstracts International, 41, 3474-A.

Hamilton, E. J., & Anderson, S. C. (1983). Effects of leisure activities on attitudes toward people with disabilities. Therapeutic Recreation Journal, 3, 50-57.

Hayes, G. A. (1969). The integration of mentally retarded and non-retarded in a day camping program: A demonstration program. Mental Retardation, 7, 14-16.

Hus, J. (1979). The socialization process of hearing-impaired children in summer day camp. Volta Review, 81, 146-156.

Jansma, P., & Shultz, B. (1982). Validation and use of a mainstreaming attitude inventory with physical educators. American Corrective Therapy Journal, 36, 150-158.

Johnson, R. E., & Robinson, M. R. (1983). Physical functioning levels of learning disabled and normal children. American Corrective Therapy Journal, 37, 56-59.

Kahn, L. E. (1983). Self-concept and physical fitness of retarded students as correlates of social interaction between retarded and non-retarded students. (Doctoral dissertation, New York University, 1982). Dissertation Abstracts International, 43, 2275-A.

Karper, W. B., & Martinek, T. J. (1982). Differential influences of various instructional factors on self-concepts of handicapped and non-handicapped children in mainstreamed physical education classes. Perceptual and Motor Skills, 54, 831-835.

Karper, W. B., & Martinek, T. J. (1983). Motor performance and self-concept of handicapped and non-handicapped children in integrated physical education classes. American Corrective Therapy Journal, 37, 91-95.

Knowles, C. J., Aufderheide, S. K., & McKenzie, T. (1982). Relationship of individualized teaching strategies to academic learning time for mainstreamed handicapped and non-handicapped students. The Journal of Special Education, 16, 449-456.

Marston, R., & Leslie, D. (1983). Teacher perceptions from mainstreamed versus non-mainstreamed teaching environments. Physical Educator, 40, 8-15.

Martinek, T. J., & Karper, W. B. (1981). Teachers' expectations for handicapped and non-handicapped children in mainstreamed physical education classes. Perceptual and Motor Skills, 53, 327-330.

Martinek, T. J., & Karper, W. B. (1982). Entry-level motor performance and self-concepts of handicapped and non-handicapped children in mainstreamed physical education classes: A preliminary study. Perceptual and Motor Skills, 55, 1002.

Mason, W. C. (1983). Attitude changes of undergraduate students toward handicapped individuals in a physical education practicum (Doctoral dissertation, Peabody College, 1983). Dissertation Abstracts International, 44, 1021-A.

Minner, S. H., & Knuston, R. (1982). Mainstreaming handicapped students into physical education: Initial considerations and needs. Physical Educator, 39, 13-15.

Rarick, G. L., & Beuter, A. (1981). Social and motor outcomes in normal and mentally retarded children exposed to a mainstreamed physical education instruction program. Abstract of Invited Papers at the NASPSPA Annual Conference.

Reynolds, R. P., & Arthur, M. H. (1982). Effect of peer modeling and cognitive self-guidance on the social play of emotionally disturbed children. Therapeutic Recreation Journal, 16, 30-40.

Rizzo, T. L. (1983). Attitudes of physical educators toward teaching handicapped pupils (Doctoral dissertation, University of Illinois, 1983). Dissertation Abstracts International, 44, 1725-A.

Santomer, J., & Kopczuk, W. (1981). Facilitation of interactions between retarded and non-retardedstudents in a physical education setting. Education and Training of the Mentally Retarded, 16, 20-23.

Spragens, J. E. (1979). Inservice training of teachers to work in mainstreamed physical education settings. Unpublished doctoral dissertation, Texas Women's University, Denton.

Vickery, R. M., McCabe, J. F., & Field, C. (1983). Play material and social interaction between disabled and non-disabled preschoolers. Therapeutic Recreation Journal, 17, 43-51.

Wess, P. I. (1983). Factors used to determine mainstreaming of mentally handicapped and learning disabled students into elementary school physical education programs (Doctoral dissertation, University of Oregon, 1983). Dissertation Abstracts International, 44, 2087-A.

West, P. C. (1984). Social stigma and community recreation participation by the mentally and physically handicapped. Therapeutic Recreation Journal, 18, 40-49.

Overview

Auxter, D. (1981). Equal opportunity for the handicapped through physical education. Physical Educator, 38, 8-14.

Bird, P. J., & Gansneder, B. M. (1979). Preparation of Physical Education teachers as required under Public Law 94-142. Exceptional Children, 45, 464-466.

Broadhead, G. D. (1982). A paradigm for physical education for handicapped children in the least restrictive environment. Physical Educator, 39, 3-12.

Cushing, D. (1980). Physical Education: Integrating the handicapped. The Physician and Sports Medicine, 8 (1), 16-18.

DePaepe, J. L. (1984). Mainstreaming malpractice. Physical Educator, 41, 51-56.

Dixon, J. T. (1980). Mainstreaming and leisure education for the mentally retarded. Therapeutic Recreation Journal, 14, 30-35.

Dunn, J. M. (1976). Mainstreaming: Definition, rationale and implications for physical education. Mainstreaming Physical Education: Briefings. NAPE for College Women and NCPEA for

Men, 4, 3.

Eichstaedt, C. (1980). Is mainstreaming in physical education appropriate for all handicapped students? Illinois Journal of Health, Physical Education, and Recreation, 2, 17-19.

Goodwin, L. (1976). Arguments against mainstreaming: Are we ready? Mainstreaming Physical Education Briefings. NAPE for College Women and NCPEA for Men, 4, 30-33.

Gunn, S. L. (1976). Mainstreaming is a two-way street. Journal of Physical Education and Recreation, 47 (7), 48-49.

Jansma, P., & French, R. (1982). Law and the physical educator. Journal of Physical Education, Recreation & Dance, 53, 70, 72-73.

Matthews, P. R. (1977). Recreation and the normalization of the mentally retarded. Therapeutic Recreation Journal, 11, 112-114.

McClenaghan, B. A. (1981). Normalization in physical education: A reflective review. Physical Educator, 38, 3-7.

Miller, A. G., & Sullivan, J. V. (1982). Teaching Physical Activities to Impaired Youth: An Approach to Mainstreaming. New York: John Wiley & Sons.

Morreau, L. E., & Eichstaedt, C. B. (1983). Least restrictive programming and placement in physical education. American Corrective Therapy Journal, 37, 7-17.

Putoff, M. (1976). Instructional strategies for mainstreaming. Mainstreaming Physical Education, Briefings. NAPE for College Women and NCPEA for Men, 4, 34-35.

Pyfer, J. (1982). Criteria for placement in physical education experiences. Exceptional Education Quarterly, 3, 10-16.

Rich, S. M., & Wuest, D. A. (1983). Self-confidence and the physically handicapped mainstreamed child. Physical Educator, 40, 163-165.

Rider, R. A. (1979). Mainstreaming the young moderately retarded child into the regular physical education class. The North Carolina Journal, 15 (1), 1-4.

Rider, R. A. (1980). Mainstreaming moderately retarded children in the elementary physical education program. Teaching Exceptional Children, 12, 150-152.

Rink, J. E. (1982). The key is the learning environment. Profiles/ Luann Alleman. Journal of Physical Education, Recreation and Dance, 53 (7), 44, 46.

Schleifer, M. J. (1977). Mainstreaming: We did a terrible thing in sending Ed to camp. Exceptional Parent, 7, 21-26.

Sherill, C. (1976). Arguments for mainstreaming: A humanistic rationale. Mainstreaming Physical Education Briefings, NAPE for College Women and NCPEA for Men, 4, 19-29.

Shriver, E. K. (1976). Physical education: Shortest road to success for the handicapped. Science and Children, 13, 24-26.

Soulek, M. (1975). A look at stigmas and the roles of recreators and physical educators. Journal of Physical Education and Recreation, 46 (5), 28-29.

Stein, J. (October, 1977). Sense and nonsense about mainstreaming. Sixth National Conference on Physical Activity for the Exceptional Individual. Los Angeles, CA, 161-165.

Stein, J. (1978). Physical education and sports as required by PL 94-142 and Section 504. American Corrective Therapy Journal, 32, 145-151.

Stewart, C. (1980). Integrating the physically handicapped child into the physical education classroom. Journal of Physical Education and Recreation, 51 (4), 17.

Weiss, R. A., & Karper, W. B. (1980). The preparation of non-physical education teachers to teach physical education to handicapped students. American Corrective Therapy Journal, 34, 137-141.

Weiss, R. A., & Karper, W. B. (1980). Teaching the handicapped child in the regular physical education class. Journal of Physical Education and Recreation, 51 (2), 32-35, 77.

Practical Applications

Austin, D. R., & Powell, L. G. (1981). What you need to know to serve special populations. Parks and Recreation, 16, 40-42.

Danaher, P. M. (1983). Handicap awareness program. Journal of Physical Education, Recreation and Dance, 54 (3), 67-68.

Dummer, G. M., & Windham, G. M. (1982). Mainstreaming in physical education: An insurance teacher training model that works. Physical Educator, 39, 16-20.

Eichstaedt, C. B., & Seiler, P. J. (1978). Signing. Journal of Physical Education and Recreation, 49, 19-21.

Folio, M., & Norman, A. (1981). Toward more success in mainstreaming: A peer teacher approach to physical education. Teaching Exceptional Children, 13, 110-114.

French, R. (1979). Direction or misdirection in physical education for mentally retarded students. Journal of Physical Education and Recreation, 50, 22-23.

Gorelick, M. C. (1974). What's in a label? Journal of Physical Education, Recreation and Dance, 45 (7), 71-72.

Grosse, S. (1978). Mainstreaming the physically handicapped student for team sports. Practical Pointers, 1 (8), 1-8.

Jansma, P. (1977). Get ready for mainstreaming. Journal of Physical Education and Recreation, 48, 15-16.

Jansma, P., & Krasnavage, P. (1982). Progressive inclusion of the handicapped into community youth football. Physical Educator, 39, 30-35.

Kraft, R. E. (1981). Movement experiences for children with auditory handicaps. Physical Educator, 38, 35-38.

Liddle, J., & Breihan, S. (1980). What is it like to be handicapped? Journal of Physical Education and Recreation, 51 (3), 36-38.

Long, E. et al. (1980). Journal of Physical Education and Recreation, 51, 28-29.

Melograno, V. (1978). Status of curriculum practice- Are you a consumer or designer? Journal of

Physical Education and Recreation, 49, 27-28.

Mizen, D. W., & Linton, N. (1983). Guess who's coming to PE: Six steps to more effective mainstreaming. Journal of Physical Education, Recreation and Dance, 54, 63-65.

Owen, B. H. (1978). Mainstreaming at Doe Valley Camp. Journal of Physical Education and Recreation, 49, 28-30.

Owens, M. F. (1981). Mainstreaming in the Every Child a Winner Program. Journal of Physical Education and Recreation, 52, 16-18.

Priest, L. (1979). Integrating the disabled into aquatics programs. Journal of Physical Education and Recreation, 50, 59.

Winnick, J. P. (1978). Techniques for integration. Journal of Physical Education and Recreation, 49, 22

References & Resources
in
Special Physical Education

REFERENCES & RESOURCES IN SPECIAL PHYSICAL EDUCATION

A REFERENCE GUIDE IN SPECIAL PHYSICAL EDUCATION

Reprinted with permission from: Lavay, B. & Dart, S. (1988). A resource guide for special physical educators in Kansas. <u>Kansas Association for Health Physical Education Recreation and Dance Journal, 55</u> (2),14-17;38. * This material has been updated to 1992.

The 1980's have witnessed an explosion of resource materials available to professionals providing physical education for students with special needs. Too often professionals, especially practitioners, are unaware of the current information and where it can be obtained. Availability of these materials can improve teacher instruction and ultimately enhance programming for students with special needs. Therefore, the purpose of this guide is to expose the reader to a variety of resources in the following areas: (a) professional personnel specific to each state, (b) nationally disseminated packaged programs, (c) assessment instruments, (d) literature including textbooks and journal articles, (e) professional organizations and journals, and (f) state department curriculum guides and materials. *This article has been updated since its initial publication date.

Professional Personnel:

Individuals with varied backgrounds exist such as State Department and University Personnel that can help provide direction to information regarding physical activity programming for the handicapped.

Public School Teachers/Programs:

A number of excellent adapted/ special physical education teachers and programs exist throughout each state. Many of these professionals possess certification and varied training expertise in adapted/ special physical education. The reader can begin by checking with the special education services in their district to determine if programs are available and the professionals to contact.

Nationally Disseminated Packaged Programs:

Large scale assessment and curriculum models are usually developed through federally funded grants and may eventually become nationally disseminated. These projects can be a helpful addition to an already existing adapted/ special physical education program. The following is a brief description of some of the most widely known and used models.

Project ACTIVE

Dr. Thomas Vodola, Researcher. Township of Ocean School District, Dow Avenue, Oakhurst, New Jersey. Contact Person: Mr. Joe Karp, 13209 NE 175th, Woodenville, Washington 908072. Population: Designed for children with special needs related to one of the following conditions: 1) low motor ability, 2) low physical vitality, 3) postural abnormalities, 4) nutritional deficiencies, 5) communication disorders, 6) motor disabilities/ limitations, 7) breathing problems, or 8) mental retardation and learning disabilities. Purpose: The entire teacher training program focuses on the acquisition and demonstration of specific skills that are necessary for effectively teaching children with a variety of disabilities. Guidelines for initiating the diagnostic-prescriptive process as well as procedures for evaluation and organization of student learning experiences are detailed in a series of program manuals for each of the above eight conditions.

Project I'M SPECIAL

Dr. Louis Bowers and Dr. Steven Klesius, Researchers. University of South Florida. Population: For use primarily by elementary and special physical educators as well as classroom instructors responsible for teaching physical education to children with disabilities in grades K-6. Purpose: This program consists of a set of 15 videotapes and print materials covering various topics related to physical education for the disabled. All videotapes are color/ sound presentations and use a variety of techniques to heighten viewer interest and to illustrate the content. The print materials include a synopsis of each videotape, discussion questions, and participation experiences. The modules are quite versatile and can be used in preservice university courses, inservice education presentations, and/or educational or public access television broadcasts. These materials are also available on videodisc.

Project I CAN

Dr. Janet Wessel, Researcher. PRO:ED Publications, Austin TX. also contact: Dr. Luke Kelly, Department of Physical Education, University Virginia. Population: Specifically for children whose overall developmental growth is slower than average; those with mental retardation, learning disabilities, social or emotional adjustment difficulties, and/ or economic or language disadvantages. Purpose: Provides for a criteria/ achievement-based approach with emphasis in the following instructional areas: plan, assess, prescribe, teach, and evaluate. A developmental skills program from primary through sport-leisure that accommodates each learner at his own pace and level of performance.

Project PEOPEL

Larry Irmer, Researcher. Phoenix High School District, 2910 North 19th Ave., Phoenix, Arizona. Population: Designed for children with disabilities who are capable of functioning in a mainstreamed physical education setting at the secondary level of education. Purpose: Uses the concept and practice of peer-tutoring, where trained nondisabled student aides work and play with children with disabilities who have unique needs in physical education. The teacher's guide contains 35 units, each task analyzed to provide individualized student learning and progress.

Project UNIQUE

Dr. Joseph Winnick and Dr. Francis Short, Researchers. Human Kinetics Pub., Chaimpaign Ill. Population: Designed for individuals between the ages of 10-17 classified as sensory (visual and auditory) or orthopedically impaired. The fitness test can also determine the status of nondisabled individuals. Purpose: normal physical fitness development is discussed and modifications are suggested for individuals with sensory and orthopedic handicapping conditions. Test administration and assessment along with age-group norms specific to the Project UNIQUE Physical Fitness Test are detailed in a testing manual. A training system, fitness activities, and sport modifications which are appropriate for individuals with sensory and orthopedic impairments are included in the training program manual.

Data-Based Gymnasium

Dr. John Dunn and Dr. James Moorehouse, Researchers. PRO:ED Pub., Austin TX. Population: Specifically for youngsters with severe mental, emotional, and sensory impairments. The program is designed to help the teacher effectively instruct even those individuals who are non-ambulatory. Purpose: A sequenced, task-analyzed,and data-based curriculum provides a bridge between therapeutically-oriented motor programs and the more advanced physical education gymnasium experiences. A systematic behavioral teaching approach formulated at baseline allows for individualized objectives to be established with each student. A text presents task-analyzed skills in four major movement domains.

Assessment Instruments:

Proper assessment procedures with regard topersons with a disability are important for a number of reasons. Primarily, these procedures are necessary to determinine the individual student's present level of performance in order to make sound placement and programming decisions. The instructor must realize that no single test is available to adequately measure the movement needs of all individuals with a disability . A variety of standardized assessment instruments exists and should be considered by the instructor during test selection.

Numerous textbooks offer listings and brief descriptions of various standardized assessment instruments. Three of these textbooks are:

Folio, R. M. (1986). Physical education programming for exceptional learners. Rockville, Maryland: Aspen Publishers.

Sherrill, C. (1986). Adapted physical education and recreation: A multidisciplinary approach. Dubuque, IA: Wm. C. Brown.

Werder, J. K., & Kalakian, L. H. (1985). Assessment in adapted physical education. Minneapolis, MN: Burgess Publishers (no longer in print).

The following is a list of some widely used assessment instruments along with a brief description and address of each. The listing is divided into three sections: physical fitness, motor ability, and posture.

Physical Fitness

the first four fitness tests described can be purchased through the American Alliance for Health, Physical Education, Recreation & Dance, 1900 Association Dr., Reston, VA 22091.

1. AAHPERD Physical Best (1988): This test measures the physiological parameters of health-related physical fitness such as: cardiorespiratory function, body composition, and abdominal and low back-hamstring muscoleskeletal function. Minimal standards were established with nondisabled students 5-18 years of age.

2. AAHPERD Health Related Physical Fitness (1980): This test measures the physiological parameters of health-related physical fitness such as: cardiorespiratory function, body composition, and abdominal and low back-hamstring muscoleskeletal function. The norms were established with nondisabled students 5-17 years of age (no longer in print).

3. AAHPER Special Fitness Test for Mildly Mentally Retarded (1976): The items on this test are similar to the AAHPER Youth Fitness Test with some slight modifications. The norms were established for individuals with mild mental retardation 8-18 years of age. (No longer in print.)

4. AAHPER Motor Fitness Test for the Moderately Mentally Retarded: Johnson & Londeree (1976): This test measures the motor fitness of moderately mentally retarded individuals ages 6-20 years. The test manual consists of 13 items with the first six items similar to the Special Fitness Test for the Mildly Mentally Retarded.

5. Project UNIQUE Physical Fitness Test: Winnick & Short (1985): Human Kinetics, Champaign, Il. this test measures the physical fitness of sensory (blind and deaf) and orthopedically impaired individuals. The test battery consists of 7 items with many similar to the Health-Related Physical Fitness Test. Slight test modifications were made when the impairment prevented the group from completing that particular test item.

Motor Ability

1. Basic Motor Ability Test: Arnheim & Sinclair (1979). The clumsy child: A program of motor therapy. St. Louis:C. V. Mosby. this test was designed to evaluate the motor ability of children 4-12 years of age. It is a norm-referenced test consisting of 11 items which primarily measure fine and gross motor ability of individuals with mild disabilities. (No longer in print.)

2. Bruininks-Oseretsky Test of Motor Proficiency: Bruininks (1978). American Guidance Services, Circle Pine, MN 55014. The test is designed to measure the overall motor proficiency of children 4.5-14.5 years old. This norm-referenced test must be individually administered and consists of 46 test items (long form) and 14 test items (short form). The curriculum guide Body Skills is also available with this test.

3. Ohio State University Scale of Intra Gross Motor Assessment: Loovis & Ersing (1979). College Town Press P.0. Box 669, Bloomington, IN 47402. A criterion-referenced test which measures the fundamental motor skills of preschool, elementary and young mentally retarded children. The test

consists of 11 items with a four point performance rating level for each fundamental skill.

4. Test of Gross Motor Development: Ulrich (1986). PRO-ED Publishers. 5341 Industrial Oaks Blvd., Austin, TX 78735. This test measures 12 fundamental skills (locomotor and object control) in children 3-10 years of age. This test is unique from others in that results can be interpreted by means of both criterion-referenced and norm-referenced standards.

Posture

New York State Posture Rating Test: Revised (1976). Project Active. Township of Ocean School District, Oakhurst, NJ. Mr. Joe Karp, 13209 NE 175th, Woodenville, Washington 908072. This test is used to measure the posture of children in grades 4-12. A posture chart is used by the examiner to rate 13 areas of the individual's body.

Literature:

Literature in the form of textbooks and journal articles can be a valuable source of information to the practitioner seeking effective strategies to provide physical activity to the disabled. Special Physical Education Textbooks consist of various topics dealing with physical education for the disabled as well as follow the particular philosophy of the author(s). Therefore, it is important to read from a variety of textbooks in order to keep abreast with the most current information regarding program instruction. The following is an annotated list of current textbooks on special physical education.

1. Auxter, D. & Pyfer, J. (1989). Principles and methods of adapted physical education and recreation. St. Louis, MO: C. V. Mosby. This text stresses a process approach in determining the unique needs of students with disabilities. Topics on integration of assessment, programming, and implementation procedures that can maximize motor development of the disabled are described in detail. The text contains perhaps the most comprehensive information on behavior management to be written in any special physical education textbook.

2. Dunn, J. M & Fait, J. F. (1989). Special physical education: adapted, individualized, developmental. Philadelphia, PA: W. B. Saunders Company. This text provides attention to individualized education programming which parallels the major thrusts of special education. Two significant additions to this edition are appropriate physical education instruction for the severely handicapped as well as the role of competitive sports for individuals with disabilities.

3. Eichstaedt, C. B. & Kalakian, L. H. (1987). Developmental/ Adapted physical education: Making ability count. Minneapolis, MN: Burgess Publishing. This text places a major focus on "Making ability count" among all individuals. The text presents in-depth information regarding each disability in order to complement the intent of P.L. 94-142 in determining who is eligible for special services.

4. Folio, M. R. (1986). Physical education programming for exceptional learners. Rockville, MD: Aspen Publishing. This textbook serves as a "cookbook" to the practitioner faced with the challenge of developing and/or implementing physical education programs for their handicapped

students with disabilities. A chapter on assessment which outlines and details 27 assessment tools is offered.

5. Seaman, J. A. & Depauw, K. P. (1989). <u>The new adapted physical education: A developmental approach</u>. Palo Alto, CA: Mayfield Publishing. The authors of this text provide a noncategorical approach to viewing and tailoring instruction to each individual with special needs. The concept of developmental programming is stressed in order to prepare the teacher to challenge students to progress along a natural as well as individual movement continuum. the text devotes a large section to the process of assessment.

6. Sherrill, C. (1986). <u>Adapted physical education and recreation: A multidisciplinary approach</u>. Dubuque, IA: Wm. C. Brown. Perhaps the most comprehensive textbook in the area of special physical education. The text is organized in three sections emphasizing the three instructional approaches to teaching special physical education. A unique chapter on dance therapy and adapted dance is offered.

Other textbooks which offer specific programming information as well as general referencing in the area of special physical education are:

1. Adams, R. C., & McCubbin, J. A. (1990). <u>Games, sports and exercises for the physically handicapped</u>. Philadelphia, PA: Lea & Febiger. This text contains information regarding remedial exercise programs primarily for the physically disabled.

2. Arnheim, D. D. & Sinclair, W. A. (1979). <u>the clumsy child: A program of motor therapy</u>. St. Louis, MO: C. V. Mosby. This text provides a review of the factors and strategies for implementing a therapy program for students displaying motor dysfunction (this text is no longer in print).

3. Arnheim, D. D. & Sinclair, W. A. (1985). <u>Physical education for special populations: A developmental, adapted & remedial approach</u>. Englewood Cliffs, NJ: Prentice-Hall.

4. Bishop, P. (1988). (Ed.) <u>Adapted physical education: A comprehensive resource manual</u>. Kearney, NE: Educational Systems Associates Inc.

5.Eichstaedt, C. B. & Lavay, B. (1992). <u>Physical activty for persons with mental retardation: Infant to adult</u>. Champaign, IL: Human Kinetics.

6. French, R. W. & Jansma, P. (1992). <u>Special physical education</u>. Englewood Cliffs, NJ: Prentice-Hall.

7. Horvat, M. (1990). <u>Physical education and sport for the exceptional child</u>. Dubuque, IA: Wm. C. Brown.

8. Winnick, J. P. (1990). <u>Adapted physical education and sport</u>. Champaign Ill., Human Kinetics.

For additional information on certain content information, the following references are cited and divided into major areas of content.

Motor and Perceptual Development

Gallahue, D. L. (1989). Understanding motor <u>development in infants, children and adolescents</u>. Indianapolis IN: Benchmark Press

Gallahue, D. L. (1982). <u>Developmental movement experiences for children</u>. New York: John Wiley & Sons.

Horvat, M. (1989). <u>A manual of activities to improve perceptual motor skills</u>. Kearney NE: Educational Systems Associations Inc.

Payne, G.V. & Issac, L.D. ((1991). <u>Human motor development: A lifespan approach</u>. Mountain View CA: Mayfield.

Wickstrom, R. L. (1983). <u>Fundamental motor patterns</u>. Philadelphia: Lea & Febiger.

Williams, H. G. (1983). <u>Perceptual and motor development</u>. Englewood Cliffs, NJ: Prentice-Hall.

Mainstreaming

Dunn, J. M. & Craft, D. H. (1985). Mainstreaming issue. <u>Adapted Physical Activity Quarterly</u>, <u>2</u>, 263-356.

Lavay, B. & DePaepe, J. (1987). The harbinger helper : Why mainstreaming in physical education doesn't always work: . <u>Journal of Physical Education, Recreation and Dance</u>, <u>58</u> (7), 98-103.

Mainstreaming and the least restictive environment issue (1991). <u>Palaestra, 7</u> (2), 30-53.

Mizen, D. W. & Linton, N. (1983). Guess who's coming to P.E.: Six steps to more effective mainstreaming. <u>Journal of Physical Education, Recreation and Dance</u>, <u>54</u> (8), 63-65.

Stewart,C. C. (1980). Integrating the physically handicapped child into the physical education classroom. <u>Journal of Physical Education and Recreation</u>, <u>51</u> (4), 17.

Weiss, R. & Karper, W. B. (1980). Teaching the handicapped child in the regular physical education class. <u>Journal of Physical Education and Recreation</u>, <u>51</u> (2), 32-35 & 77.

Behavior Management

Dunn, J. M. & French, H. W. (1982). Operant conditioning: A tool for special physical educators in the 1980's. <u>Exceptional Education Quarterly</u>, <u>3</u>, 42-53.

French, R., & Lavay, B. (1990). <u>Behavior management skills for physical educators and recreators</u>. Kearney , NE: Educational Systems Associations Inc.

French, R., Lavay, B. & Henderson, H. (1985). Take a lap. <u>The Physical Educator</u>, <u>42</u>, 180-185.

Hellison, D. R. (1985). <u>Goals and strategies for teaching physical education</u>. Champaign, Il: Human KineticsPublishers.

Lavay, B. (1986). Behavior management in physical education, recreation and sport: A bibliography. <u>Physical Educator</u>, <u>43</u> (2),103-112.

Aquatics

Christie, I. (1985). Aquatics for the handicapped: A review of literature. <u>The Physical Educator</u>. <u>42</u>, 24 -33.

Horvat, M., & Forbus, W. R. (1989). <u>Using the aquatic environment fro teaching handicapped children</u>. Kearney , NE:Educational Systems Associations Inc.

Killian, K. J., Arena-Ronde,S., & Bruno, L. (1987). Refinement of two instruments that measure water orientation of atypical swimmers. <u>Adapted Physical Activity Quarterly</u>, <u>4</u>, 25-37.

Langendorfer, S. (1989). Aquatics for young children with handicapping conditions. <u>Palaestra</u>, <u>5</u> (3), 17-19;37-40

Peganoff, S. A. (1984). The use of aquatics with cerebral palsy adolescents. <u>American Journal of Occupational Therapy</u>, <u>7</u> (38), 469-473.

YMCA of the USA (1987). <u>Aquatics for special populations</u>. Champaign, IL: Human Kinetics.

Professional Organizations

<u>The American Alliance for Health, Physical Education, Recreation and Dance</u> (AAHPERD) is comprised of state and district chapters devoted to promoting and enhancing health, physical education, recreation and dance at all levels of education. The substructures specific to the disabled have merged into one body under the governance of ARAPCS. This new structure, the Adapted Physical Activity Council, advances educational policy favorable for the disabled as well as conducts conferences at which the members are able to share theory and practices. The official publication for this group of professionals is Able Bodies.

<u>The National Consortium on Physical Education and Recreation for the Handicapped</u> (NCPERH) is exclusively devoted to professionals involved in training, demonstration and/ or research related to physical education and recreation for the disabled. Its membership promotes legislation and funding, disseminates information and generates a growing knowledge base for adapted physical education. This organization's professional newsletter is The Advocate.

<u>The American Kinesiotherapy Association</u> recommends standards for training facilities and the certification of professionals in the area of corrective therapy. Their publication is the Clinical Kinesiology Journal.

<u>The National Therapeutic Recreation Society</u> (NTRS) has contributed to the evolution of therapeutic recreation for the disabled. This organization publishes the Therapeutic Recreation Journal.

<u>The Association for Retarded Citizens </u>(ARC) is devoted to preventing mental retardation, finding cures, and assisting persons with mental retardation in their daily living. ARC also provides a variety of publications aimed at answering lay and professional inquiries about mental retardation.

<u>The Council for Exceptional Children </u>(CEC) advances the education of exceptional children and youth, both disabled and gifted. The organization develops a variety of professional programs and publications geared to meet the needs of the members.

Professional Journals

Adapted Physical Activity Quarterly

Palestra: The Forum of Sport, Physical Education & Recreation for the Handicapped

Journal of Physical Education, Recreation and Dance (AAHPERD)

Research Quarterly for Exercise and Sport (AAHPERD)

The Physical Educator (Phi Epsilon Kappa)

American Journal of Mental Deficiency

Exceptional children

Journal of Applied Behaviorlal Analysis

Mental Retardation

The Special Educator

Curriculum Guides/ Materials

A variety of excellent curriculum guides and resource materials are available in various states. The interested reader can inquire about available materials by contacting the special education or physical education director in each particular state department. For example, in the state of Kansas the following resource manual is available:

Johnson, R. & Lavay, B. (1988). Adapted/Special Physical Education Test Manual. 120 East 10th Street, Topeka, KS: Kansas State Department of Education.

ADAPTED/SPECIAL PHYSICAL EDUCATION TEXTBOOK REFERENCES

The following list of special physical education textbooks dates back to primarily the 1980s and will prove helpful to the student or practitioner.

Adams, R.D., & McCubbin, J. (1990). Games, sports, and exercises for the physically handicapped (5th ed). Philadelphia: Lea & Febiger.

American Red Cross. (1975). Swimming for the handicapped: An instructor's manual. Washington, D.C.: American Red Cross.

Arnheim, D. D., & Sinclair, W. A. (1985). Physical education for special populations. Englewood Cliffs, NJ: Prentice Hall.

Auxter, D., & Pyfer, J. (1989). Principals and methods of adapted physical education and recreation. St. Louis: C. V. Mosby.

Bishop, P. (1988). (Ed.) Adapted physical education: A comprehensive resource manual. Kearney, NE: Educational Systems Associates Inc.

Buell, C. (1975). Physical education for blind children. Springfield, IL: Charles C. Thomas.

Cratty., B. J. (1989). Adapted physical educationin the mainstream. Denver: Love Publishing.

Dunn, J. M., Moorehouse, J. W., Fredericks, H. D. (1986). Physical education for the severely handicapped: A systematic approach to data-based gymnasium. Austin, TX: Pro Ed.

Dunn, J. M. & Fait, H.F. (1989). Special physical education: Adapted, individualized, developmental. Philadelphia: W. B. Saunders.

Eichstaedt, C. B. & Lavay, B. (1992). Physical activty for persons with mental retardation: Infant to adult. Champaign, IL: Human Kinetics.

Eichstaedt, C. B. & Kalakian, L. H. (1987). Developmental/Adapted physical education: Making ability count. New York: MacMillan.

Folio, M. R. (1986). Physical education programming for exceptional learners. Rockville, Maryland: Aspen Pub.

French, R. W., & Jansma, P. (1992). Special physical education. Englewood Cliffs, NJ: Prentice-Hall.

French, R., & Lavay, B. (1990). Behavior management skills for physical educators and recreators. Kearney , NE: Educational Systems Associations Inc.

Geddes, D. (1981). Psychomotor individualized educational programs for intellectual, learning, and behavioral disabilities. Boston: Allyn and Bacon, Inc.

Horvat, M. (1990). Physical education and sport for the exceptional child. Dubuque, IA: Wm. C. Brown.

Hellison, D. R. (1985). Goals and strategies for teaching physical education. Champaign, IL: Human Kinetics.

Jansma, P. (Ed) (1989). The psychomotor domain and the seriously handicapped. Washington, D.C.: University Press of America.

Jones, J. A. (1988). (Ed). Training guide to cerebral palsy sports. Champaign, IL: Human Kinetics.

Lasko-McCartney, P., & Knopf, K. (1988). Adapted exercise for the disabled adult. Dubuque IA: Eddie Bowers Pub.

Masters, L. F., Mori, A. A., & Lange, E. K. (1983). Adapted physical education: A practitioner's guide. Rockville, Maryland: Aspen.

Seaman, J. A., & DePauw, K. P. (1989). The new adapted physical education: A developmental approach. Palo Alto, CA: Mayfield.

Shepard, R. J. (1990). Fitness in special populations. Champaign, IL: Human Kinetics.

Sherrill, C. (1986). Adapted physical education and recreation: A multidisciplinary approach. Dubuque, Iowa: Wm. C. Brown.

Sherrill, C. (Ed.). (1986). Sport for the disabled athlete. Champaign IL: Human Kinetics.

Sherrill, C. (Ed.). (1988). Leadership training in adapted physical education. Champaign, IL: Human Kinetics.

Werner, J. K., & Kalakian, L. H. (1985). Assessment in adapted physical education. Minneapolis, MN: Burgess.

Wessel, J. A., & Kelly, L. (1986). Achievement-based curriculum development in physical education. Philadelphia: Lea & Febiger.

Winnick, J. P. (1990). Adapted physical education and sport. Champaign Ill., Human Kinetics.

Winnick, J. P. & Short, F. X. (1985). Physical fitness testing of the disabled: Project UNIQUE. Champaign, IL: Human Kinetics.

Winnick, J. P. (1979). Early movement experiences and development: Habilitation and remediation. Philadelphia: W. B. Saunders.

Wiseman, D. C. (1982). A practical approach to adapted physical education. Reading, Massachusetts: Addison-Wesley.

YMCA of the USA (1987). Aquatics for special populations. Champaign, IL: Human Kinetics.

MOTOR DEVELOPMENT REFERENCES

Arnheim, D., & Pestolesi, R. (1983). Developing motor behavior in children. St. Louis: C. V. Mosby Company.

Arnheim, D. D., & Sinclair, W. A. (1979). The clumsy child: A program of motor therapy. St. Louis: C. V. Mosby Company.

Capon, J. (1975). Perceptual-motor lesson plans. (level 1 and 2). Alamenda, CA: Front Row Experiences.

Corbin, C. B. (Ed.). (1980). A textbook of motor development. Dubuque, Iowa: Wm. C. Brown Company.

Clark, J. E. & Humphrey, J. H. (Ed.). (1985). Motor development: Current research, Volume 1. Princeton, NJ: Princeton Book Co. Volume 2 is also in print.

Cratty, B. J. (1967). Developmental sequences of perceptual motor tasks. Freeport, New York: Educational Activities, Inc.

Cratty, B. J. (1986). Perceptual and motor development in infants and children. Englewood Cliffs, NJ: Prentice Hall.

Espenschade, A., & Eckert, H. (1980). Motor development. Columbus, Ohio: Charles E. Merrill, Publishers.

Gallahue, D. L. (1989). Understanding motor development in infants, children and adolescents. Indianapolis IN: Benchmark Press

Gallahue, D. L. (1982). Developmental movement experiences for children. New York: John Wiley & Sons.

Haywood, K. M. (1986). Life span motor development. Champaign, IL: Human Kinetics.

Horvat, M. (1989). A manual of activities to improve perceptual motor skills. Kearney, NE: Educational Systems Associations Inc.

Keogh J. & Sugden, D. (1985). Movement skill development. New York: MacMillan.

Nichols, B. (1986). Moving and learning: The elementary school physical education experience. St. Louis: Times Mirror/Mosby.

Payne, G. V. & Isaac, L. (1991). Human motor development: A lifespan approach. Mountain View, CA: Mayfield Publishing.

Rarick, L. (1973). Physical activity: Human growth and development. New York: Academic Press.

Robertson, M. A. & Halverson, L. E. (1984). Developing children their changing movement. Philadelphia: Lea & Febiger.

Ridenour, M. (1978). Motor development: Issues and applications. Princeton, N.J.: Princeton Book Co.

Sugden, D. A. & Keogh J. F. (1990). Problems in movement skill development. University of South Carolina Press.

Thomas, J. (ed.). (1983). Motor development during childhood and adolescence. Minneapolis, MN: Burgess.

Ulrich, D. (1985). Test of gross motor development. Austin, TX. Pro-Ed Pub.

Wickstrom, R. L. (1983). Fundamental motor patterns. Philadelphia: Lea & Febiger.

Williams, H. G. (1983). Perceptual and motor development. Englewood Cliffs, New Jersey: Prentice-Hall.

Wright, L. G. (1979). Wright on skills: Perceptual, motor skill guide. Rochester, New York: Heindl Press.

PROFESSIONAL ORGANIZATIONS

The following is a list of various professional organizations involved in providing physical activity to persons with disabilities. Included is the profession, address of the organization, & journal publication(s) specific to that organization.

Profession: **Special Physical Education**
Organizations: Association for Research, Administration, Professional Councils (a Branch of The American Alliance for Health, Physical Education, Recreation, and Dance), 1900 Association Drive, Reston, VA 22091
National Consortium on Physical Education and Recreation for the Handicapped
Journal(s): Journal of Physical Education, Recreation & Dance
Adapted Physical Activity Quarterly
Palaestra: The Forum of Sport, Physical Education and Recreation For the Disabled

Profession: **Occupational Therapy**
Organization: The American Occupational Therapy Association Inc., 1383 Picard Drive, P.O. Box 1725, Rockville, MD 20850
Journal(s): The American Journal of Occupational Therapy

Profession: Physical Therapy
Organization: American Physical Therapy Association, 111 North Fairfax Street, Alexandria VA 22314
Journal(s): Physical Therapy
Clinical Management

Profession: **Therapeutic Recreation**
Organization: The National Therapeutic Recreation Society (a Branch of the National Recreation and Park Association), 3101 Park Center Drive, 12th floor, Alexandria, VA 22302
Journal(s): Therapeutic Recreation Journal
Journal of Leisurability

Profession: **Special Education**

Organization: The Council for Exceptional Children,
                              1920 Association Drive, Reston, VA 22091

Journal(s):   Exceptional Children
                              Teaching Exceptional Children
                              Education in Mental Retardation

Profession: **Mental Retardation**

Organization: American Association of Mental Deficiency, 1719 Kalorama,
                              Road NW Washington DC 20009

Journal(s):   Mental Retardation

Modfied from: Eichstaedt, C. & Lavay, B. (1992). <u>Physical activity for persons with mental retardation: Infant to adult</u>. Champaign IL: Human Kinetics.

JOURNAL PUBLICATIONS

The following is a list of journal publications in physical education and special education. When appropriate professional organizations proceed the listed journal(s).

Physical Education

American Alliance for Health, Physical Education, Recreation and Dance (AAHPERD)
Journal of Physical Education, Recreation and Dance
Strategies
Research Quarterly for Exercise and Sport

American Kinesiotherapy Association
Clinical Kinesiology

National Association for Physical Education in Higher Education (NAPEHE)
Quest

National Consortium Physical Education and Recreation for the Handicapped (NCPERH)
Advocate

Phi Epsilon Kappa
The Physical Educator

Other Journals
American Journal of Dance Therapy

Adapted Physical Activity Quarterly

Journal of Motor Behavior

Journal of Sports Psychology

Journal of Teaching Physical Education

Motor Skills: Theory into Practice

Palestra: The Forum of Sport & Physical Education and Recreation for the Handicapped

Perceptual and Motor Skills

The Physician & Sports Medicine

Sports n' Spokes

Special Education

American Association on Mental Retardation (AAMR)
American Journal of Mental Deficiency
Mental Retardation

Association for Children with Learning Disabilities (ACLD)

The Association for Severely Handicapped (TASH)
The Journal of the Association of the Severely Handicapped

Council for Exceptional Children (CEC)
Exceptional Children
Teaching Exceptional Children
Education and Training in Mental Retardation

American Annuals of the Deaf

Behavior Modification

Exceptional Educational Quarterly
1983, Volume 3 No. 1, Adapted Physical Education Issue

Journal of Applied Behavioral Analysis

Journal for Special Educators

The Journal of Special Education

The Special Educator

Rural special Education Quarterly (1990 issue pertains to SPE)

Related Services

The American Journal of Occupational Therapy

Journal of Leisurability

Journal of Orthopedics, Sport, & Physical Therapy

Physical Therapy

Clinical Management

Therapeutic Recreation Journal

SPORT ORGANIZATIONS FOR ATHLETES WITH DISABILITIES

The following sport organizations for athletes with a disabilities were organized in the 1980s under group E membership by the United State Olympic Committee (USOC) on sport:

American Athlete Association for the Deaf (AAAD)
1134 Davenport Dr., Burton MI, 48529

Dwarf Athletic Association of America (DAAA)
3725 West Holmes, Lansing MI, 48911

National Handicapped Sport & Recreation Association (NHSRA)
Farragut Station, P. O. Box 33141, Washington D. C., 20033

National Wheelchair Athletic Association (NWAA)
3617 Betty Dr. Suite S, Colorado Springs, CO, 80907

Special Olympics International (SOI)
1350 New York Ave., N. W., Washington D. C., 20005

United States Amputee Athletic Association (USAAA)
P. O. Box 210709, Nashville, TN, 37221

United States Association for Blind Athletes (USABA)
33 N. Institute, Brown Hall, Suite 015, Colorado Springs, CO, 80903

United States Cerebral Palsy Athletic Association (USCPAA)
34518 Warren Rd. Suite 264, Westland MI, 48185

ADAPTED/SPECIAL PHYSICAL EDUCATION TERMINOLOGY

The following is a list of words and terms used frequently in adapted/special physical education students should be familiar with

Individuals with Disabilites Edcuation Act (IDEA) (P L 101-476)

Education of Handicapped Act (P L 94-142)

P L 99-457, the Education of Handicapped Act ammendment of 1986

Rehabilitation Act Section 504

Individualized Educational Program (IEP)

Mainstreaming

Least Restrictive Environment

Developmental Approach (DA, CA, MA, IQ)

Motor Development

Perceptual Motor Development

Impaired

Disabled

Handicapped

Mental Retardation (MR, EMR, Mild, TMR, Moderate, Down syndrome)

Atlantoaxial Dislocation Condition (ADC)

Orthopedically Impaired (OI)

Paraplegia

Quadriplegia

Cerebral Palsy (CP)

Muscular Dystrophy (MD)

Behavioral or Emotional Disorder (BD or ED)

Learning Disabled (LD)

Attention Span Deficit Disorder (ADS)

Severely Multihandicapped (SMH)

Contraindicated

Assessment

Norm-referenced

Criterion-referenced

Objective

Subjective

Validity

Reliability

Appendices

APPENDIX A

INTRODUCTORY ADAPTED PHYSICAL EDUCATION COURSE SYLLABUS

California State University, Long Beach
Physical Education Department

PED 320 (3 units)
ADAPTED PHYSICAL EDUCATION

"Too Often the handicapped are more handicapped by attitudes
and misbelief than there own handicapped condition"
(Stewart,1980)

COURSE OUTLINE
Fall 1991

I. **Course Description**

Prerequisites: A/P 202. This course is designed to prepare physical
education majors to meet the physical activity program needs of persons
with a disability. Designed primarily to understand the etiology and
characteristics of persons with mental, physical, emotional, sensory,
health, learning and/or multiple disabilities. When appropriate be able
to successfully integrate the individual with a disability into the physical
education mainstream. (lecture/laboratory)

II. **Expected Outcomes**

At the conclusion of the course, the student will be able to:

1. Define and understand the philosophy of special physical
    education and justify the importance of physical activity for persons
    with a disability.

2. Identify and discuss the impact of current legislation pertaining
    to the education for persons with a disability.

3. Define and understand the difference between the categorical
    and noncategorical approach when programing for persons with a disability.

4. Understand the definitions, etiology, characteristics, and
    developmental programming considerations for persons

with mental, physical, emotional, sensory, health, learning and/ or multiple disabilities.

5. Effectively write an individualized educational program (IEP) for persons with a disability.

6. Understand the principles of learning in physical education and how they can be effectively applied to meet the instructional needs for persons with a disability.

7. Determine an appropriate program plan of physical activity by identifying a variety of activities persons with a disability can safely and successfully participate in.

8. Determine equipment needs and modifications when necessary in order to allow persons with a disability to successfully participate.

9. Describe assessment instruments used to test individuals with various disabilities.

10. When appropriate be able to successfully integrate the individual with a disability into the regular physical education mainstream.

III. Required Readings

Eichstaedt, C. B., & Kalakian, L. H. (1987). Developmental/adapted physical education: Making ability count. New York: Macmillan.
Lavay, B (1992). Special physical education: A resource guide for professionals & students. Dubuque IA: Kendell Hunt Publishing.

The student is responsible to read the material assigned each week and be prepared to discuss this information during lectures. Check the course outline on the next page regarding reading assignments! If students come to class unprepared than we will begin to have quizzes.

IV.	Course Outline: fall, 90/ Mon 1-2:40 (PE1-62), Wed 1-2:40 (AS1 330) Practicums/Labs are on Mon, All assignments are due on Mon. Quizzes/Exams are on Wed except for Exam 2.

Week of:	Topic	Reading
Sept 4	Labor Day Course Overview	
Sept 9	PE Benefits for the Disabled Who is the Disabled Individual(videotape) Categorical-Noncategorical Approach	CH 1, HB 6-15 HB 50 HB 51-52
Sept 16	Adjusting to a Handicap Lab What is APE?	CH 4 HB 57-58 HB 16-33
Sept 23	Group Practicum Assignment Lab P L 94-142 (videotape)	CH 2 HB 53-56
Sept 30	Developmental Teaching Approach Lab **Quiz 1** (videotape) **CABA State Games (Oct 5)**	CH 5,6 HB 117-122; 131-133
Oct 7	Writing the IEP Lab **Exam 1**	CH 8 HB 123-130
Oct 14	Practicum Exp. Lab (A) Combining Students of Different Abilities Movement Response Disorders	CH 3 HB134-140 CH 7, HB 59
Oct 21	Practicum Exp.Lab (B) Mental Retardation Learning Disabilities (Apraxia) **IEP Due**	 CH 9; HB 60-69 CH 10; HB 89-92
Oct 28	Group Practicum Assignments Obesity/ Behavior Disorder **Breath Games (Nov 2) Contact Mike LaCourse**	CH 11&12, HB 72-88 CH 13; HB 101-103

Week of:	Topic	Reading
Nov 4	Practicum Exp. Lab **Group 1**	
	Sensory Deficits More	CH 18,19
	Quiz 2	HB 93-98
Nov 11	Practicum Exp. Lab **Group 2**	CH 17; HB104-106
	Neuromuscular Disabilities (CP & MD)	CH 15, 350-5;
		HB 113-114
Nov 18	Practicum Exp. Lab **Group 3**	
	Seizure Disorders	CH 16; HB 107-108
	Exam 2	
Nov 25	Practicum Exp. Lab **Group 4**	CH 14,372-374
	Postural Deviations (OSD,LCP)	HB 99-100
	SPE Trivial Pursuit Due	
Dec 2	Practicum Exp. Lab **Group 5**	
	Asthma	CH 21;HB 111-112
	Diabetes	CH 22, HB 109-110
	APE Observations Due	
Dec 9	Assessment Lecture/Lab	CH 5, 8 173- 85,HB 34-50
	Orthopedically Impaired	CH15, 346-50 HB115-116
	Final exam review SPE trivial pursuit	
Dec 16	**Final Exam Time: 12:30 - 2:30 Monday**	

Key
CH = Eichstaedt, C. B., & Kalakian, L. H. (1987). Developmental/adapted
  physical education: Making ability count. New York: Macmillan.
HB =Lavay, B (1992). Special physical education: A resource guide for
  professionals & students. Dubuque IA: Kendell Hunt Publishing.

V. Methods of Presentation

A. Lecture/discussion/audiovisual aids
B. Practicum and observations
C. Student presentations.
D. Written assignments and readings.

VI. Method of Evaluation

Weighting of Assignments:

Quiz 1	25pts.
Exam 1	75pts
Quiz 2	25pts
Exam 2	75pts
Final Exam	100pts
Written IEP	30pts
Group Practicum Exp	30pts
Observation of APE	20 pts
SPE trivial Pursuit	20 pts
	400pts

See course calendar for **due date** of each assignment listed.
See **The Special Physical Education Resource Guide** for an explanation of each the assignment listed.

Grade Scale:

400-360	A
359-320	B
319-280	C
279-240	D
Below 239	F

Note: No early or late exams may be taken unless there is a medical emergency (verification required) or athletic team travel. Advanced notice of absence must be given for the latter.

Course Work Requirements:

All submitted work/projects must be typed and submitted on the prescribed due dates. Course work submitted after the prescribed due date will result in the following grade deduction. Two days or less **10%**, three days or more **20%**. No work will be accepted after the last day of class! **Assignments will not be accepted during finals week !**

Attendance

Please make every effort to attend all scheduled class meetings and be punctual upon arriving. There are many experiences shared in class meetings which can not be made up by reading the text or by copying a classmates notes. In addition, arriving late to lecture & labs disrupts class! **Excessive absenteeism and/or tardiness will result in a meeting between professor and student.**

VII. Instructor

Dr. Barry Lavay
AAS 307
(213) 985-4077
Office Hours: Posted outside of the office. When this time are
                          not convenient, come see me and I will arrange
                          to meet with you.

Professors should have high expectations of their students. They should expect students to exhibit a commitment to learning and skill development that often goes beyond routine expectations. Grades and standard of performance for papers, readings, discussion, and other activities must reflect these high expectations. The benefits received from this course will be derived from both of our efforts. Have a good and productive learning experience. Barry Lavay

APPENDIX B

UNIVERSITY STUDENT ACTIVITY
FOR COURSE ASSIGNMENTS

UNIVERSITY STUDENT ACTIVITY ASSIGNMENTS

The following is a list of activities that will serve as a learning experience for university students enrolled in a special physical education course. These assignments are developed to assist university students to foster a better appreciation as well as gain experiences regarding the role of physical activity for persons with disablities.

A. OBSERVATIONS IN SPECIAL PHYSICAL EDUCATION ASSIGNMENT

Lecture and instruction will become more applicable and meaningful by observing programs of physical activity for persons with a disability. Therefore, class members will accumulate 4 hours of time outside of class observing programs of physical activity for persons with a disability. You must conduct at least two seperate observations. You will be provided a list of various programs on-campus and in the community that are available and acceptable (if you have another program in mind you must come see me first). Examples are programs such as the CABA State Track Meet and the Breath Games held on the CSULB campus each year. You will be responsible to arrange this time outside of class meetings. Each outside practicum must be signed by the immediate supervisor of the program on the description activity sheet you develop and hand in. A seperate description activity sheet must be typed and handed in for each seperate observation. Turn in all description sheets together on the due date or earlier. Type the description activity sheet beforehand so you will have it with you when you go to the observation.

Each activity description sheet must include the following information (to be typed and answered with complete sentences).
1. Name of the program
2. Type of disability observed (age, grade, particular disability).
3. A brief description of the particular program implemented.
4. A description of what you felt was effective and not effective about the particular program you observed.
5. Discipline problems if any that occurred and how they were handled.
6. Unique teaching approaches you observed throughut the program.
7. A description of what you learned by observing this particular program.

Questions 3-7 should be explained in detail each consisting of at least 3-4 sentences. Each <u>activity description sheet</u> must include proper sentence structure.

One option is to choose to spend one of the observations in a wheelchair (2 hrs of credit toward observation time), during this time you may travel around campus or go to to a shopping mall. Submit a two page paper outlining your experiences.

B. GROUP PRACTICUM EXPERIENCE ASSIGNMENT

The group you are assigned to work with will be responsible for teaching the rest of the class a particular lesson. As a group you will develop a lesson which consists of the following:

1. The lesson plan should be typed and submitted to me one week before your group is scheduled to teach. This way I can provide your group with feedback before teaching.

2. The group is responsible for organizing the activity area with all necessary equipment beforehand. Arrive early and be ready to teach. The class practicum may be held in the class activity room or outside.

3. The lesson plan should include; the date, names of the students assigned to teach in your group, equipment needs, a detailed description of what will take place during the lesson including a 2-3 behavioral objectives (each consisting of behavior, condition, and criteria), warm-up, the actual lesson, diagrams for formations, and a cool-down.

4. All students should be dressed in proper teaching attire and ready to teach.

5. Each person in the assigned group is responsible for teaching a part of the lesson (ie. warmup, skill work, a particular station, leading an activity). Teaching assignments of each group member are the decision of the group. Group members are expected to share the lesson responsibility!

6. During the practicum certain students in the class will assimilate certain disabilities: 2 persons in wheelchairs; a person who is blind; and there may be 2-3 adults with mental retardation from the CSULB Transition Program.

7. Each student will be graded individually as well as within the group. Grading will be on a 30 point basis; lesson plan (10pts); organization (5pts); equipment (5pts); instruction (5pts); modifications (5pts).

C. WRITTEN IEP ASSIGNMENT

You will be responsible to develop an IEP from the information provided on the student described in this manual on page 130. You may follow the IEP program sheet on page 129 or develop your own. Before the assignment is due the instructor will lecture on the IEP Development information on pages 123-130.

D. TRIVIAL SPECIAL PHYSICAL EDUCATION PURSUIT ASSIGNMENT*

* This assignment was modified from an idea developed by Michael Blazey, CSULB. Develop 10 individual study test questions. Each individual card is to be completed on a 4 x 6 index card and should contain either a multiply choice or short answer test question. Questions should be taken from course content (course lecture and reading material). Follow the format provided below:
1. Each card should include your name in the upper right hand corner.
2. The front of the card should contain the individual question. Selection of each question should be based on material from course lectures and reading materials. Verification of the question should include the page number from the material where it can be found.
3. Select questions from a variety of areas studied throughout the semester (e. g. the law, various disabilities, assessment, developmental approach).
4. The back of the card should include the correct answer to that particular question. Type the answer upside down so that it can not be read by the person across from you when playing special physical education trivial pursuit.
5. The cards will be used during a study sessions for the final exam.
An example of special physical education trivial pursuit card:

Front of card	Back of card
By definition approximately ___ percent of the population consists of persons with mental retardation. A. 1% B. 2% C. 3% D. 4% E. None of the above Eichstaedt & Kalakian, CH 9, pg 193.	C. 3%

E. ACTIVITY CARDS FILE ASSIGNMENT

Develop a card file of activities that can be effectively used for persons with special needs. Develop 10 individual activity cards, each typed on a 5 x 8 index card. Use your creativity and imagination when developing the activities, however each card should follow the format provided below.

Activity Title: develop a catchy title that would excite the person(s) who will be participating in the activity.

Disability: list the disability or disabilities this activity can be used with and be sure it is appropriate for that particular disability. For example you would not play power volleyball with a group of children with severe mental retardation.

Level: activity is appropriate for particular age group; elementary, secondary or adult.

Activity Description: be specific in your description of the activity. A person should be able to pick up the card and teach the activity from your directions.

Skills Reinforced: what type of skills are being reinforced. For example in the activity of "twister" the skills of body awareness and nonlocomotor skills such as bending and twisting are reinforced.

Modifications: what type of modifications are necessary to effectively meet the needs of the group performing the activity. Include modifications that would make the activity successfully as well as more challenging for certain individuals.

The following is an example of an activity card:

Activity: Parachute   Tina Johnson

Disability: Visually impaired

Level: elementary

Activity Description: have the children constantly hold the parachute and perform certain activities such as; shake the chute different ways, shake the chute with various balls, have them kneel and stand up with the chute, perform different locomotor skills while holding the chute, traveling clockwise and counter clockwise, and different children travel under the chute while it is raised.

Skills Reinforced: various locomotor skills, upper body strength.

Modifications: Balls with bells can be used, and partners can assist persons who are visually impaired to travel under the chute.

F. EQUIPMENT MODIFICATION ASSIGNMENT

Select and research a piece of equipment (or material) that has been designed to assist professionals in providing physical activity to individuals with special needs. This assignment should be typed, double spaced, and not exceed three pages. In your report provide the following information: name of the equipment, address of where to obtain the equipment, report the cost (is this the best buy for the money?), if possible provide a picture or diagram of the equipment, state the advantages and disadvantages (durability, versatility, user-friendly) to users (ie. teachers), review any relevant research concerning the equipment, provide examples of activities and any necessary modifications of the equipment, and interview one individual if possible who has used the equipment.

G.   JOURNAL/ PERIODICAL REVIEW ASSIGNMENT

Select a current issue of a journal/periodical in the area of physical education or special education that contains information pertaining to physical activity for persons with disabilities. A list of these journal/periodicals are located on pages 201-203 of this manual. Review the entire issue or more than one issue and critique the contents to include the information provided below. This assignment should be typed double spaced and not exceed three pages in length.
1. Name of journal
2. Editor
3. Editorial board (choose a few names and institutions)
4. Publisher
5. Subscription cost
6. Frequency of publication
7. Information on procedure and format for submitting an article
8. Nature of advertisements and target consumer
9. Nature of articles (original research, position papers, applied, reviews)
10. Other contents (announcements, conference abstracts, book reviews)
11. Would you subscribe to this journal? What are the strengths and weaknesses of the journal?

H. TERMINOLOGY ASSIGNMENT

A list of terms discussed in class are provided on pages 205-206 of this manual. Define each term and provide an example of how this term is used in special physical education

I.   COURSE NOTEBOOK ASSIGNMENT

Develop a Special Physical Education course notebook. The notebook should be neatly organized and have a table of contents which includes the categories of the notebook. For organization purposes use a 3-ring notebook so that papers can be added throughout the semester. Include the following information:

1. Outline the chapters of your introductory Special Physical Education Textbook that are listed on your course syllabus. Be detailed in your outline so that you can study from these outlines.
2. Include a section of all key and new terms from lectures and readings. Define each of these terms.
3. Include a section of daily class lectures. Include two or three questions from each daily lecture or discussion topics covered in the lectures.
4. Include all coursework assignments and projects
5. Include any additional information such as class handouts and information you find throughout the semester such as journal or newspaper articles.

J.   INDIVIDUALIZED TEACHING ASSIGNMENT

Develop and implement a program of physical activity for a person with a disability. Choose an individual that is pertinent to your own teaching interests or experiences. The final report of your experiences is to be typed double spaced and include the following information:

1. Title page
2. An introductory paragraph stating the justification for developing this program and choosing the individual.
3. A background information paragraph or two stating the persons specific disability, medical and developmental history, age, physical characteristics, and general behavior.
4. Conduct an assessment on the individual. Discuss what tests were administered and provide a brief description of each test. Discuss your findings and how they will assist you in your program development.
5. Based on your assessment develop and write long term goals and

behavioral objectives you wish to accomplish with the individual. Similar to an IEP.

6. Develop a list of instructional strategies as well as a variety of age appropriate activities for this individual which are designed around the long term goals and behavioral objectives. Be creative in your design and write up of instructional strategies and activities.

7. Implement the actual program and write about your experiences. What was effective and not effective in the administration of the program.

8. Discuss future goals and objectives for the individual and provide suggestions for how they can be implemented once your program has stopped.

EXPERIENCES IN SPECIAL PHYSICAL EDUCATION

1. Visit a special physical education program in the public schools or at a hospital setting.

2. Take lecture notes or string beads while wearing a cloth glove that has some of the fingers sewn together.

3. Spend time in a wheelchair attending classes on campus or going to a shopping mall.

4. Walk with a partner while blindfolded through various buildings on campus such as the physical education complex.

5. Participate in an actual game or sport designed for persons with a disability such goal ball, wheelchair tennis or basketball.

6. Volunteer to assist at a local sporting event for persons with disabilities such as Special Olympics or a wheelchair road race.

7. Select and read a current issue of a journal/periodical pertaining to physical activity for persons with disabilities.

8. Attend a professional conference or seminar regarding physical activity for persons with disabilities. For example, attend the adapted physical edcuation section meetings of your state AAHPERD conference.

9. Make a piece of home-made physical activity equipment with modifications for a certain disability group.

10. View videotapes from the IM SPECIAL videotape series and write a reaction paper to each videotape you watch.

11. Write to a sports organization for the disabled requesting information about their organization.

12. Videotape and analyze a person with a disability performing a movement activity or sport.

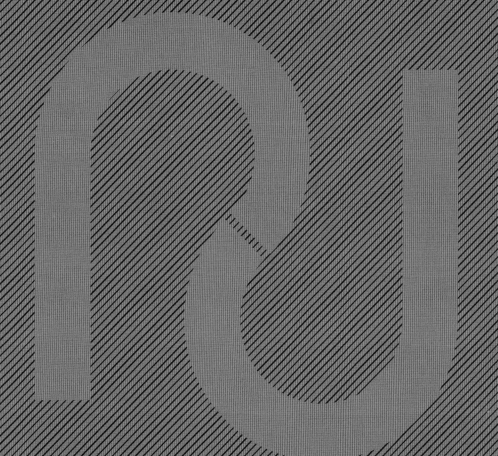

Package Design In Italy: Phase One

First published 2004 by Red

book design by Kalimera.it

cover photo and section photos by Stefano Camellini

print by Grafiche dell'Artiere

ISBN 88 - 88492 - 02 - X

Package
Design In Italy
:Phase One

Air-bag, Anti-static Materials,
Beecore©, Bubble Wrap, Canvas,
Grey Board, Cork, Corrugated Board,
Denim, Fake Fur, Felt, Foam, Glass,
Glow-edge Acrylic, Hessian, Kinetic
Pvc, Leather, Liquid-filled Plastic, Metal
Sheet, Mirriboard, Perspex,
Polypropylene, Pulp-carton Mouldings,
Pvc, Rubber, Space-age Materials,
Styrofoam, Tyvek.
Closures, Die Cutting, Dip Moulding,
Injection Moulding, Thermoforming,
Welding, Welding Continued.

Packaging: protagonista del brand design
Packaging: leading actor of brand design

Che il rivestimento, di una persona non meno che di una cosa, sia innanzitutto un messaggio rivolto all'esterno, benché apparentemente concepito in funzione delle esigenze di chi o cosa lo indossi, è consapevolezza antica. D'altronde, è la natura stessa che, abbigliando animali e piante di forme e colori variopinti, persegue le sue imprescindibili necessità comunicative al fine di garantire la sopravvivenza e la riproduzione delle specie.

Nel tempo in cui la categoria della merce è diventata onnipervasiva e lo sviluppo dei consumi è la condizione stessa della produzione non sorprende che il rivestimento dei prodotti, il packaging insomma, abbia una importanza crescente e addirittura strategica per gli obiettivi di massimizzazione dei consumi stessi. Esso garantisce innanzitutto l'identità di marca (brand identity), ormai necessaria per fronteggiare, tramite azioni che rendano forti, unici e inconfondibili un marchio o una linea di prodotti, la concorrenza su scaffali sempre più affollati e il potere montante della grande distribuzione organizzata come abitudine al consumo. "L'imballaggio di un prodotto - insomma - è l'incarnazione fisica (e spesso anche emotiva) dei valori di una marca", come ha scritto Siebert Head, agenzia londinese specializzata in packaging e brand design.

Una delle peculiarità del packaging è quella di agire con una continuità e una reiterazione sconosciuta alle altre forme di comunicazione. La pubblicità tradizionale, ad esempio, agisce a monte dell'acquisto con una forza persuasiva potenzialmente superiore a quella offerta dalla visual identity, ma esaurisce il suo effetto in un'unica soluzione; il pack, invece, comunica - senza costi aggiuntivi - i valori positivi di una marca all'interno del punto vendita, ma anche tutte le volte che il prodotto viene aperto, chiuso, consumato, cioè per tutta la sua vita utile. Per questo, un packaging di alta qualità per un'azienda o per un marchio rappresenta un investimento a medio-lungo termine più che un costo d'esercizio: a fronte di un esborso iniziale per l'ideazione, la progettazione e la realizzazione, è possibile ottenere ritorni economici prolungati nel tempo, che a volte possono cominciare già dopo pochi mesi dal "lancio".

Per il suo elevato contenuto di tecnologia, studio dei materiali, industrializzazione dei processi produttivi, un packaging realizzato in modo professionale e innovativo può veramente rappresentare un investimento strategico da valutare in termini di analisi costi/benefici più complessi del semplice "ritorno pubblicitario": un intervento di packaging può avere effetti sul lancio di una novità, sulla riproposta di un prodotto maturo, sui costi dei materiali per il confezionamento, sugli stampi e sulle attrezzature da utilizzare, sulle operazioni di imballaggio e staccaggio, sull'ambiente.

La potenza del packaging come mezzo di marketing e comunicazione assume un particolare rilievo soprattutto in periodi di crisi. Il beneficio ottenuto da una corretta azione sul packaging può risultare alquanto vantaggioso, anche rispetto ad altri interventi di pubblicità classica, a patto di accostarsi ad essa con una visione globale ed una metodologia scientificamente definita. Anche da sola, un'azione di packaging particolarmente azzeccata può contribuire sensibilmente all'aumento della quota di mercato e della penetrazione commerciale

It is an old-as-time awareness that when people put on clothes, first of all they want to send a message to other people rather than satisfy, as it would seem, a basic need. The same applies to objects.
Besides, nature itself, by dressing animals and plants in vivid colours, pursues it vital communicative aims, that will allow the survival and reproduction of the species.

Nowadays, with the widespread presence of goods and the massive consumption, the way we "dress" goods, that is packaging, is not surprisingly of strategic importance, when planning to maximize consumption, since consumption itself is the living condition for production.
Packaging guarantees the brand identity and makes a line of products and trademarks unique and outstanding, which is essential to meet competition on increasingly packed shelves and to face the mounting power of large-scale distribution, whose strength lies in fostering a consumption-oriented attitude. Siebert Head, a London agency specialized in packaging and brand design, on this issue remarked: "Packaging is the physical (and emotive as well) embodiment of the values of a brand".

In comparison to other forms of communication, packaging displays two peculiarities: continuity and reiteration.
Traditional advertising, for example, may affect purchasing at an earlier stage, with a potential for persuasion virtually higher that that communicated through visual identity, but its effect is limited in time; packaging, on the other hand, communicates – without any further costs – the positive values of a trademark throughout the lifespan of a product, that is, both in the point of purchase and every time the product is opened, closed, used.
For this reason, a company should deem a high-quality packaging as a long-term investment rather than a running cost: the initial expenses for the project and its realization bring long-lasting profits, which can start right after a few months from launching.

For its relevant content of technology, study of materials, industrialization of production processes, a professional and innovative packaging should be evaluated as a strategic investment in terms of cost-benefit analysis rather than of simply "advertising gain": a packaging project can have positive effects on launching a new product, on restyling an already known one, on the costs of package materials, on the tools to be used, on the packing and storage operations, on the environment.

The importance of packaging stands out particularly in times of economical crisis.
A coherent packaging project may bring in more benefits than classic advertising would do, provided that the project is undertaken on a global level and through a scientific methodology. Thanks to a well-aimed packaging project, even if not supported by other means, some consumables and trademarks may undergo a steep increase in market shares and in market

di alcuni marchi e prodotti di largo consumo.

Specie in periodi di riduzione dei consumi e di conseguenti tagli ai budget pubblicitari (come è avvenuto ad esempio durante la crisi mondiale della prima metà degli anni '90), molte aziende hanno avuto immediati e insperati incrementi nelle vendite tramite appropriati restyling delle confezioni o specifici progetti di rafforzamento visivo della marca. E' capitato che alcune aziende che avevano già investito budget elevati nell'immagine e nella pubblicità prima della crisi sono uscite da un periodo di contingenza negativa completando la loro strategia di comunicazione con investimenti nel package design.

Insomma, presentarsi bene sul punto vendita, avere buona visibilità, può dare buoni risultati, anche per le aziende che non investono in pubblicità tradizionale.

La selezione percettiva si manifesta in ogni evento conoscitivo e comunicativo e ha il suo momento cruciale nella scelta da parte del consumatore, all'interno dei fantasmagorici templi della grande distribuzione. Allora la capacità di suggestione e di seduzione del packaging si manifesta in tutta la sua potenza sottile e versatile, utilizzando tutti i toni di una scala di richiami, dai più espliciti a quelli più dissimulati.

Il packaging, dunque, in un contesto di grande distribuzione di beni a largo consumo è veramente "un venditore silenzioso": se la tecnologia rende i beni di consumo sempre più efficaci, sofisticati e simili tra loro (omologati) e la concorrenza tra una varietà sempre nuova di prodotti è ancora più agguerrita, la pubblicità da sola non è più sufficiente a rimarcarne le differenze. La scelta spesso è tra le confezioni, non tra i prodotti. Tanto più che la maggioranza dei consumatori entra nel negozio incerto e possibilista e decide l'acquisto all'ultimo momento: il packaging, l'involucro, la busta, il barattolo sono in questi casi la forma di promozione più efficace, una sorta di pubblicità dell'ultimo momento, quando non c'è più tempo per i ripensamenti. Al packaging, insomma, si deve riconoscere il ruolo di realizzatore di una autentica "comunicazione integrata" tra la pubblicità vera e propria e le altre discipline (pubbliche relazioni, promozioni, direct marketing, corporate identity, ecc.) che vi entrano in gioco.

Ma si potrebbe dubitare che un eccesso di packaging nel mondo della produzione e della distribuzione crei alla lunga gravi problemi di smaltimento. D'altronde, il problema dell'inquinamento e della protezione dell'ambiente è all'ordine del giorno e non è più sollevato soltanto dai movimenti ecologisti, ma da tutti i governi interessati alla salvaguardia dei propri cittadini. Gli imballaggi, secondo le ultime stime, costituiscono una percentuale rilevante dei rifiuti solidi, arrivando a superare il 35% del totale. Anche se in ritardo e in modo ancora non organizzato, in Europa e in Italia le principali aziende produttrici e distributrici di beni di largo consumo, di concerto con le principali agenzie coinvolte nella realizzazione di nuove soluzioni di packaging, stanno orientandosi – spinti anche dalle nuove normative comunitarie – verso il cosiddetto ecopackaging. La sfida di molti operatori del mercato che progettano ed adottano strategie di packaging innovative

penetration.
It has happened in the past (especially during the worldwide crisis of the early Nineties) that, even in circumstances of a drop in consumption and subsequent cutbacks in advertising budgets, many companies have unexpectedly increased their sales, through appropriate restyling of the packaging of their products or through specific projects aiming at reinforcing the visual identity of a particular brand.
It has also happened that some companies, after significant investments in image and advertising, have come out of the crisis investing in the package design, thus completing their communication strategy.

In short, a broad and effective visibility in the point of purchase can give excellent results even to those companies that do not invest in traditional advertising.

The perceptive selection reveals itself anytime a communicative event takes place; it reaches its climax when the consumer chooses a product in the phantasmagorical temples of large-scale distribution. It is then that packaging displays its powerful fascination at the utmost level, using all the tones of a "scale of lure", from the most explicit to the subtlest ones.

Packaging proves to be a "silent salesman", especially with regard to large-scale distribution of convenience goods. Since technology makes products increasingly effective, sophisticated and similar to each other, since competition among new products becomes tougher and tougher, advertising alone is no longer capable of pointing out the differences. Often, the choices is between packages and not products.
All the more so, as most consumers are unsure about what they will buy when entering a shop and make the final decision at the very last minute: the packaging, the wrapping, the bag, the jar… these are the most effective form of promotion, a kind of "last-minute advertising", when no time is left for second thoughts.
In short, packaging alone realizes a kind of "corporate communication", implying advertising and all other connected disciplines (public relations, promotion, direct marketing, corporate identity, etc.).

The sore point might be represented by the excess of packaging required by the production and distribution of goods and not always easy to dispose of.
As a matter of fact, pollution and protection of the environment are constant concern not only of ecological movements, but also of governments whose first aim is to safeguard their citizens. According to recent estimates, packages sum up to over 35% of all solid waste. In Italy and in Europe, despite delays and scarce organization, the main producers and distributors of consumables, together with agencies specializing in innovative packaging, and in response to new EC regulations, are opting for the so-called ecopackaging.

si stanno lentamente – ma indiscutibilmente – orientando verso soluzioni rispettose dell'ambiente: dai contenitori degradabili e riutilizzabili, a cluster più leggeri o con meno plastica; dalle confezioni con ricariche e refill, alla carta riciclata e al recupero di imballi usati.

Il packaging – per la sua specifica caratteristica di stretta interazione con le tecniche, i materiali e i processi produttivi – è uno dei pochi strumenti di marketing che può concretamente contribuire a ridurre l'attuale impatto ambientale delle attività industriali, fornendo nello stesso tempo al consumatore spunti e modelli etici ed educativi.

Tutto questo ha naturalmente un importante risvolto economico, dal momento che l'ecopackaging va interpretato anche come una valida opportunità di marketing, capace di provocare forti guadagni in termini di immagine per aziende e marchi eco-consapevoli presso le fasce di consumo più colte, più sensibili e più dinamiche.

Forse il complesso rapporto che si istituisce tra il consumatore e la merce, mediato dal packaging, rinvia ad una questione più complessa. Si tratta del fatto che, proprio come i nostri primitivi antenati, tutti noi tendiamo a personificare animisticamente le cose con cui entriamo in contatto. Non solo le forme viventi dunque, animali e piante, subiscono un processo più o meno inconscio di antopomorfizzazione. Anche le cose inanimate (appunto) possono diventarne oggetto.

Le fiabe per l'infanzia usano comunemente tale espediente, che risponde a bisogni profondi di rassicurazione consolatoria. Psicologicamente parlando, l'invenzione animistica del mondo ci sottrae all'angoscia della solitudine esistenziale. Ci illude, noi tutti umani, piccole particelle organiche sperdute casualmente in un immenso cosmo inorganico, di non essere una anomalia destinata ad essere rapidamente espulsa, mediante l'incessante opera della morte, da una realtà a noi comunque indifferente e insensibile. Ecco perchè anche gli oggetti e le merci vanno abbigliate. Non solo per un'ovvia esigenza denotativa e funzionalmente conservativa, ma proprio per introdurle nel nostro universo simbolico e potere con esse intrattenere delle relazioni umanamente comparabili.

C'è qualcosa di infantile dunque e, se protratto nel tempo oltre l'età evolutiva, anche di patologico in tale approccio. Ma d'altra parte, è proprio grazie a questa assidua tentazione di onnipotenza creativa, a questa irrazionale forza immaginativa che si rispecchia nelle cose, che l'umanità afferma la sua umanità e non si identifica solo organicamente nel grembo della natura. Non diversamente dall'arte, dalla poesia, le suggestioni dell'imballaggio compongono l'inconsapevole scenografia del teatro dell'esistenza di ogni singolo uomo. In una sorta di perenne work in progress noi smontiamo e rimontiamo il palcoscenico su cui recitiamo la nostra piccolissima parte, comparse sempre, anche se ci illudiamo di essere protagonisti.

*Giovanni Brunazzi**
Docente di design industriale all'Università di Parma
e di packaging al Politecnico di Torino

A great many dealers projecting innovative packaging strategies are, slowly but no doubt firmly, leading towards eco-friendly solutions: reusable and biodegradable packages, light clusters containing less plastic, refillable containers, recycled paper and packages.

Due to its close interaction with techniques, materials and production processes, packaging proves to be one of the few marketing instruments that can give a clear contribution to reducing the environmental impact of industrial production, and at the same time can lead consumers towards new ethic models and approaches.

The other side of the coin is the economic implication, as ecopackaging can turn out to be a valid opportunity for marketing, especially for those eco-conscious companies that can appeal to educated and dynamic consumers, thus realizing higher profits.

The complex packaging-mediated relation between consumers and goods is possibly to be connected with a more complex matter.
Exactly like our primitive ancestors did, we tend do personify the things we get in touch with.
Not only do we anthropomorphise animals and plants, even if unconsciously, but we do that with inanimate objects as well. This expedient, widely exploited in fairy tales, responds to our profound need for consolation and reassurance.
From a psychological point of view, the animistic invention of the world protects us from the anguish for existential solitude. It creates for us, little human beings, small particles roaming in an immense inorganic universe, the illusion that we are not an anomaly, whose destiny is to be thrown out of this uninterested and unmoved reality, by the unceasing work of death. This is the reason why things and goods need to be "dressed": it is not so a matter of denoting and preserving them, as it is a way of letting them into our symbolic universe, so to establish humanly comparable relations with them.

There is something childish or even pathologic in this approach, when we go far beyond childhood.
But it is in fact through this constant temptation to creative almightiness, through the irrational imaginative force which is mirrored in things, that humankind affirms its humanity beyond its mere organic nature.
Similarly to art and poetry, the evocative power of packaging creates the unconscious setting of the theatre of life, for every single man. Through a sort of perennial work in progress, we do and undo the stage where we play our tiny walk-on part, still flattering ourselves that we are the main character on stage.

Giovanni Brunazzi
Professor of industrial design at the University of Parma
and of packaging at Turin Polytechnic

Index

 :Living:**010**

 :Wine:**026**

 :Beauty:**050**

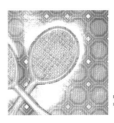 :Sport:**072**

 :Food:**084**

 :Corporate:**142**

Dall'arredamento ai vestiti dagli orologi ai
computer, dalle penne stilografiche agli occhiali,
tutto quanto è utile per vivere in confort, praticità
e bellezza viene ora anche "impacchettato" per
essere più riconoscibile, più trasportabile, più
coinvolgente.
Le confezioni di questa enorme varietà di prodotti
ne propogono l'identità di marca e la
desiderabilità.
Proprio per il valore economico generalmente
medio alto, il packaging è realizzato con materiali
e tecniche cartotecniche e di assemblaggio tali
da fare di queste confezioni un contenitore di
alta comunicabilità.

From furniture to clothes, from watches to
computers, from fountain pens to glasses, all
that adds comfort, beauty and convenience to
our life is nowadays "wrapped", thus looking
more appealing, recognizable and easy to take
away.
The very packages of this great variety of products
stress brand identity and desirability.
Given the relevant value of this kind of products,
packaging is realized with paper-transformation
materials and with assembling techniques that
lend products a high degree of communicability.

Project   "L'Indispensabile" by Vinicio Capossela

- **Customer**   CGD – Compagnia Generale del Disco – Warner Music Italia
- **Agency**   Inside BTB – Dentro la comunicazione
- **Author**   Francesco Nicoletti (art director) - Andrea Forlani - Francesca Leoncini
- **Year**   2003
- **Materials**   CD packaging (leaflet, booklet, CD cover), MC packaging (booklet)

Notes   the project received a mention at the Italian Music Awards as the best graphic project

Project	Private show Vol. II
– Customer	La Perla
– Agency	Mixage
– Author	Maria Pia Lenzi
– Year	2004
– Materials	PPN + silver film

Notes UV offset + silver film, die cutting and assembling. CD and bracelet are inserted in the relevant spaces.

paq >>

making media movable

Project	PAQ – CD case
– Customer	Isia
– Agency	Isia
– Author	Giuditta Matteucci – Jan Mast
– Year	2002/03
– Materials	PP

Notes It contains 2 CDs. It can be used alone and "worn" through a lace, or piled up to form a tower.

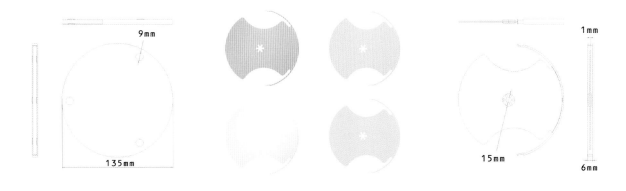

Project	Relay – pencil case	//
– **Customer**	Isia	
– **Agency**	Isia	
– **Author**	Giulia Ancarani – Nico Strobbe	
– **Year**	2002/03	
– **Materials**	silicone rubber	

Notes it consists of one single printed piece.
The pencils are wrapped up.

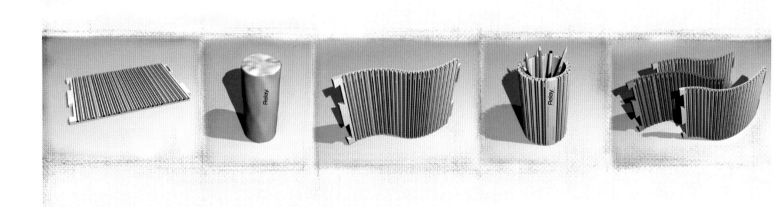

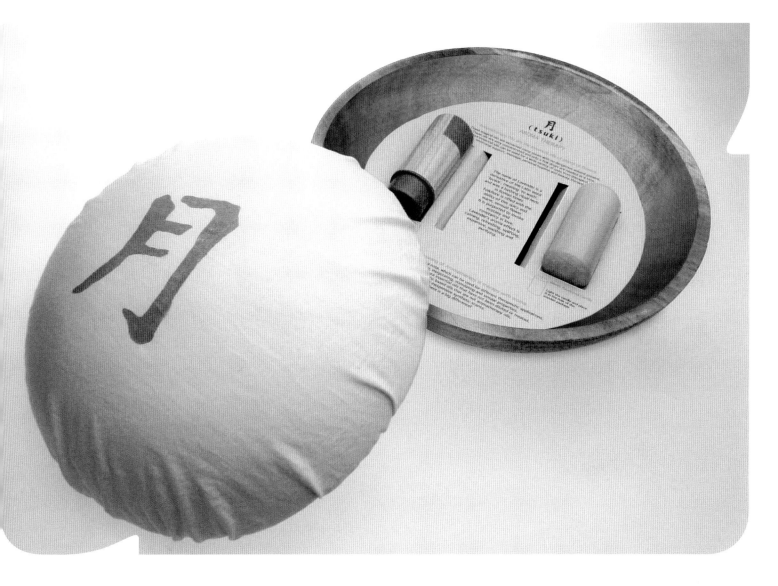

Project	Tsuki – packaging for perfume and candle
– Customer	Isia
– Agency	Isia
– Author	Elena Freddi – Lucie Cara
– Year	2002/03
– Materials	wood, board, cloth, foam polyurethane

Notes: packaging for psychophysical wellbeing. The lid becomes a pillow and the wooden part a tray or a candle stick.

Project	Night Comfort Kit
– Customer	Starhotels
– Agency	The Ad Store Italia
– Author	Rachel Wild e Natalia Borri (creative direction)
	Rachel Wild (art direction)
– Year	2002
– Materials	plastic

Project	Mandarina Duck jewelry box
– Customer	Plastimoda (Mandarina Duck)
– Agency	The Ad Store Italia
– Author	Creative Direction: Rachel Wild and Natalia Borri - Art Director: Rachel Wild
– Year	2001
– Materials	carton and elastic band

Project	Display stand for silver jewels
– Customer	Effetto Oro
– Agency	no.parking
– Author	Caterina Romio
– Year	2000
– Materials	silk screen on opal blue PVC

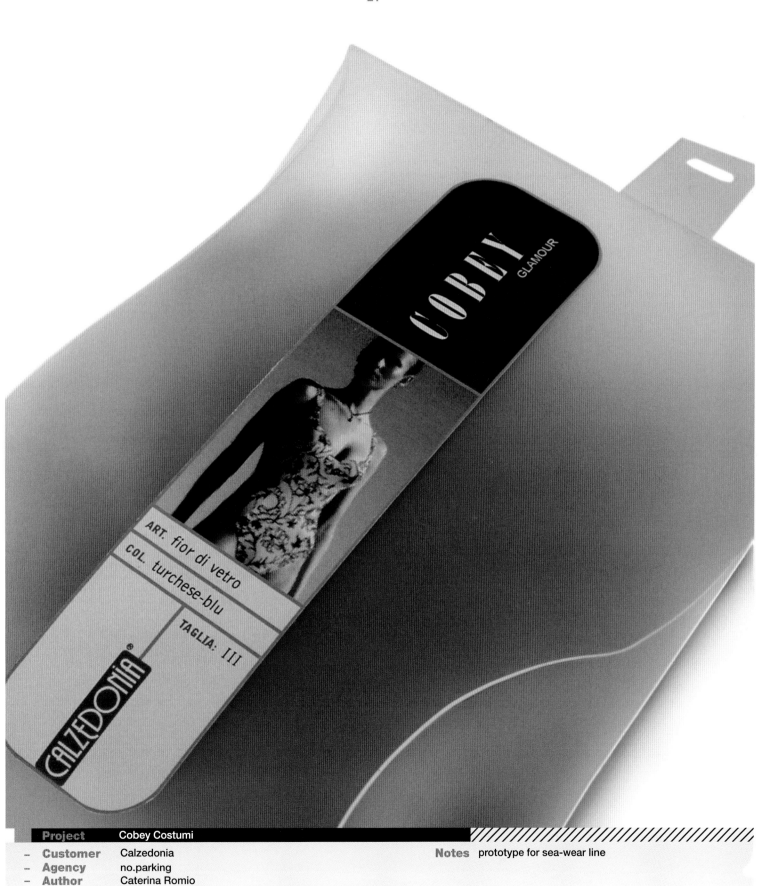

Project	Cobey Costumi		
– Customer	Calzedonia	Notes	prototype for sea-wear line
– Agency	no.parking		
– Author	Caterina Romio		
– Year	2001		
– Materials	opal blue PVC – offset-printed sticky label		

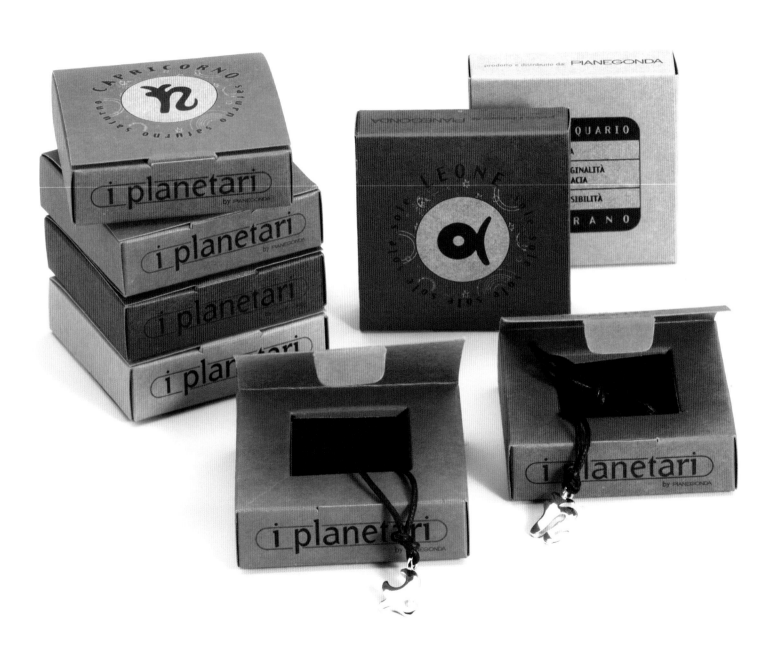

Project	I Planetari		
– Customer	Pianegonda Gioielli	**Notes**	packaging for a line of silver jewels related to the zodiacal signs
– Agency	no.parking		
– Author	Caterina Romio		
– Year	1999		
– Materials	light brown kraft paper – silk screen		

Project	Bioproject by Albatros – hydro-massage bathtub
– Customer	Domino Spa –Albatros trademark
– Agency	Le Design by Elena Squalizza and Luisa Sparavier Snc
– Author	Elena Squalizza
– Year	1999
– Materials	pack containing a CD and a box of essential oils, pack containing a brochure and a CD, shopping bags

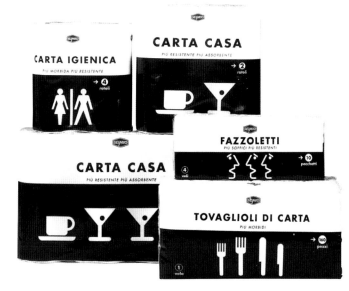

Project	Paper for the Seimio company
– Customer	MDO - Moderna distribuzione organizzata
– Agency	Tangram Strategic Design Srl
– Author	Enrico Sempi (creative director) - Enrico Sempi (art director)
	Enrico Sempi - Andrea Sempi (designer) - Guido Rosa (illustrator)
– Year	2001
– Materials	two special colour + white flexography

Project	Belli e Forti – kitchen utensils made of plastic for large-scale department stores
– Customer	Treti Srl
– Agency	Carré Noir Italia
– Author	Enrico Maria Pecchio (art director)
– Year	2003
– Materials	corrugated board printed with five-colour offset printing + machine varnishing

Notes the brand identity of this product is designed by Carré Noir Italia. This packaging has an original opening on the sides so that customers can touch the utensils, as usual in big stores.

Graficabgc

Project	Agricultural products
- Customer	Demetra
- Agency	Grafica BGC
- Author	Beatrice Gandolfi Colleoni
- Year	2000

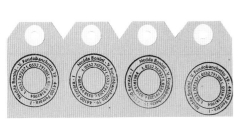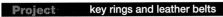

Project	key rings and leather belts
- Customer	Arte e comunicazione by Nedda Bonini
- Agency	Arte e comunicazione by Nedda Bonini
- Author	Nedda Bonini
- Year	2003-2004
- Materials	Sirio-Fedrigoni board, synthetic leather and string

Il settore dei vini sta conoscendo a livello mondiale una crescita, non solo quantitativa ma anche qualitativa.
Il packaging dei vini è soprattutto definito dall'etichetta, anche se recentemente si sta assistendo ad una ricerca sul design delle bottiglie, in modo da renderle riconoscibili nei sempre più affollati scaffali delle enoteche e dei supermercati.
Il design delle etichette sta praticamente esplorando tutte le forme visive e materiche possibili: dalla grafica più tradizionale, classica, a quella minimalista.
Il problema per il designer è progettare un sistema di etichette che identifichi la marca, il vino e quanto di edonistico può essere visualizzato. Questo spiega come il settore dei vini sia tra quelli più vivaci in termini di progettazione.

The wine branch is undoubtedly undergoing a worldwide increase both in quality and in quantity. In this case, the packaging concentrates mostly on the label, even though recently there has been a mounting interest for bottle design, so that wines can be easily recognized on the packed shelves of supermarkets and wine shops.
The label design is currently exploring all possible visual and matter forms: from traditional to classical graphics, to minimalist approaches.
Designers are called to project a system of labels which identify the brand, the wine and all the hedonistic elements that can be translated visually.
This accounts for the great vivaciousness of this branch in terms of projecting.

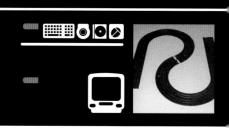

Package
Design In Italy
:Wine

Brunazzi&Associati

Project	**Corporate profile and packaging for Arbiola wines labels**
– **Customer**	Azienda Agricola Arbiola
– **Agency**	Brunazzi & Associati - Turin
– **Author**	Andrea Brunazzi (creative director)
	Roberto Necco (art director)
– **Year**	2002

Notes The redesign of the visual identity of Arbiola wines constitutes the starting point of the definition of a new corporate identity for the whole firm. The design, which involved the brand and logo, makes provision for marked differentiantion within the framework of a strictly coherent graphic system. The labels are all in one format that adapts to bottles of different sizes. Organised around a square module that guides the composition of the graphic elements, the labels are given different colour schemes each time to indicate the many different types of wines. The quality of the paper and the inks /serigraphic and material) are part of the design details that have the capacity to increase the product's communicative potential.

SiebertHead BRAND DESIGN CONSULTANTS

Project	Turin bottle
– Customer	Province of Turin
– Agency	SiebertHead (London) Brunazzi Associati (Turin)
– Author	Alistair Russell
– Account	Tim Corvin, Ada Brunazzi
– Year	2003
– Materials	glass

Notes The aim of this design was to create an object with a strong connotation and a high profile, suitable for becoming an emblem of the excellence of the wines of Turin and for constituting a tool for promoting them. The bottle has a crooked, irregular, asymmetric shape: a sculptural bottle that rests on a raised pedestal that is also useful as a location for the logo.
Made of old green for white wines and dark brown for red wines, the bottle maintains semantic contents coherent with the tradition of wine-making in the Turin area, while at the same time relating to contemporary meanings. The bottle can be developed as a theme and is flexible to use; it is suitable for different wines and is easely distinguished from the standard types of bottle already on the market, such as the Bordeaux and the Alba bottles.

Project	"Motus Vitae" - Il brut di Giuliano
– Customer	Bortolomiol
– Agency	Caseley Giovara
– Author	Caseley Giovara
– Year	2003
– Materials	Bottle, labels, tissue paper, cylinder case; labels and collar are printed in offset with gold dust. Tissue paper is printed in two colors - Cylinder case is printed in offset with gold foil blocking and screen printed varnish.

Notes Packaging - A high profile bottle dedicated to the late founder (who died in 2000). On the case and on the label are printed the notes he himself wrote down for the creation of Brut Prosecco.

claudio
cristofori
eassociati

Project	Aromatic grape juices
– Customer	Gavioli Antica Cantina
– Agency	Claudio Cristofori e Associati Srl
– Author	Claudio Cristofori (creative director) - Laura Pasqualino (designer)
– Year	1998
– Materials	stick-on paper

Project	**Boxes of wines**
– **Customer**	Gruppo Mezzacorona – Feudo Arancio wine producers
– **Agency**	Luisa Sparavier
– **Author**	Luisa Sparavier - Elena Squalizza
– **Year**	2003
– **Materials**	- box for two bottles of wine - box for three bottles of wine - cylinder case containing a sommelier smock

Project	Sole
– Customer	Tenuta S.Piero D'Uzzano
– Agency	DBV Advertising
– Author	DBV staff
– Year	2003
– Materials	stick-on label, hot stamped ribbon, offset printing

Project	Bottle packaging for stores
– Customer	Le Cantine di Greve in Chianti
– Agency	DBV Advertising
– Author	DBV staff
– Year	2001
– Materials	corrugated board, hot stamped ribbon, offset printing

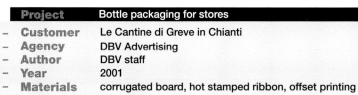

no.parking

Project	Box of wines	
– Customer	Cortepack (packaging contest)	
– Agency	no.parking	**Notes** prototype for 6 bottles of Bordeaux wine for large-scale retail outlets
– Author	Elisa Dall'Angelo	
– Year	2002	
– Materials	corrugated board – silk screen	

::studiomagni

Project	Arte Industria Natura	
– Customer	FOR	Notes collector's wines
– Agency	Studio Magni	
– Author	Laura Magni (art direction)	
	Elisa Serra (graphic design)	
	Sergio Toppi (illustration)	
– Year	2000	

Project	"Emozioni" wine label
– Customer	Leone Conti Viticoltore
– Agency	Casa Walden Comunicazione
– Author	Giuseppe Tolo
– Year	2003
– Materials	lithographic print on paper

Notes scrapeboard illustration

Project	Montenato Griffini wine – label design
- Customer	Montenato Griffini Estate
- Agency	Advance
- Author	Enrico Malinverni (creative director)
- Year	2002
- Materials	paper labels printed in 2 colours and varnished

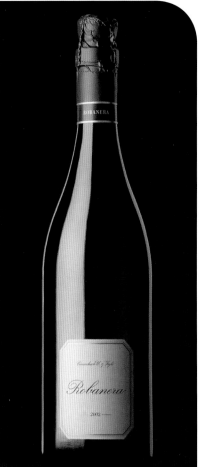

Project	Packaging for a bottle of Robanera wine
– Customer	Cantine Cavicchioli U. & Figli - San Prospero (Modena)
– Agency	Basaglia.com
– Author	Fausto Basaglia
– Year	2003

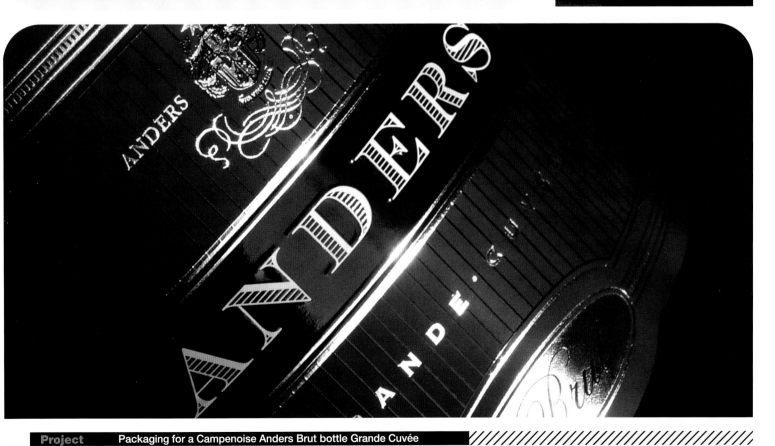

Project	Packaging for a Campenoise Anders Brut bottle Grande Cuvée
– Customer	Åkesson A.B. - Sweden
– Agency	Basaglia.com
– Author	Fausto Basaglia
– Year	1999

Project   Packaging for Italian wines from the 1998 vintage (aged in barriques)
- **Customer**   Åkesson A.B. - Sweden
- **Agency**   Basaglia.com
- **Author**   Fausto Basaglia
- **Year**   2000

Project   Cabernet Sauvignon bottle from the 1998 vintage (aged in barriques)
- **Customer**   Åkesson A.B. - Sweden
- **Agency**   Basaglia.com
- **Author**   Fausto Basaglia
- **Year**   2000

Project	Packaging for a Monogram Franciacorta Millesimato
– Customer	Castel Faglia Spa - Franciacorta (Brescia)
– Agency	Basaglia.com
– Author	Fausto Basaglia
– Year	2003

	Project	**Valle di Cembra - Dos Caslir**	
–	**Customer**	La Vis and Valle di Cembra winery	**Notes** brand and product identity
–	**Agency**	RBA design	
–	**Author**	Nicola Mincione	
–	**Year**	2003	

Project	Malgrà - Export red wine
– Customer	Malgrà wine producers
– Agency	RBA design
– Author	Nicola Mincione
– Year	2000

Project	Charmant by Cesarini Sforza
– Customer	Cesarini Sforza sparkling wines
– Agency	RBA design
– Author	Nicola Mincione
– Year	2002
– Notes	product identity

Project	Gancia - Tenute dei Vallarino
– Customer	F.lli Gancia & Co. Spa
– Agency	RBA design
– Author	Nicola Mincione
– Year	2003
– Notes	brand identity and packaging image

Project	La Vis wines
– Customer	La Vis and Valle di Cembra winery
– Agency	RBA design
– Author	Nicola Mincione
– Year	2003
– Notes	new product range identity

Project	Valle di Cembra - Vineyard	
– Customer	La Vis and Valle di Cembra winery	**Notes** brand identity and product packaging and image
– Agency	RBA design	
– Author	Nicola Mincione	
– Year	2003	

STRATEGIC BRAND DESIGN
PACKAGING
CORPORATE IDENTITY
RETAIL DESIGN

Project	Malgrà - red wine		
– Customer	Malgrà Wine producers	Notes	brand identity and product packaging and image
– Agency	RBA design		
– Author	Nicola Mincione		
– Year	2000		

studio Padovani
packaging & graphic design

Project	Terre del Cevico, Trebbiano and Sangiovese del Rubicone IGT wines
– Customer	Cevico (Coltiva Group)
– Agency	Studio Padovani
– Author	Luciano Padovani
– Year	2000
– Materials	label and upper band with transparent closure

Project	Valdobbiadene prosecco – Jacopo Maestri wine line
– Customer	San Geminiano
– Agency	Studio Padovani
– Author	Luciano Padovani
– Year	2002
– Materials	sticky label

Cosmetici, profumi, prodotti e accessori per la cura del corpo e per solleticare il desiderio di bellezza e di fascino di donne e uomini si rivelano, come oggetti e come portatori di emozioni, attraverso le confezioni.
Il settore beauty è quello che, più di ogni altro, utilizza in modo creativo materiali e forme innovative, sia nel package che negli espositori/campionari da banco.
I progetti delle confezioni devono tener conto contemporaneamente a) delle esigenze di visibilità e di appealing richiesti per il punto vendita b) dello stile che ogni marca possiede e deve sviluppare costantemene per garantire la riconoscibilità della marca e dei suoi prodotti.
In questo senso il valore di un package design innovativo e coerente incide sull'immaginario evocato dalle marche e dai prodotti.

Cosmetics, perfumes, products and accessories for body care: all these tickle men's and women's desire for beauty and charm and, through packaging, carry not only a content but also emotions.
The beauty branch is the most creative one in using original materials and forms, both for package, display stands and counter displays.
Packaging projects must take into account the needs for visibility and appeal in the point of purchase and, at the same time, they cannot fail to reformulate the peculiar style that makes each trademark and its products immediately recognizable.
In this sense, the value of an innovative and coherent package design adds to the imagery trademarks and products recall.

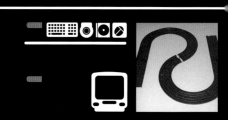

Project	**Perfume case for Theorema perfume by Fendi**	
– Customer	Florbath/Profumi di Parma - Parma	**Notes** The project has proved hugely successful. The whole line won the International Oscar in London and the Cosmprof 1999 as the best packaging for female products.
– Agency	Studio Brozzi Snc- Parma	
– Author	Giacomo Brozzi	
– Year	1999	
– Materials	"Fedrigoni" black board, glossy board, golden hot foil stamping, pre-printed corrugated board, fastened with a wooden stick	

Project	HQ mini-quantities of cosmetic products

–	Customer	Paglieri Sell System
–	Agency	Tangram Strategic Design Srl
–	Author	Enrico Sempi (creative director)
		Antonella Trevisan - Enrico Sempi (art director)
		Antonella Trevisan - Enrico Sempi (designer)
		Angelo Annibalini (photographer)
–	Year	2002
–	Materials	3 kinds of material glued together: PET, aluminium, PE

Notes four + 1 special colour gravure + pearly varnish

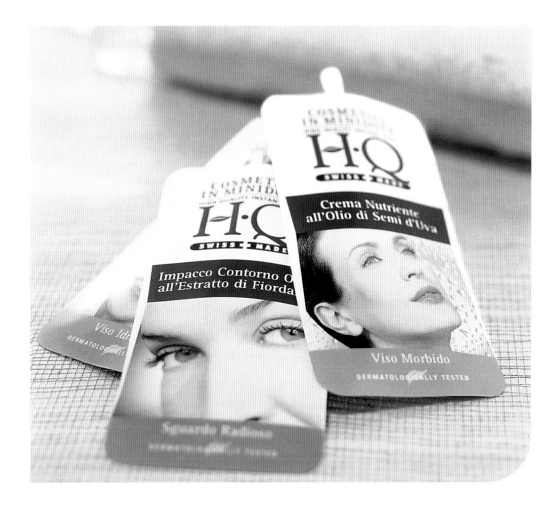

54

Project	Comfort Zone Action Sublime
– Customer	Davines
– Agency	The Ad Store Italia
– Author	Rachel Wild e Natalia Borri (creative direction)
	Rachel Wild (art direction)
– Year	2000
– Materials	plexiglass

[comfort zone]
[comfort zone]
action sublime
cream SPF12
anti-aging skin saver
bio-complesso protettivo anti-età

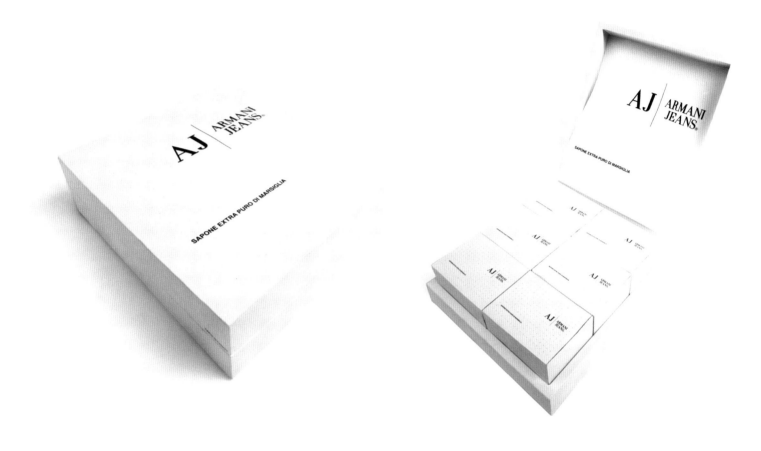

Project	Armani Jeans pack
– **Customer**	Simint Spa
– **Agency**	Unjust
– **Author**	Paolo Santosuosso – Francesco Roncaglia
– **Year**	2001
– **Materials**	hemp paper

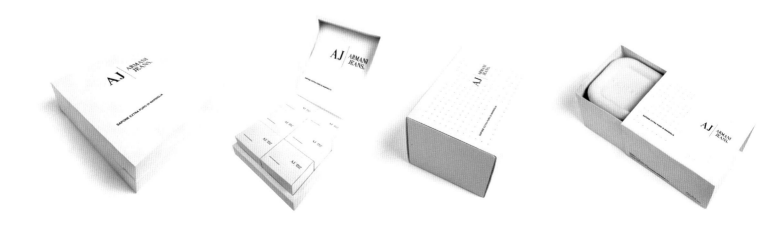

Project	Hiwa Cosmetics
– Customer	Premio Internazionale Cosmopack
– Agency	no.parking
– Author	Caterina Romio
– Year	1994
– Materials	corrugated board

Notes prototype for bottle and jar. It can be used both as packaging and as a dispenser

Graficabgc

Project	Design of chemist's logo and new cosmetic/ wellbeing line /////////
– Customer	Di Zollino chemist's - Imola
– Agency	Grafica BGC
– Author	Beatrice Gandolfi Colleoni
– Year	2003
– Materials	clear calendered PVC

Project	Erbe Rare - herbal products for professional beauty treatment /////////
– Customer	Principi attivi
– Agency	Grafica BGC
– Author	Beatrice Gandolfi Colleoni
– Year	2001

Project	Oli Rari: oils for massaging
– **Customer**	Principi attivi
– **Agency**	Grafica BGC
– **Author**	Beatrice Gandolfi Colleoni
– **Year**	2003

Project	I Professionali - products for professional beauty treatment
– **Customer**	Principi attivi
– **Agency**	Grafica BGC
– **Author**	Beatrice Gandolfi Colleoni
– **Year**	2001
– **Materials**	PVC droppers – boxboard – matt plastic-coating

Project	Four different lines of cosmetic and herbal products
– **Customer**	Herbella - Florence
– **Agency**	Pascucci D.sign - Grafica BGC
– **Author**	Daniela Pascucci - Beatrice Gandolfi Colleoni
– **Year**	2000

GIŌ MINOLA

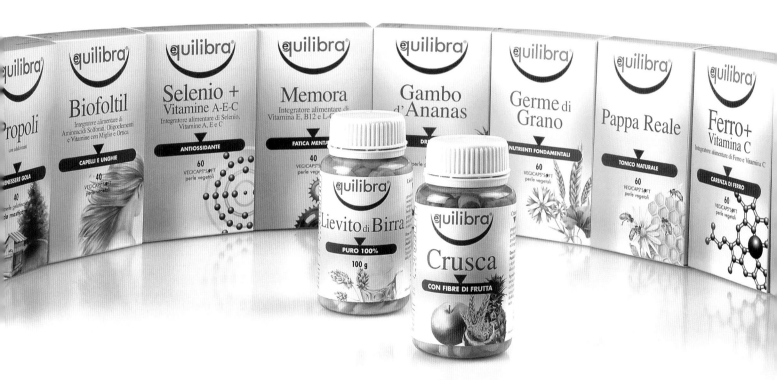

Project	**Equilibra – nutritional supplements**
– Customer	Equilibra Srl
– Agency	Giò Minola - Torino
– Author	Alovisi Cèline
– Year	2003
– Materials	cases made of pure cellulose paper, printed with CMYK and UV-coated labels

Notes the line is made up of 40 different items

Project	Solè dispenser
- Customer	2G Beauty Communications Srl
- Agency	Image Studio Snc
- Author	Luigi Brivio - Stefania Brivio
- Year	2002
- Materials	corrugated board glued together with "Ensarote" board, matt plastic coating

Project	Oligoline
- **Customer**	2G Beauty Communications Srl
- **Agency**	Image Studio Snc
- **Author**	Luigi Brivio - Stefania Brivio
- **Year**	2003
- **Materials**	"Ensarote" board, 1+1 colour printing, matt plastic coating

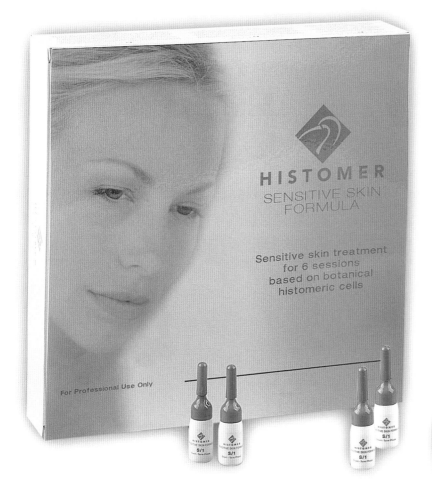

Project	Histomer
– Customer	Valetudo Srl
– Agency	Image Studio Snc
– Author	Stefania Brivio - Luigi Brivio
– Year	2003
– Materials	glossy plastic coated Bindakote board (400 gm)

Project	Essence
– Customer	Emmebi Italia Snc
– Agency	Image Studio Snc
– Author	Stefania Brivio - Luigi Brivio
– Year	2004
– Materials	PB bottles, PP jars

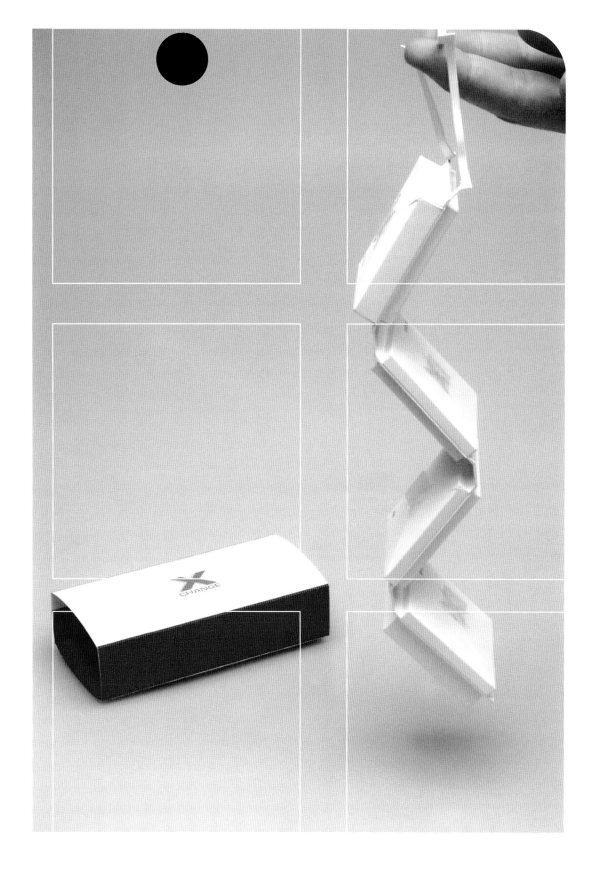

Project   **XChange – travel kit for female hygiene** //

– **Customer**   Isia
– **Agency**   Isia
– **Author**   Fabiana Farneti - Wendy Guns
– **Year**   2002/03
– **Materials**   Tyveck (DuPont product)

Notes the kit is dedicated to women travelling.
It contains: refreshing tissues, toothpaste
lozenges, sanitary towels, etc.

STRATEGIC BRAND DESIGN
PACKAGING
CORPORATE IDENTITY
RETAIL DESIGN

Project	Carlo Erba Leviogel
- Customer	Carlo Erba Otc Spa
- Agency	RBA design
- Author	Massimo Cecchi
- Year	2002
- Notes	new product identity

Project	Beiersdorf - Nivea hand Night
- Customer	Beiersdorf Spa
- Agency	RBA design
- Author	Nicola Mincione
- Year	2003
- Notes	packaging design

Project	Beiersdorf - Nivea Body Q10 Plus	
- Customer	Beiersdorf Spa	Notes packaging design and image
- Agency	RBA design	
- Author	Nicola Mincione	
- Year	2003	

Project	Arca Verde – beauty line
– **Customer**	Regard
– **Agency**	Kalimera srl
– **Author**	Kalimera
– **Year**	1998
– **Materials**	board

Notes three beauty lines (for body, hair, face), each displaying its own colour and symbol, which is die cut on the sides of the relevant box.

Project	Sunsé – Sun products
– Customer	C.R.B.
– Agency	Il Telaio Advertising
– Author	agency's staff
– Year	2001
– Materials	two-colour printing + glazed varnishing on a copper-coloured metallised base

POLAROLO
IMMAGINE E COMUNICAZIONE

Project	Relassime skin-toning lifting cream by Sant'Angelica
– Customer	Sant'Angelica
– Agency	Polarolo Immagine e Comunicazione
– Author	Felice Polarolo – Cristina Garello
– Year	2003
– Materials	case, jar

::studiomagni

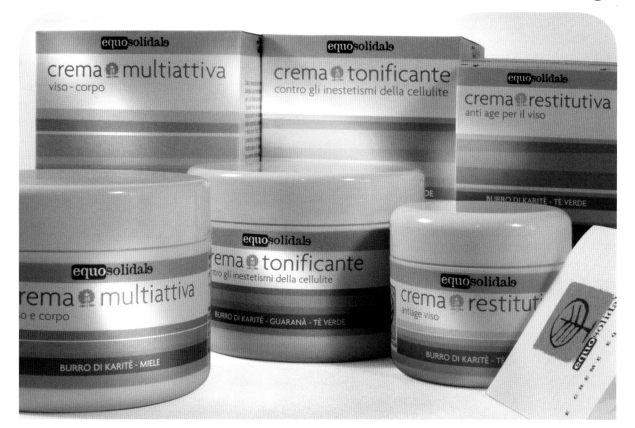

Project	Crème corpo - Fair Trade body cream		Notes	beauty pack containing three jars of karite cream with enclosed information sheet
– Customer	Cooperativa Commercio Alternativo			
– Agency	Studio Magni			
– Author	Laura Magni (art direction) Sara Cimarosti (graphic design)			
– Year	2002			

Project	Linea Vivissima by Sant'Angelica
– Customer	Sant'Angelica
– Agency	Polarolo Immagine e Comunicazione
– Author	Felice Polarolo Cristina Garello
– Year	2004
– Materials	jars, tubes, bottles

Notes silk screen on a pearly base

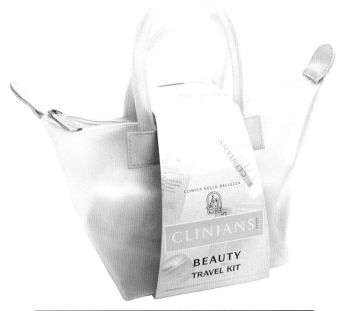

Project	Clinians beauty travel kit
– Customer	Mirato
– Agency	Polarolo Immagine e Comunicazione
– Author	Felice Polarolo – Sonia Ambroggi
– Year	2003

Project	Clinians
– Customer	Mirato
– Agency	Polarolo Immagine e Comunicazione
– Author	Felice Polarolo – Sonia Ambroggi
– Year	2003

Project	Axenia – Post color line
- Customer	Soco
- Agency	Polarolo Immagine e Comunicazione
- Author	Felice Polarolo – Sonia Ambroggi
- Year	2003
- Materials	bottle, jar

Project	Clinians – anti-aging products
- Customer	Mirato
- Agency	Polarolo Immagine e Comunicazione
- Author	Felice Polarolo – Sonia Ambroggi
- Year	2003

Project	Hexance - creams
- Customer	Medint
- Agency	Polarolo Immagine e Comunicazione
- Author	Felice Polarolo – Cristina Garello
- Year	2003
- Materials	cases, jars, tubes

Lo sviluppo, ma non solo a livello agonistico degli sport ha generato una enorme varietà di prodotti, dagli attrezzi agli equipaggiamenti, agli abiti e calzature disegnate appunto per ogni specifico sport.
L'importanza di questo settore è enorme come pure quello della sua identità. Se si pensa alla Nike, ad esempio, si può capire come sia possibile per una marca diventare, attraverso i prodotti, la sua esposizione e il suo packaging, un modo di essere e di vivere.
La ricerca nel design dei prodotti si accompagna a quella della loro presentazione in modo da presentare sul mercato un'idea vincente di marca.

The growth of sports, both on a competitive and on an amateur level, has produced a considerable variety of products (accessories, gymnastic apparatus, sportswear and shoes designed for specific sports).
This branch and its identity are of great importance. Think of Nike just to realize how a brand can become a way of life through its products, their merchandising and their packaging.
The research, then, focuses both on the design of products and on their introduction onto the market: in this way it is possible to enter the market with a winning brand idea.

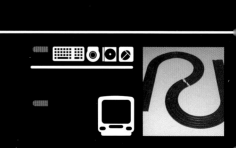

Project	Extreme Sports Promotional
– Customer	Extreme Sports Event
– Agency	Temecula Design
– Author	Cristiano de Veroli
– Year	2002/03
– Materials	Digital print on glossy paper (120 gr), opaque plasticization, set on forex and spiral-bound

Project	Rossignol safety line
– Customer	Rossignol Ski Poles Vallèe D'Aoste Spa
– Agency	Giò Minola - Torino
– Author	Piera Luisolo
– Year	2003
– Materials	- helmet box in varnished cardboard CMYK; - box for body armor in varnished cardboard CMYK; - U-bolt for bags

	Project	Briko Helmets bike
–	Customer	Brico Srl
–	Agency	Tangram Strategic Design Srl
–	Author	Enrico Sempi (creative director)
		Antonella Trevisan (art director)
		Antonella Trevisan – Anna Grimaldi (designer)
–	Year	1998
–	Materials	craft cardboard

Notes four colour offset printing + car varnish

Project	Briko Underwear
– Customer	Brico Srl
– Agency	Tangram Strategic Design Srl
– Author	Enrico Sempi (creative director)
	Enrico Sempi (art director)
	Antonella Trevisan - Enrico Sempi - Andrea Sempi (designer)
	Edoardo Mari (photographer)
– Year	1998
– Materials	single-side coated paper

Notes four + one special colour offset printing + plastic coating. Die-cut logo to allow product visibility

Project	Briko Ski Goggles
– Customer	Brico Srl
– Agency	Tangram Strategic Design Srl
– Author	Enrico Sempi (creative director)
	Antonella Trevisan (art director)
	Antonella Trevisan (designer)
– Year	1998
– Materials	cellulose acetate

Notes three special colour flexography

79

Project	**Briko Turbo Ski Wax**	///
– Customer	Brico Srl	**Notes** four colour offset printing
– Agency	Tangram Strategic Design Srl	
– Author	Enrico Sempi (creative director)	
	Enrico Sempi - Antonella Trevisan (art director)	
	Antonella Trevisan – Anna Grimaldi (designer)	
	Hiro Kawai (industrial design)	
– Year	1998	
– Materials	stick-on label and HDPE box containing the ski wax	

no.parking

Project	**Enersocks**	///
– Customer	Calzedonia	**Notes** packaging for sports socks
– Agency	no.parking	
– Author	Sabine Lercher	
– Year	2000	
– Materials	natural white kraft paper - 4-Pantone-colour offset printing	

Raineri design
immagine|comunicazione

80

Project	Underwear
– Customer	Micosport Spa
– Agency	Raineri Design
– Author	William Raineri
– Year	2002
– Materials	10 cartons, dispenser, display stand

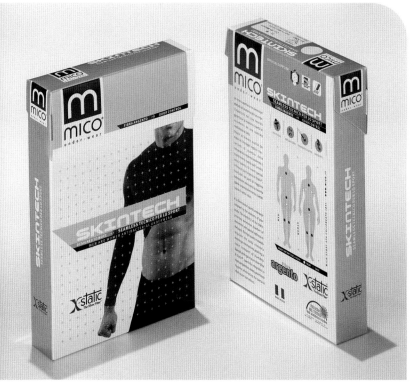

Project	Skintech - Underwear
– Customer	Micosport Spa
– Agency	Raineri Design
– Author	William Raineri
– Year	2004

Project	Akkua - Technical aqua gear
– Customer	Decortex Spa
– Agency	Raineri Design
– Author	William Raineri
– Year	2004

Project	Spin – Skates and fittings
– Customer	Dal Bello
– Agency	Il Telaio Advertising
– Author	agency's staff
– Year	1998
– Materials	flexography on light brown cardboard

Il settore Food è da sempre quello in cui la progettazione di packaging si deve misurare per rendere forte e desiderabile il prodotto.
Negli ultimi anni, ai prodotti di marca (da sempre attenti alle evoluzioni del gusto) si sono affiancati i prodotti a marchio (private label) che hanno abbandonato l'aria dimessa dei primi anni d'introduzione sul mercato, per entrare in diretta competizione con i prodotti di marca e rendere così più interessante le proposte sullo scaffale.
L'avvento recente di prodotti biologici o senza grassi o colesterolo ecc. ha permesso di sviluppare progetti di packaging molto comunicativi, attraverso forme, colori, immagini e rendere così più allettante e facile scegliere il prodotto giusto.
In molti casi il packaging del food deve anche tenere conto di sterotipi sedimentati nel tempo, ma la tendenza recente è quella di tenerli in considerazione ma senza essere troppo vincolati.

The food branch has always been the most challenging for packaging, whose aim here is to make products outstanding and appealing.
In the last years, private labels have gained increasing importance on the market, beside brand products (which have always been attentive to changes in taste). Once unobtrusive on the market, private labels are now in open competition with brand products, which results in a richer and more interesting offer for the consumer.
The recent newcomers, i.e. organic, fat-free, cholesterol-free products, have fostered strongly communicative packaging projects, through forms, colours, images that make it easier for consumers to choose the right product.
In most cases, as far as food packaging is concerned, it may be necessary, even though not binding, to take into account existing stereotypes.

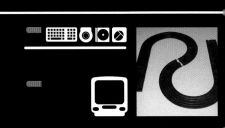

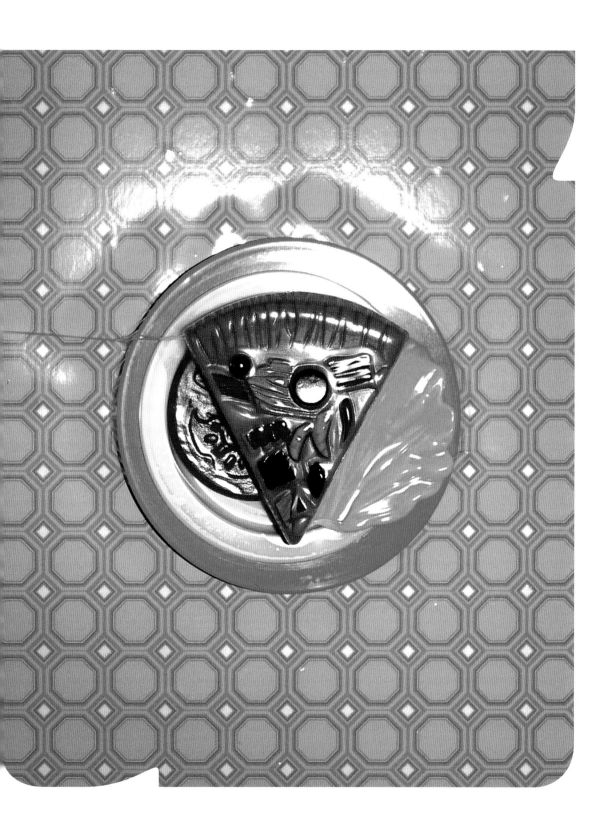

Project	Biosanafrutta Gipsy – PET bottle for fruit juice
– Customer	Biosanafrutta Gipsy
– Agency	Equilibrisospesi - Design e comunicazione
– Author	Sara Pasini
– Year	2002-2003
– Materials	PET

Notes this project has never been realized practically. It was designed as part of a university degree.

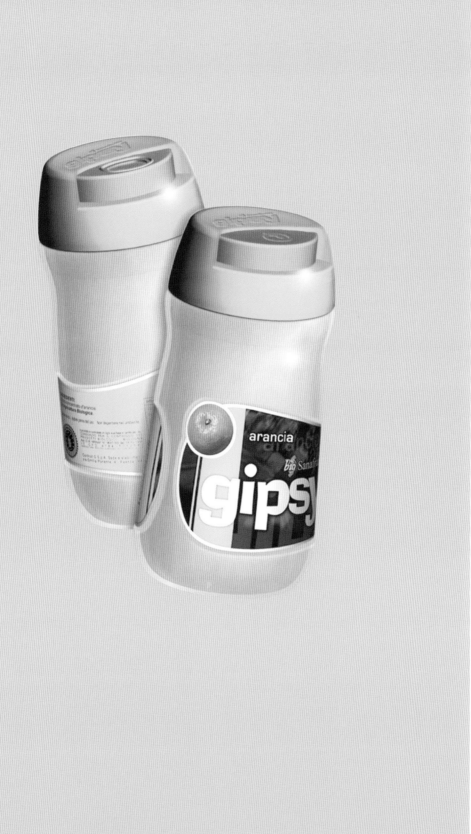

ADVERTISING

88

brand appeal®

Project	**Deep-frozen products**
– Customer	Antica Macelleria Falorni
– Agency	DBV Advertising
– Author	DBV staff
– Year	2002
– Material	cardboard, offset printing, hot stamped ribbon

Project	**Mazzetti L'originale - Modena balsamic vinegar**
– Customer	Mazzetti D'Altavilla
– Agency	Advance
– Author	Enrico Malinverni (creative director) - Anna Albini (illustrator)
– Year	2002-2003
– Materials	paper labels and carton box

(:R:) CarloRaffaelliComunicazione

Project	Extra-virgin olive oil Calia
– Customer	Olio de' Pardi
– Agency	CarloRaffaelliComunicazione
– Author	Carlo Raffaelli
– Year	2003
– Materials	paper, glass, corrugated board

Notes corporate image: name, logo, brand, label and bottle

Project	A line of presents
– Customer	Foresteria Casentinese
– Agency	Immedia
– Author	Veronique Michalski - Piero Lanini
– Year	1999

Notes Awards: Packaging Stars 99; equal second prize for structural design; award in the food category; Special Stars

Project	Caterina's recipes
– Customer	Boscovivo
– Agency	Immedia
– Author	Giuseppe Scapigliati
– Year	1999
– Materials	"Sugo pronto" jars and tubs

claudio
cristofori
eassociati

Project		Gift products Parma d'Or
–	**Customer**	System Food
–	**Agency**	Claudio Cristofori e Associati Srl
–	**Author**	Claudio Cristofori (creative director) - Laura Pasqualino (designer)
–	**Year**	1998
–	**Materials**	corrugated board

Project	Tomato soups and ready-made sauces
– Customer	Azienda Agricola Terre di San Giorgio
– Agency	Claudio Cristofori e Associati Srl
– Author	Claudio Cristofori (creative director) - Laura Pasqualino (designer)
– Year	2002
– Materials	stick-on paper

Project	Gioia Gold margarine
– Customer	Unigrà Spa
– Agency	Claudio Cristofori e Associati Srl
– Author	Claudio Cristofori (creative director) - Laura Pasqualino (designer)
– Year	2001
– Materials	aluminium paper, PP

RICREATIVI
IMAGE FACTORY

Project	Soleado – Coordinate image for a coffee line
– Customer	Attibassi Co.Ind Scarl
– Agency	Ricreativi Srl
– Author	Anna Maria Govoni – Michele Oca
– Year	2002
– Materials	aluminium foil for food wrapping – five-colour printing

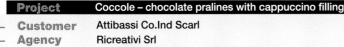

Project	Coccole – chocolate pralines with cappuccino filling
– Customer	Attibassi Co.Ind Scarl
– Agency	Ricreativi Srl
– Author	Anna Maria Govoni – Michele Oca
– Year	2002-2003
– Materials	four-colour stiff paper, 6-colours printed PVC, four-colour printed can

NOUVELLE
Comunicazione & Marketing

Project   Organic products L'albero buono (extra-virgin olive oil and sunflower oil)
- **Customer**   Olitalia
- **Agency**   Nouvelle Srl
- **Author**   agency's staff

Project   Le Cultivar - local extra-virgin olive oils (from Riviera Ligure, Terra di Bari, Toscano, Umbria, Valli Trapanesi)
- **Customer**   Olitalia
- **Agency**   Nouvelle Srl
- **Author**   agency's staff

95

Project	Condishake dressings - Modena aromatic vinegar (500ml) - Special for meat, Special for fish, Special for salads (250 ml)
– **Customer**	Olitalia
– **Agency**	Nouvelle Srl
– **Author**	agency's staff

Project	Oro - extra-virgin olive oil
– **Customer**	Olitalia
– **Agency**	Nouvelle Srl
– **Author**	agency's staff

Project	Frumenta - wheat flour (for home-made pasta, bread, all-purpose flour - 1-kg- packs)
- Customer	Grandi Molini Italiani
- Agency	Nouvelle Srl
- Author	agency's staff

Project	Flour for discount shops (flour for cakes, pizzas, all-purpose flour 1-kg- packs)
- Customer	Grandi Molini Italiani
- Agency	Nouvelle Srl
- Author	agency's staff

Project   Evolution - yeast and leaven products

- **Customer**   Grandi Molini Italiani
- **Agency**   Nouvelle Srl
- **Author**   agency's staff

Project	Packaging for crisps
– Customer	Derwent Valley Foods – PHILEAS FOGG, UK
– Agency	SiebertHead (London)
– Year	1999

Notes

The graphic design study redefined the Phileas Fogg logo character making it more approachable and ironic. The treatment of the core graphic communication was to make the product and flavour the hero.

The pack was a success from launch.
Derwent Valley Foods sales figures tracked the product at 100% up on forecast over the first 9 months of its launch. This increase in sales is purely down to the design as there was no advertising support.

Project	Unicom Bols	
– **Customer**	Bols Excellent, Poland	
– **Agency**	SiebertHead (London)	
– **Year**	1999	

Notes

To create a premium vodka brand within the Bols portfolio, combining brand naming, 3D and graphic design was developed an elegant slim bottle with a domed shoulder to help define a clear silhouette for the brand.

The graphics are printed directly onto the bottle, further enhancing the premium values and expressing the purity of the product.

The dynamic wrap-around bottle in ice used for the gift carton created a powerful in-store display.

–	**Customer**	Industrie Alimentari Cinara
–	**Agency**	Brunazzi & Associati (Turin) – SiebertHead (London)
–	**Author**	Giovanni Brunazzi (creative coordinator)
		Matteo Marucco (graphic designer)
–	**Year**	2001-2002
–	**Materials**	paper glued on tinplate or glass

Notes

Centrone is leader in the Italian market as for the food preservation industry. For over 30 years now, it has always had a special concern for quality.
The visual identity of Centrone and of its distribution company Cinara has been designed so to:
- reposition their existing image on a higher level (according to the high quality of their products)
- underline the wish for a change which nevertheless continues and confirms their positive and comforting tradition to their final customers.

The first phase dealt with the basic elements of the visual identity: trademark, logo, colours, characteristic elements. The colour codes (two different tones of bright green), the lettering (modern and different for each brand), the new graphic patterns, all these have improved the quality of the image, which has come out exclusive and international.

The second phase dealt with the redesign of the whole packaging (3D-design, graphics, development) which aimed at defining/making uniform the two product lines, "retail" and "catering".

–	**Customer**	Pasticceria Maggi - Bene Vagienna (CN)
–	**Agency**	Brunazzi & Associati (Turin)
–	**Author**	Andrea Brunazzi (art director)

Notes

For these fine sweets, based on recipes of the old days, a simple and low-cost package has been designed (the printing is in one or two colours).
The Bodoni type mirrors the image of the town, Bene Vagienna, full of memories of the Neoclassic and of the Augustan periods.

Project	Boom Stick - chips
– Customer	Salati Preziosi – Mitica food
– Agency	Officina Comunicazione
– Author	Luca Manfredini – Andrea Marchesi
– Year	2003
– Materials	double metallised PP

Project	Fruit juice line		
– Customer	Juice Mambo	Notes	creation of bottle design, name, logo and brand
– Agency	Officina Comunicazione		
– Author	Andrea Marchesi		
– Year	2001		

Project	Ciocosnack		Notes	packaging of box and brand design
– Customer	Ciocosnack			
– Agency	Officina Comunicazione			
– Author	Andrea Marchesi			
– Year	2003			

Project	Biancosarti Aperitif	
– Customer	Davide Campari	
– Agency	Tangram Strategic Design Srl	
– Author	Enrico Sempi (creative director)	
	Antonella Trevisan - Enrico Sempi (art director and designer)	
	Sergio Quaranta (illustrator)	
– Year	2001	
– Materials	paper	

Notes four colour gravure + golden hot foil stamping

Project	Ehrmann Yogurt	
– Customer	Ehrmann Italia	**Notes** four colour offset printing + car varnish
– Agency	Tangram Strategic Design Srl	
– Author	Enrico Sempi (creative director) - Antonella Trevisan (art director)	
	Antonella Trevisan (designer) - Vittorio Zucchelli (photographer)	
– Year	2001	
– Materials	paper	

Project	Biffi Auter Sauces	
– Customer	A. Vismara by Antonio Biffi	**Notes** four + one special colour offset printing + car varnish
– Agency	Tangram Strategic Design Srl	
– Author	Enrico Sempi (creative director)	
	Enrico Sempi + Antonella Trevisan (art director)	
	Enrico Sempi + Antonella Trevisan (designer)	
	Sergio Quaranta (illustrator)	
– Year	1998	
– Materials	paper	

Project	Seimio olive oil and extra-virgin olive oil
– Customer	MDO – Moderna distribuzione organizzata
– Agency	Tangram Strategic Design Srl
– Author	Enrico Sempi (creative director)
	Antonella Trevisan (art director)
	Antonella Trevisan – Andrea Sempi (designer)
	Sergio Quaranta (illustrator)
– Year	2001
– Materials	paper

Notes four + one special colour offset printing + car varnish

	Project	Consilia Cereals
–	**Customer**	Gruppo SUN
–	**Agency**	Tangram Strategic Design Srl
–	**Author**	Enrico Sempi (creative director)
		Antonella Trevisan (art director)
		Antonella Trevisan – Anna Grimaldi (designer)
		Vittorio Zucchelli (photographer)
		Guido Rosa (illustrator)
–	**Year**	1998
–	**Materials**	stiff paper

Notes four colour offset printing + car varnish

	Project	Seimio pet food
–	**Customer**	MDO – Modena distribuzione organizzata
–	**Agency**	Tangram Strategic Design Srl
–	**Author**	Enrico Sempi (creative director)
		Antonella Trevisan (art director)
		Antonella Trevisan – Andrea Sempi (designer)
		Kenji Sumura (illustrator)
–	**Year**	2001
–	**Materials**	paper

Notes four colour offset printing

Studio Brozzi
Packaging Design . Pubblicità.

Project	Tomato products
– Customer	Izdihar (Morocco) and Germafinance Trader Sa
– Agency	Studio Brozzi Snc- Parma
– Author	Giacomo Brozzi (art designer and designer) Manuel Bolzoni (computer graphics)
– Year	2003
– Materials	PET bottle and sleeves

Notes this line is made up of a series of products based not only on tomato but also on mayonnaise, mustard and harissa. The whole line has been created by Studio Brozzi

Studio Brozzi
Packaging Design . Pubblicità.

108

	Project	Tuna in olive oil by Rizzoli
–	**Customer**	Rizzoli Emanuelli - Parma
–	**Agency**	Studio Brozzi Snc- Parma
–	**Author**	Giacomo Brozzi (art designer)
–	**Year**	1998
–	**Materials**	tuna in a jar with wooden hand-made cap - 6-colour printing, golden hot foil stamping and plastic coating for the packet, which contains two jars

Notes the really original cap makes this jar stand out among the products on display. It has been appreciated so much that has become leading product in its section (i.e. tuna in jars)

Studio Brozzi
Packaging Design . Pubblicità.

Project	Le Rizzoline – Voglia di alici
– Customer	Rizzoli Emanuelli - Parma
– Agency	Studio Brozzi Snc- Parma
– Author	Giacomo Brozzi (art designer) Studio Brozzi (photographs)
– Year	2001
– Materials	PVC tubs with metal lids – box of 6-colour-printed cardboard, matt plastic coating

Notes the project develops a totally new idea: two anchovies in each tub, in olive oil and hot sauce. Big seller in supermarkets.

Project	Kyboom - pack of sports products
- Customer	Gevisport – food division by Geviplast
- Agency	Turconi & Co.
- Author	Davide Pratesi
- Year	2004

Project	Il GelatoFresco - Ice-cream line
– **Customer**	Carnini
– **Agency**	Turconi & Co.
– **Author**	Alessia Ghezzi
– **Year**	2002

OA+/-•

the portable glass of water

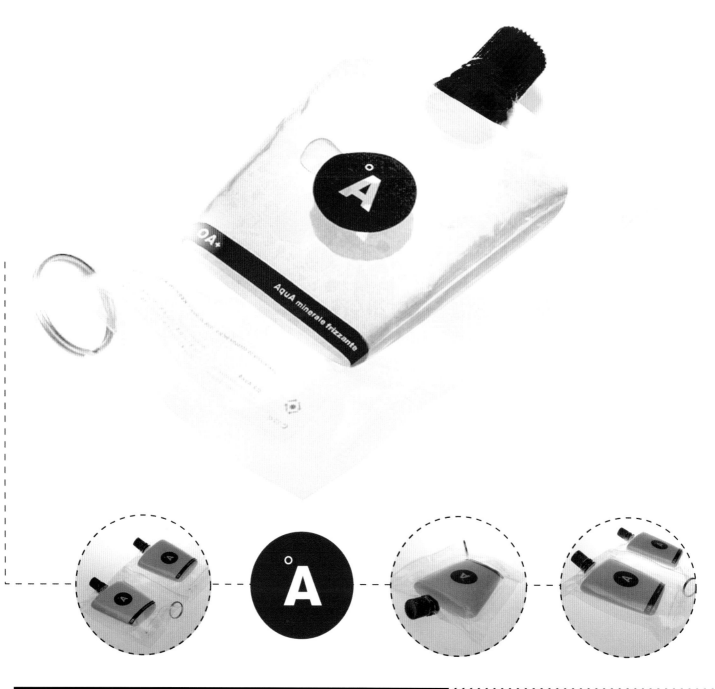

Project   OA+/-

- **Customer**   Isia
- **Agency**   Isia
- **Author**   Silvia Cogo - Bernd Van De Voorde
- **Year**   2002/03

Notes   water glass in two versions: for mineral and sparkling water

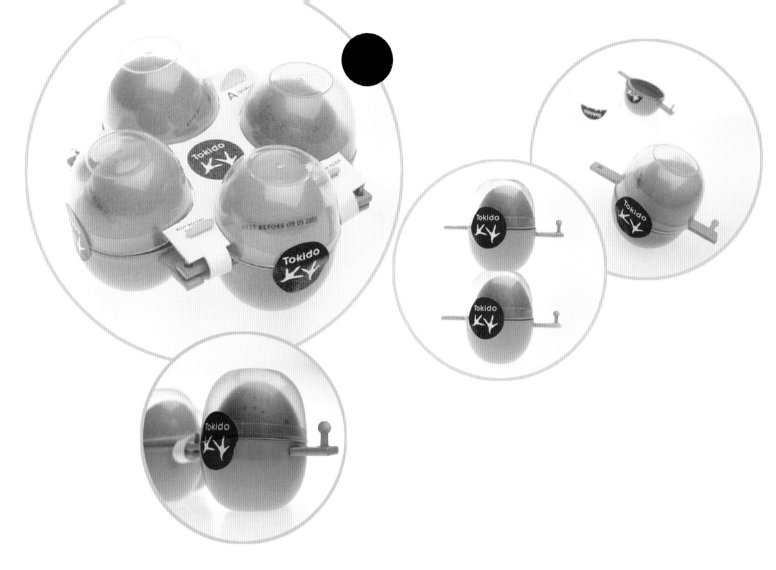

Project	Tokido – refillable egg box
- Customer	Isia
- Agency	Isia
- Author	Anna Bardovagni - Ellen Adam
- Year	2002/03
- Materials	PP

Notes: after purchasing the 6-egg box, the customer can refill it with loose eggs

Project   Food packaging

- **Customer**   A'Nanda ka'nan - (organic fresh food)
- **Agency**   Studio Knecht Sottile
- **Author**   Daliah Sottile (graphic and layout)
                  Massimiliano Bisetto (copywriting and photography)
- **Year**   2003
- **Materials**   Fedrigoni paper, white Woodstock (285 gm/sq m), stamps
                  with wooden handgrips, straw paper

Notes   a set of packaging labels to be used for
wrapping fresh food by hand

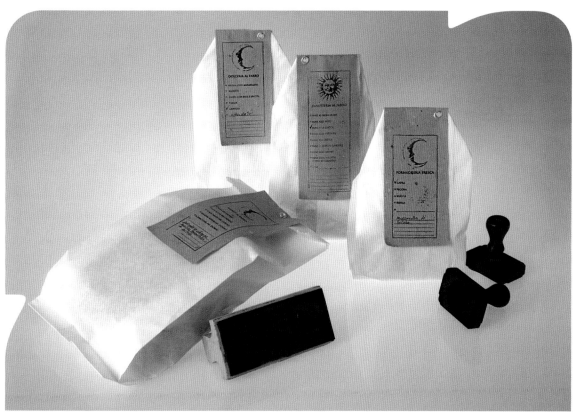

Project	Feedstuff sacks
– **Customer**	Sun Company Srl
– **Agency**	Charta Sas
– **Author**	Danilo Stifano
– **Year**	2003
– **Materials**	three-layer paper for food sacks

Project	Pre-cooked products ("cotechino")
– Customer	Vismara Spa
– Agency	Charta Sas
– Author	Danilo Stifano
– Year	2002
– Materials	stiff paper

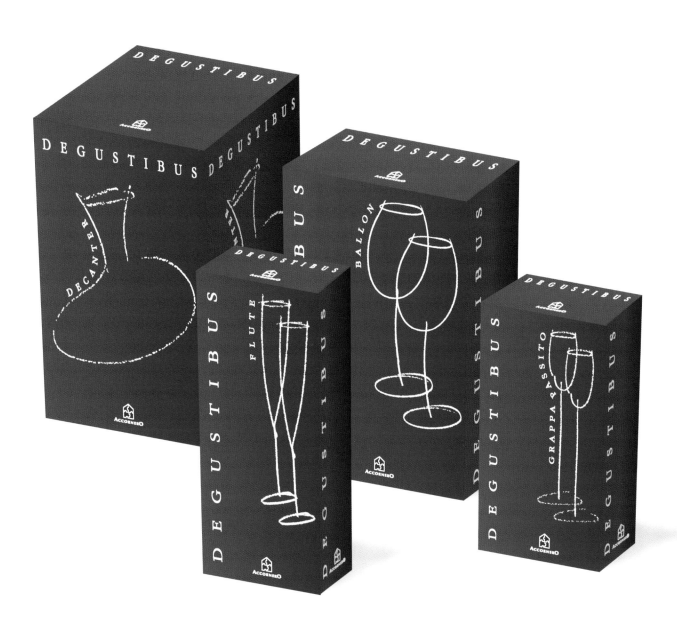

Project	Packaging of packs for wine tasting
– Customer	Accornero Srl
– Agency	Charta Sas
– Author	Danilo Stifano
– Year	2001
– Materials	stiff paper

Project	Yoga – restyling of label of fruit juice bottles for bars
– Customer	Conserve Italia
– Agency	Carré Noir Italia
– Author	Enrico Maria Pecchio (art director)
– Year	2002
– Materials	die-cut, single-side coated paper; six-colour printing

Notes the typical green bottle has been maintained in line with tradition. The 16 different labels (one for each type) are in all colourful without being childish. The elegant lettering remarks the historic importance of this brand.

120

Project	Parmalat UHT milk
– Customer	Parmalat Spa
– Agency	Carré Noir Italia
– Author	Enrico Maria Pecchio (art director)
– Year	2002
– Materials	five-colour printed Tetra Pack PET bottle with five-colour printed label

Notes the project aimed at a conservative restyling and at the same time at conveying a more friendly and emotional image. The restyling has been made also for UHT milk in bottles and Tetra Pack.

Project	**Nesquik Syrup – Shape and label restyling**
– Customer	Nestlé Italia
– Agency	Carré Noir Italia
– Author	Enrico Maria Pecchio (art director)
– Year	2003
– Materials	five-colour printed sleever

Notes The shape of the top down bottle is ergonomic for children's hand. The label has been substituted by a sleever where the distinctive Nesquik yellow mixes with the tones of chocolate, hence conveying an appetizing look. The playful mascot Quiky completes the joyful image.

Project — **Dietorelle next – new line of Dietorelle sugar-free dragées**

- **Customer** — Leaf Italia
- **Agency** — Carré Noir Italia
- **Author** — Enrico Maria Pecchio (art director)
- **Year** — 2003 – launching in Feb. 2004
- **Materials** — pure cellulose (280 gm/sqm), polythene (20 gm/sqm), six-colour offset printing + varnish

Notes — The sub-brand Next displays a young and appetizing look, thanks to the vivid colours (yellow, orange, red) and the three-dimensional lettering recalling the spray art. The writing Next stands out in comparison to Dietorelle, so to remark the innovation of this product.

Project	Tre Marie - Christmas 2002
– Customer	Gran Milano Spa
– Agency	Carré Noir Italia
– Author	Enrico Maria Pecchio (art director)
– Year	2002
– Materials	Classic Line: whitish cardboard, six-colour offset printing, watery matt varnishing; Collection Line: whitish cardboard, nine-colour offset printing + golden hot foil stamping + watery matt varnishing

Notes the project aimed at preserving the historic brand elements and, at the same time, at giving it more brightness. As a result, the packaging is in one more appealing and perfectly recognizable in its constituent elements.

Project	Tè in vimini – Fair Trade tea	
– **Customer**	Cooperativa Commercio Alternativo	**Notes** printed in Sri Lanka
– **Agency**	Studio Magni	
– **Author**	Laura Magni (art diroction)	
	Sara Cimarosti (graphic design)	
– **Year**	2001	
– **Materials**	6 wicker packets + paper label containing organic tea or spices	

Project	Fair Trade tropical fruit juices	
– Customer	Cooperativa Commercio Alternativo	**Notes** printed in Philippines
– Agency	Studio Magni	
– Author	Laura Magni (art direction) Federico Borghi (graphic design)	
– Year	2002	
– Materials	cans with paper label	

Project	Coordinate image for the Italian espresso coffee Goppion Caffè
– Customer	GoppionCaffè Spa
– Agency	Ubis Design e Comunicazione
– Author	Violetta Boschiero - Luca Facchini
– Year	2002

Notes the line is made up of: a coffee tin (250 g), coffee cups, a mug, saucers, napkin dispenser, napkins

Project	Cases containing bottles (0,20l) of Canella Cocktail	
- **Customer**	Cantine Canella Spa	
- **Agency**	Ubis Design e Comunicazione	
- **Author**	Violetta Boschiero – Nicoletta Linguanti	
- **Year**	2004	

Project	Coordinate line Bellini: Venice's cocktail
- **Customer**	Cantine Canella Spa
- **Agency**	Ubis Design e Comunicazione
- **Author**	Violetta Boschiero - Luca Facchini
- **Year**	2001 - 2002 - 2003

Notes Venice's Bellini cocktail has been the first product to carry the logo "Un marchio per Venezia" (A trademark for Venice)

Project	Home line - tins and vacuum-packets of ground coffee (three blends)
– **Customer**	Mokarabia Spa
– **Agency**	Cba Progetti - Ubis Design e Comunicazione
– **Author**	Cristina Zanato
– **Year**	2003

design e comunicazione

Project	Cases containing single-dose bags of cocoa, camomile, barley and tea (two blends)
– Customer	Mokarabia Spa
– Agency	Cba Progetti - Ubis Design e Comunicazione
– Author	Cristina Zanato
	Valentina Dotto (illustrator) - Venticento Studio (photo)
– Year	2003

Project	Tin (250 g)		
– Customer	Cipriani Industria	**Notes**	for Cipriani's outlets only
– Agency	Ubis Design e Comunicazione		
– Author	Violetta Boschiero		
– Year	2003		

Project	Frozen Sicilian croquettes
– Customer	Riso Gallo Spa
– Agency	Show Box
– Author	Cristina Cordani
– Year	2003
– Materials	paperboard

Project	Organic rice
– Customer	Riso Gallo Spa
– Agency	Show Box
– Author	Cristina Cordani
– Year	2001/02
– Materials	paperboard

STRATEGIC BRAND DESIGN
PACKAGING
CORPORATE IDENTITY
RETAIL DESIGN

Project	Iper private label corn flakes
– Customer	Finiper
– Agency	Rba design
– Author	Orsola Aldemagni
– Year	2003

Notes packaging design

Project	Iper private label honey
– Customer	Finiper
– Agency	Rba design
– Author	Massimo Cecchi
– Year	2003

STRATEGIC BRAND DESIGN
PACKAGING
CORPORATE IDENTITY
RETAIL DESIGN

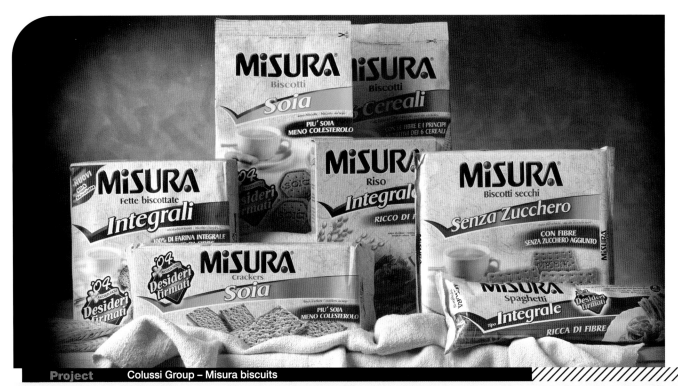

Project	Colussi Group – Misura biscuits	Notes	creation of new product identity
– Customer	Colussi Spa		
– Agency	Rba Srl		
– Author	Ivano Zito		
– Year	2003		

Project	Sosalt	Notes	creation of brand identity and product image
– Customer	Sosalt Spa		
– Agency	Rba Srl		
– Author	Nicola Mincione – Fiona Martin		
– Year	2003		

Project	Allied Dorecq – Ballantine's tin-plated case
– **Customer**	Allied Dorecq Italia Spa
– **Agency**	Rba Srl
– **Author**	Nicola Mincione
– **Year**	2001

Notes Creation of image and packaging design for a gift pack

Project	Allied Dorecq – Ballantine's case
– **Customer**	Allied Dorecq Italia Spa
– **Agency**	Rba Srl
– **Author**	Nicola Mincione
– **Year**	2001

Notes creation of shape and image of case

LEONARD
Design

Project	Acqua Gerasia - water
– Customer	Reale Srl - Messina
– Agency	Leonard Design - Verona
– Author	Giulio Rocco – Giovanni Sguazzardo
– Year	2003
– Materials	PET

LEONARD
Design

Project	Torte & Torte Bauli		
– Customer	Bauli Spa - Verona	Notes	packaging for cakes
– Agency	Leonard Design - Verona		
– Author	Giulio Rocco		
– Year	2003		
– Materials	stiff paper		

Project	Grandi Classici Bauli		
– Customer	Bauli Spa - Verona	Notes	packaging for cakes
– Agency	Leonard Design - Verona		
– Author	Giulio Rocco		
– Year	2003		
– Materials	paper		

Project	Amarena Toschi (fruit and syrup - 700 gr)
– Customer	Toschi – Vignola (MO)
– Agency	Studio Padovani
– Author	Paolo Ruini
– Year	2002
– Materials	non-enamelled can

Project	Gavioli Nocino di Modena (700 ml and 500 ml bottles)
– Customer	Liquori Gavioli
– Agency	Studio Padovani
– Author	Roberta Ferrarini
– Year	2001
– Materials	sticky labels, dark glass

Project	Amarena Toschi (1 kg can)
– Customer	Toschi – Vignola (MO)
– Agency	Studio Padovani
– Author	Paolo Ruini
– Year	2002
– Materials	non-enamelled can

studio Padovani
packaging & graphic design

Project	Le Monelle - (small bologna sausages)
– Customer	Ibis (Cremonini Group) - salami from Emilia
– Agency	Studio Padovani
– Author	Paolo Ruini
– Year	2002
– Materials	plastic film, flexography

Project	Probiotic – Organic food for pets: rabbits and hamsters)
– Customer	Progeo – Petfood
– Agency	Studio Padovani
– Author	Luciano Padovani (art director) - Roberto della Vite (photographer)
– Year	2003
– Materials	resealable envelope, plastic film, 45-line flexography

Project	Balmì - dressing made of aromatic vinegar and hot pepper
– Customer	Toschi – Vignola (MO)
– Agency	Studio Padovani
– Author	Luciano Padovani - Paolo Ruini
– Year	2002
– Materials	label

Project	Gavioli Grappa (700 ml bottle)
– Customer	Liquori Gavioli
– Agency	Studio Padovani
– Author	Roberta Ferrarini
– Year	2000
– Materials	metallised sticky labels, black glass

Project	Packaging for myrtle liqueur
– Customer	Arcaffè Spa
– Agency	Skatto.com
– Author	Susanna Cerri – Luca Bachini
– Year	2003

skatto.com

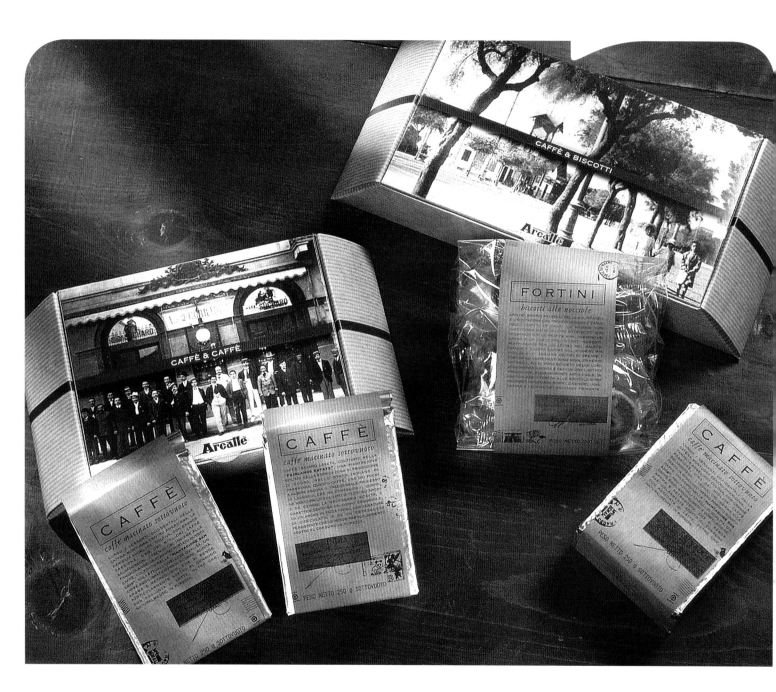

Project	Gift packs
- Customer	Arcaffè Spa
- Agency	Skatto.com
- Author	Susanna Cerri – Luca Bachini
- Year	2001

skatto •.com

Project	Pack of estate coffee (500 gm)
– Customer	Arcaffè Spa
– Agency	Skatto.com
– Author	Susanna Cerri – Luca Bachini
– Year	2002

Il packaging è un elemento determinante nella identità visiva di marche e di prodotti ed in molti casi condiziona o modifica la comunicazione realizzata attraverso i mezzi tradizionali (loghi, cataloghi, pieghevoli, espositori, inserti, shopper, ecc.).
Il brand design diventa un'occasione per enfatizzare i vari momenti in cui il prodotto e la marca si presentano e comunicano al potenziale cliente.
Gli esempi sono sempre più numerosi e sottolineano l'importanza di un coordinamento dell'identità visiva, che ha nel packaging un elemento trascinatore.

Packaging plays a crucial role in the visual identity of trademarks and products. In most cases it can influence or even modify communication, if communication is realized through traditional means such as logo, catalogues, brochures, display stands, shoppers, etc.
Brand design becomes then a precious occasion to emphasise the steps through which product and brand have been introduced to consumers and communicate with them.
There are plenty of examples which underlie the importance of creating a coordinate visual identity, which finds in packaging its leading element.

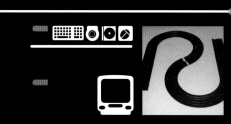

Project	Company profile
– Customer	Grafiche Pioppi
– Agency	Kalimera
– Author	Kalimera
– Year	2004
– Materials	Transparent PVC, polystyrene cover, mosquito net, paper

Notes Each page of the catalogue is printed with different techniques. The catalogue is contained in a polystyrene cover, which is then wrapped in PVC, this one being printed with white serigraphy.

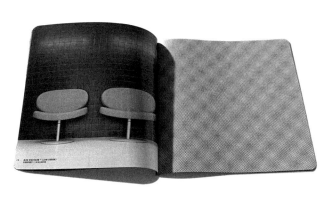

Project	Kit and Catalogue Colori Marazzi
- **Customer**	Marazzi Ceramiche
- **Agency**	Kalimera
- **Author**	Kalimera
- **Year**	2001
- **Materials**	Kit: PVC cover welded in the inside
	Catalogue: paper, wall paper

Notes The kit is a bag containing pieces of tiles representing the whole production

KƏLIMERƏ

Project	Catalogue and box containing an Uki hair-press
– **Customer**	Uki international
– **Agency**	Kalimera srl
– **Author**	Kalimera
– **Year**	2004
– **Materials**	black PVC, box in corrugated board

Notes Wrapping case in black PVC. The material is the same used for bin liners

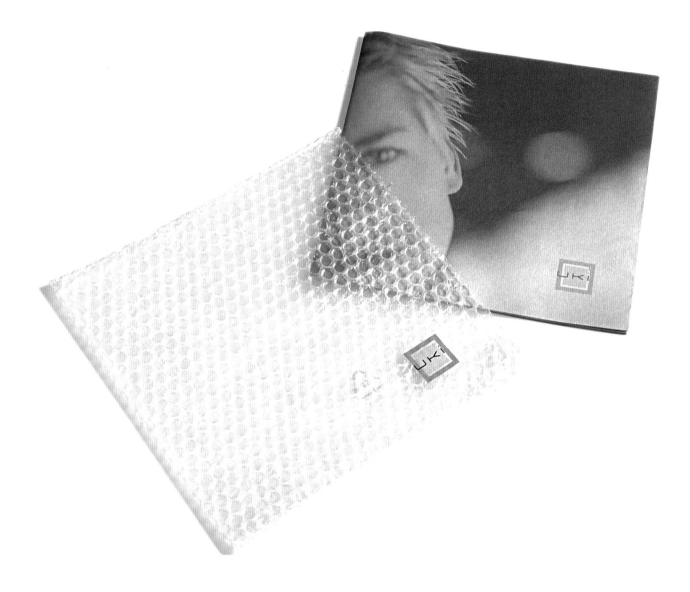

Project	Catalogue
– Customer	Uki International
– Agency	Kalimera
– Author	Kalimera
– Year	2001
– Materials	Silver bubble warp

Notes Bubble warp cover containing the catalogue

Project	Company profile
– Customer	Kalimera
– Agency	Kalimera
– Author	Kalimera
– Year	2002
– Materials	Paper, electrostatic envelope, cardboard cover with foam rubber inside

Project	Gadget for the opening of a new shop

-	Customer	E-35
-	Agency	Kalimera srl
-	Author	Kalimera
-	Year	2004
-	Materials	PVC

Notes vacuum-packed T-shirt

KALIMERA

Project	Software case
– Customer	Emmegigroup
– Agency	Kalimera srl
– Author	Kalimera
– Year	2003
– Materials	carton case

Brunazzi&Associati
Image·Communication

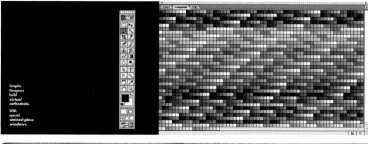

Project	Double Face series – book presentation packaging
– **Customer**	Cartiere Burgo
– **Agency**	Brunazzi & Associati - Turin
– **Author**	Giovanni Brunazzi (art director) - Roberto Necco (designer) Matteo Marucco (graphic designer)
– **Year**	2003-2004
– **Materials**	corrugated board glued together with four-colour printed art paper

Notes The Double Face series is a Burgo project dedicated to visual fascinations spreading out of the theme of the double. The first volume, Black&White/Colors, is dedicated to the dualism between black and white and color. The second volume, Natural/Artificial, goes through the concepts of "natural" and "artificial" with a joyful and fresh attitude. In both volumes, a paraphernalia of visual materials play tag on a surreal path, departing from opposite sides and rejoining into the centre: photographs, pieces of design and contemporary art, graphic signs, statements, word games, reinterpretations of famous symbols, quotations, Dadaist experiments.

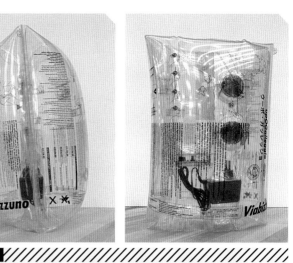

Project	Packaging for the lamp "Upogalleggio"

- **Customer** Viabizzuno
- **Agency** Viabizzuno
- **Author** UpO Viabizzuno
- **Year** 2003

Notes LED lamp switching on when in contact with water. The packaging has been devised so to contain 2 lamps + battery charger + transformer + guarantee papers. The instructions are printed on the inside of the inflatable PVC. To take the lamp out, deflate the container.

Project	**Switzerland Radio Mouse**	
– Customer	La table bijoux/Promotion incentive	
– Agency	Cilindrina/Creative consulting	
– Author	Georgia Matteini Palmerini/Sergio Bogino	
– Year	2003	
– Materials	cardboard printed in CMYK	

Notes This project was realised for promoting and launching in store promotion. After buying a small quantity of product, any customer could take part in a game and win some prizes. Among these, there was the radio mouse, which was contained in a cheese-shaped box.

Project	Invitation for man & woman on the opening of the new season	
– Customer	Sophia Dinner Club	
– Agency	Matteo Guidi	
– Author	Matteo Guidi	
– Year	2003	
– Materials	Paper: Fedrigoni Splendor Lux Covers: polypropylene for vacuum-packed products	

Notes Printing in 3 colors: black + p225 + p185. The invitation has been sent without envelopes, just stamped on

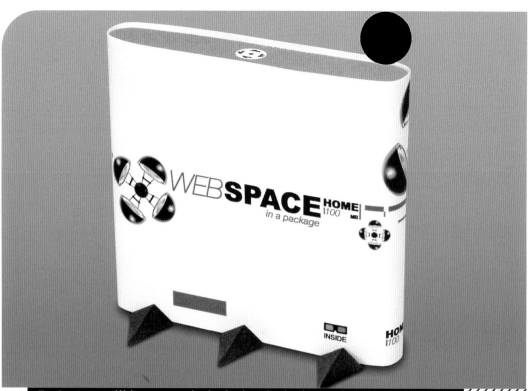

Project	Webspace – packaging for the sale of webspace through a self-installing CD

- **Customer**   Isia
- **Agency**   Isia
- **Author**   Gianantonio Gattarello - Tim Van Houtte
- **Year**   2002/03
- **Materials** paperboard

Project	Rescue box

- **Customer**   Isia
- **Agency**   Isia
- **Author**   Erika Cicognani - Stijn Vermeersch
- **Year**   2002/03
- **Materials** paperboard

Notes survival kit for students arriving for the first time in a foreign town or country. It contains a dictionary of slang, a city map, condoms and aspirins.

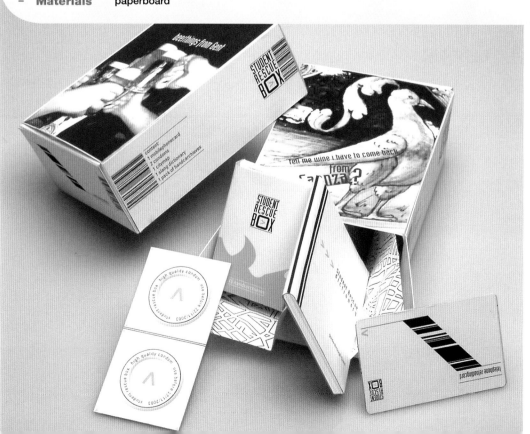

LUCA, 19 ANNI
LA MIA ARMA SEGRETA
È IL SORRISO.

ABILE
SERVIZIO CIVILE IN CARITAS

✤ caritas
italiana
organismo pastorale della CEI

Project	National campaign for the community service		
– Customer	Caritas Italia	Notes	cardboard box in booklet format containing a brochure.
– Agency	Officina Comunicazione		
– Author	Andrea Marchesi - Luca Manfredini		
– Year	2002		

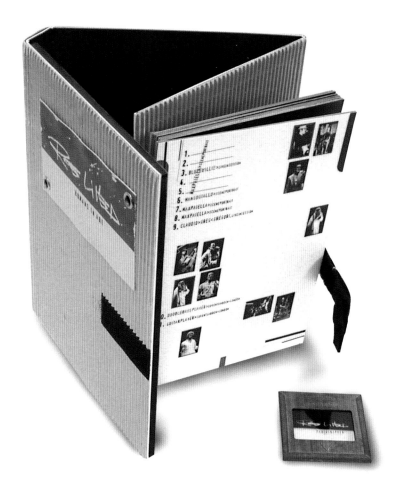

Project	Human in art
– Customer	Roe Lived (photographer)
– Agency	Temecula Design
– Author	Cristiano de Veroli
– Year	2003
– Materials	corrugated carton, metal rivets, digital print on paper (120 gm), matt plastic coating, cardboard, sticky velcro

Notes It's an original metal slide of the Thirties. The cover has been made with Velcro sewn by hand.

Project	Creative Images	
– Customer	Roe Lived (photographer)	Notes frame and button of the blanket are handmade
– Agency	Temecula Design	
– Author	Cristiano de Veroli	
– Year	2003	
– Materials	corrugated carton, digital print on recycled paper, wood, string, metal binding	

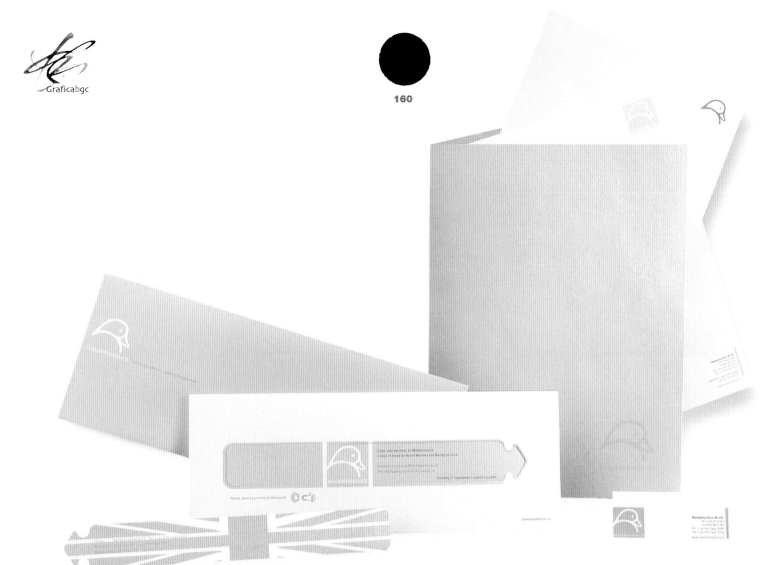

Project	Mandarina Duck
– Customer	Mandarina Duck - Bologna
– Agency	Pascucci D.sign - Grafica BGC
– Author	Daniela Pascucci - Beatrice Gandolfi Colleoni
– Year	2003

161

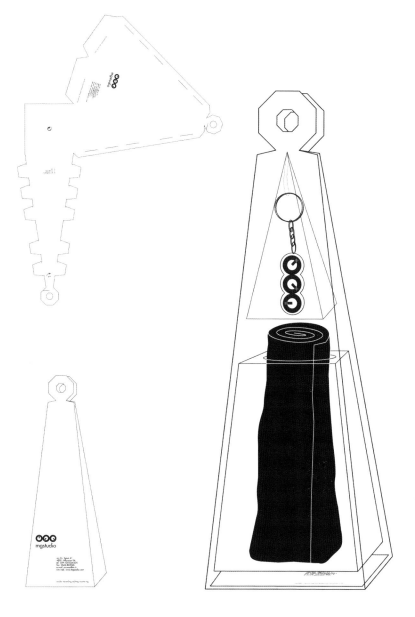

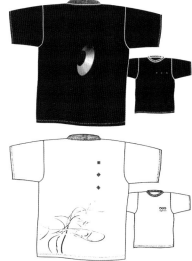

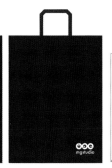
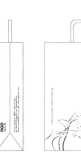

Project	Promotional packaging for gadgets (CD, T-shirt, key case)
– **Customer**	MG Studio Audio Recording – Alfonsine (RA)
– **Agency**	Equilibrisospesi – Design e comunicazione – Russi (RA)
– **Author**	Elisa Leotti
– **Year**	2003
– **Materials**	smooth white stiff paper (250 gm); clear plastic film (180 gm) for the key case

no.parking

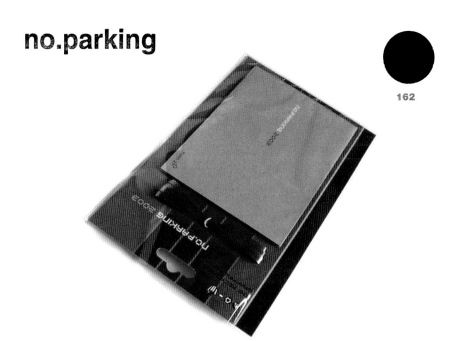

Project	Christmas card for self promotion

- **Customer**   no.parking
- **Agency**   no.parking
- **Author**   Elisa Dall'Angelo
- **Year**   2003
- **Materials**   Scheufelen gift paper (90 g), cardboard base, ribbon, cellophane

Notes the card can be recycled for gift wrapping

	Project	GE.CO – software for conferences
–	Customer	E-side
–	Agency	no.parking
–	Author	Elisa Dall'Angelo
–	Year	2003
–	Materials	Furioso matt art paper (200 gm), offset printing

Notes packaging for postal mailing with a tonguing closure

no.parking

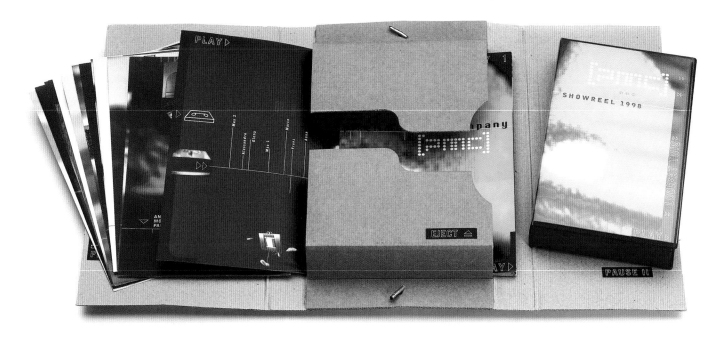

Project	PMC – Pixel Machine Company	
– Customer	PMC Video production	Notes postal mailing for self promotion
– Agency	no.parking	
– Author	Sabine Lercher	
– Year	1998	
– Materials	external packaging in corrugated board (2 mm), Magnomatt cards (170 gm), stick-on labels, videocassette	

Project   Gadgets box

- **Customer**   Siemens Spa
- **Agency**   Charta Sas
- **Author**   Danilo Stifano
- **Year**   1996
- **Materials**   stiff paper

For information on this project see page 178

For information on this project see page 178

matitegiovanotte
creatività comunicazione

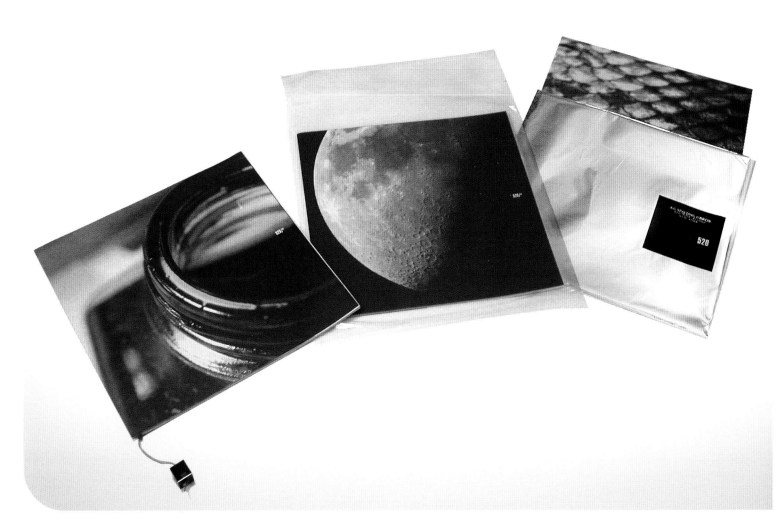

Project   520 (n. 1 – n. 2 – n. 3) – Newsletter by A.G. Spalding & Bros.

- **Customer**   A.G. Spalding & Bros.
- **Agency**   Matitegiovanotte (FC)
- **Author**   Barbara Longiardi - Sabrina Poli - Luca Rondoni - Antonella Bandoli
  Simone Verza - Claudia Button - Giovanni Pizzigati - Paolo Malorgio
- **Year**   2001-2002
- **Materials**   paper, PVC

Project	**Travel memories – literary contest**	
– **Customer**	A.G. Spalding & Bros.	**Notes** the project results from a selection of travel memories made by Alessndro Baricco's Holden School among travel diaries left by customers in A.G. Spalding & Bros shops. The company has always concerned themselves with the theme of travelling.
– **Agency**	Matitegiovanotte (FC)	
– **Author**	Antonella Bandoli - Marina Flamini Barbara Longiardi - Claudia Button	
– **Year**	2001	
– **Materials**	paper - PVC bag	

matitegiovanotte
creatività e comunicazione

Project	Va' pensiero – Christmas gift
– Customer	Matitegiovanotte (FC)
– Agency	Matitegiovanotte (FC)
– Author	Simone Verza - Antonella Bandoli
	Barbara Longiardi – Giovanni Pizzigati
– Year	2003
– Materials	wood; alveolar PC; PVC

	Project	Summer party - on-purchase gift	
–	**Customer**	A.G. Spalding & Bros.	**Notes** coordinate image for an event which would concern 50 A.G. Spalding & Bros. shops.
–	**Agency**	Matitegiovanotte (FC)	
–	**Author**	Claudia Button - Simone Verza	
		Antonella Bandoli – Barbara Longiardi	
–	**Year**	2002	
–	**Materials**	paper, cellophane, cotton (for T-shirts), polystyrene	

Project	Tombola! – Christmas gift – Christmas 2000
– Customer	Matitegiovanotte (FC)
– Agency	Matitegiovanotte (FC)
– Author	Daniele Davoli - Barbara Longiardi - Giovanni Pizzigati
	Antonella Bandoli - Stefania Adani - Cinzia Monari - Simone Verza
– Year	2000
– Materials	wood, fine felt, Algae Favini paper

Notes the most ordinary and familiar gift for the end of the millennium: a game of bingo with the dearest ones.

matitegiovanotte
creatività comunicazione

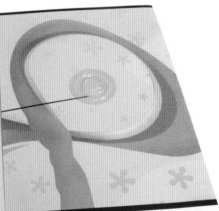

Project	N.R.G.³ – Job Dimension – Energie alternative

– Agency	Matitegiovanotte (FC)
– Author	Simone Verza
– Year	2004
– Materials	stiff paper

Notes CD pack which has been distributed to schools to promote the initiative.

– **Customer**	A.G. Spalding & Bros.
– **Agency**	Matitegiovanotte (FC)
– **Author**	Giovanni Pizzigati - Antonella Bandoli - Simone Verza
– **Year**	2003
– **Materials**	paper

Notes this invitation card, similar to a boarding baggage band, was given to passengers in the above-mentioned airports on the opening of new shops. By visiting them, passengers could receive a free gadget and a notepad.

matitegiovanotte
creatività comunicazione

176

Project	Key È Key party- Invitation card
– Customer	Matitegiovanotte (FC)
– Agency	Matitegiovanotte (FC)
– Author	Alberto Cassani - Antonella Bandoli - Simone Verza – Luca Raggi
– Year	2002
– Materials	corrugated board + glued up sheets; PVC key ring; flock-printed rubber mini-doormat

Notes this was the invitation to the opening of the agency's new office. The name plays around the word Key associated to the Who's who (in Italian "Chi è chi", same pronunciation as "Key È Key") gossip, typical of parties. The invitation card included a map and a mini-mat with a key (a doormat, exactly the place where you hide your keys for your friends).

matitegiovanotte
creatività e comunicazione

Project	Augurone – Christmas gift

///

- **Customer**   Matitegiovanotte (FC)
- **Agency**   Matitegiovanotte (FC)
- **Author**   Barbara Longiardi - Paolo Malorgio - Camilla Bruschi
  Antonella Bandoli - Giovanni Pizzigati
- **Year**   2002
- **Materials**   Toblerone chocolate bar, cardboard, sticky PVC

Notes the name of this gift recalls the sound of the agency's name and of the chocolate bar; through it, the staff wish their clients the merriest and most mouth-watering Xmas ever.

Project	Nike Vetrine News - newsletter for Nike's store managers
– Customer	Nike Italy
– Agency	Matitegiovanotte (FC)
– Author	Giovanni Pizzigati - Alberto Cassani - Antonella Bandoli Simone Verza - Elisa Sangiorgi - Barbara Longiardi
– Year	2001-2002
– Materials	Paper, PVC, wood, carbon, metal, succulent plant

Notes a fortnightly contact (with surprise) to make store managers ready to receive the new collection, together with the relevant advertising and merchandising suggestions.

Project	Merchandising Musical Rent - Towels for men/women - Perfumed black Candles
– Customer	Duke International
– Agency	Balena Corporation
– Author	Matteo Righi - Georgia Matteini Palmerini
– Year	2000
– Materials	light brown cardboard, sticky label

	Project	Promotional notepad case
–	**Customer**	Maglificio Adele
–	**Agency**	Dinamo Project - Imola (BO)
–	**Author**	Marco Bedeschi
–	**Year**	2002
–	**Materials**	stiff paper, aluminium

 DINAMO PROJECT

Project	Brochure
– Customer	Maglificio Adele
– Agency	Dinamo Project - Imola (BO)
– Author	Marco Bedeschi
– Year	2003
– Materials	paper, wool

Project   Christmas greetings

– **Customer**   Kriotrans spa
– **Agency**   Raineri Design
– **Author**   William Raineri
– **Year**   2003
– **Materials**   box, information sheets

marina turci progetti di comunicazione

Project	Writech – display-box for home and office special paper (5 types)
– Customer	Cartiere Miliani Fabriano Spa
– Agency	Unica Srl (The Republic of San Marino)
– Author	Marina Turci – Marco Tortoioli
– Year	1998
– Materials	counter display for a single product

Notes in the same year, the agency has restyled the whole Fabriano photocopy paper line

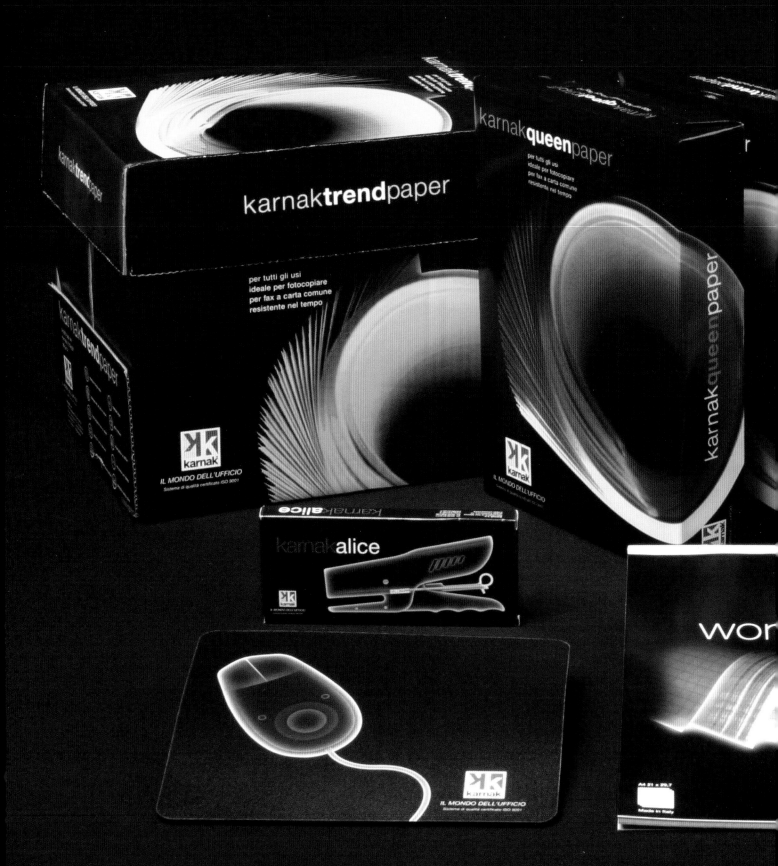

Project Coordinate line Karnak - office supplies

- **Customer** Karnak S.A. – Il mondo dell'ufficio
- **Agency** Unica Srl (The Republic of San Marino)
- **Author** Marina Turci
- **Year** 2002
- **Materials** office products

Notes the peculiarity of this project is given by the simulation of X-ray that highlights the inside of the objects.

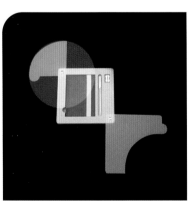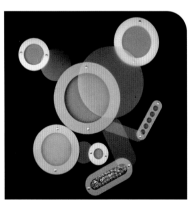

Project	STRATO®
– Customer	Ferappi Industrie Serigrafiche
– Agency	Paolo Garofalo
– Author	Paolo Garofalo
– Year	2002
– Materials	PP, cardboard

Project	Papillon shopper
– Customer	Ferappi Industrie Serigrafiche
– Agency	Paolo Garofalo
– Author	Paolo Garofalo
– Year	2003
– Materials	PP

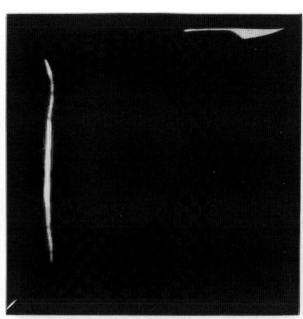

Project	Pomodoro Moonlight - Invitation card with envelope
– Customer	Pomodoro –Restaurant Theater
– Agency	Morpheus
– Author	Gian Pietro Farinelli (art director – copywriter)
– Year	2003
– Materials	clear PVC red-coloured envelope, two-colour printing for the invitation, matt plastic coating and glossy silk screen

Notes very original invitation which can be read only when in the envelope: the red envelope "deletes" the red writing and makes visible the green one only.

Project	**Opening party - Invitation cards**
– **Customer**	Meridiana - Restaurant - American bar
– **Agency**	Morpheus
– **Author**	Gian Pietro Farinelli (art director – copywriter)
– **Year**	2003
– **Materials**	red foam case, hot moulded cellophane, four-colour printed Splendolux single-side glossy paper

Notes the invitation card recalls the past promotional campaign teasers, whose format has been reduced to that of a postcard. Each case contains 7 postcards

Project	Pomodoro opening party - Invitation cards for 2002-2003 season
– Customer	Pomodoro – Disco- restaurant
– Agency	Morpheus
– Author	Gian Pietro Farinelli (art director) Stefano Pirani (copywriter) Davide Erbisti (developer)
– Year	2002
– Materials	four-colour printed matt art paper glued together with 600gm-cardboard, matt plastic coating and glossy silk screen

Notes the peculiarity of this invitation is that part of the text can be read only against the light.

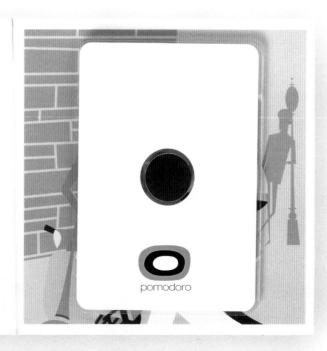

Project	Soul Shaker – gadgets (4 types)
– Customer	La Scuderia – Bologna
– Agency	Gianni Rossi Design - Cesena
– Author	Piero Casanova (art director and copywriter)
	Gianni Rossi (illustrator)
– Year	2003-2004 season
– Materials	matt art paper (250 gm), four-colour printing; cotton sticks

Notes these gadgets are part of the monthly program of La Scuderia, a well known music place in Bologna, playing Northern Soul music on Friday nights under the name Soul Shaker.

Project	Supersonico Compilation Doctor Jekyll and Mr Hyde
– Customer	Supersonico Records – Faenza (RA)
– Agency	Gianni Rossi Design - Cesena
– Author	Gianni Rossi (art director) - Andrea Rivola (illustrator) Andrea Ricci (copywriter)
– Year	2001
– Materials	- single-side matt cardboard (350 gm); three-colour printing (262,361, Rhodamine Red) - one-colour printed paper (100 gm) - clear plastic bags - CD case

Notes the customer is a CD/LP importer. The present product was realized as gadget for the opening day. It contains a compilation of independent rock music.

Project	Soul Shaker – mats
– Customer	La Scuderia – Bologna
– Agency	Gianni Rossi Design - Cesena
– Author	Gianni Rossi (art director and illustrator) Piero Casanova (copywriter)
– Year	2003-2004 season
– Materials	single-side matt paper (350 gm), four-colour printing

Notes these mats are actually entrance tickets to La Scuderia, but can be subsequently used under one's glass as a mat.

Project	Soul Shaker – die-cut brochure
– Customer	La Scuderia – Bologna
– Agency	Gianni Rossi Design - Cesena
– Author	Gianni Rossi (art director and illustrator)
	Piero Casanova (copywriter)
– Year	2003-2004 season
– Materials	matt art paper (250 gm), four-colour printing, UV silk screen glazing

Notes this brochure shows the Oct. to Dec. program of La Scuderia. It's possible to tear off the pages and collect the personalities shown on it as cards or minimats, keeping the ongoing program.

NOUVELLE
Comunicazione & Marketing

194

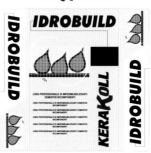

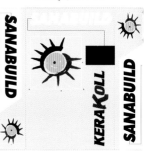

Project	Professional products for the building industry
– **Customer**	Kerakoll
– **Agency**	Nouvelle Srl
– **Author**	agency's staff

Project	Amerikana – design and image
– **Customer**	Bialetti Industrie
– **Agency**	Advance
– **Author**	Enrico Malinverni (creative director)
– **Year**	2001
– **Materials**	5-colour printed board

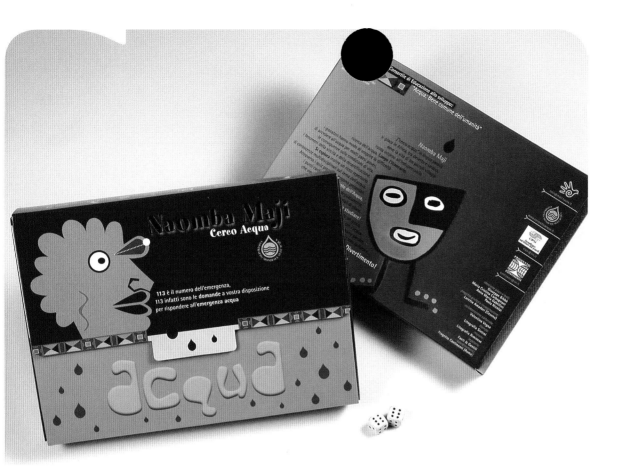

Project	Naomba maji (I'm looking for water) - game for children aged 9-12 aiming at raising awareness on the problem of water as a key resource
- Customer	ONG Progetto Continenti - Rome
- Agency	Studio Estilo – Cesena
- Author	Loretta Amadori (graphic project and video layout) - Alberto Cosentino (illustrations, board and men)
- Year	2002
- Materials	the game is made up of: a box (31x22,5 cm), a game board (42x59 cm), an inside box containing 113 cards (12x8 cm), two folders containing instructions and didactic notes (15x22 cm), a small poster displaying words related to water, three sheets (15x15 cm) containing men and other game objects, one clear plastic bag containing dice and a die-cut carton ready to contain cards, dice and men. The whole material is printed in four colours, plastic-coated and die-cut.

Project	Maurizio Pecoraio catalogue – Fall-winter 2001
– Customer	Maurizio Pecoraro
– Agency	Unjust
– Author	Paolo Santosuosso – Francesco Roncaglia
– Year	2001
– Materials	matt-coated Splendorlux for the pages printed on both sides, matt coating and UV silk screen

Project	Mandarina Duck catalogue – Spring-summer 2005
– Customer	Plastimoda
– Agency	Unjust
– Author	Paolo Santosuosso – Francesco Roncaglia
– Year	2004
– Materials	glossy coating, hybrid varnish, shrink wrapping, colour silk screen

UNjust

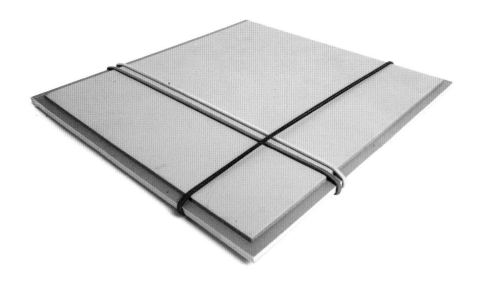

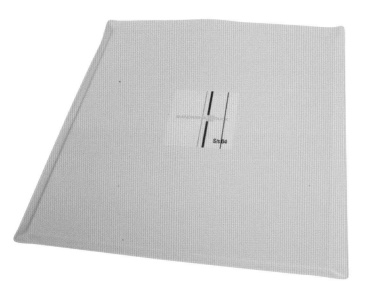

Project	Mandarina Duck catalogue – Spring-summer 2004
– Customer	Plastimoda
– Agency	Unjust
– Author	Paolo Santosuosso – Francesco Roncaglia
– Year	2004
– Materials	welded PVC, glossy and matt coating, uncoated paper

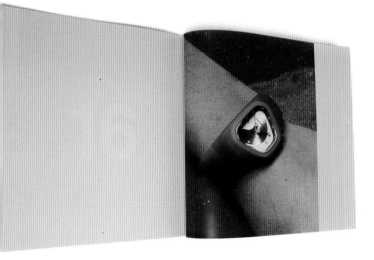

Project	Mandarina Duck catalogue – Year 2004
– Customer	Mandarina Duck - Plastimoda
– Agency	Unjust
– Author	Paolo Santosuosso – Francesco Roncaglia
– Year	2004
– Materials	raw cardboard, Yupo paper, rubber band, machine sewing

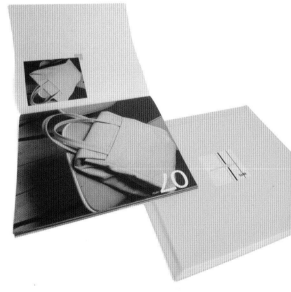

Project	**Nod invitation card – Fall-winter 2001**
– Customer	Nod – Bravo Srl
– Agency	Unjust
– Author	Paolo Santosuosso – Francesco Roncaglia
– Year	2001
– Materials	jute canvas, glossy coating, machine sewing

Project	Pitti invitation card – Fall-winter 2004
– Customer	Messaggerie GMA Srl
– Agency	Unjust
– Author	Paolo Santosuosso – Francesco Roncaglia
– Year	2004
– Materials	light brown board, multiboll envelope, two-colour silk screen, zama ring

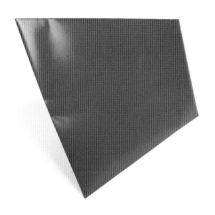 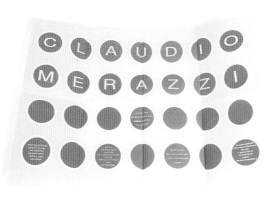 

Project	Claudio Merazzi invitation card – Spring-summer 2002
– **Customer**	Claudio Merazzi
– **Agency**	Unjust
– **Author**	Paolo Santosuosso – Francesco Roncaglia
– **Year**	2001
– **Materials**	glossy coating for the envelope, two-colour silk screen for the inside

Project	Maurizio Pecoraro catalogue – Year 2000
– Customer	Maurizio Pecoraro
– Agency	Unjust
– Author	Paolo Santosuosso – Francesco Roncaglia
– Year	2000
– Materials	die-cut black board, 18-mm rings, glossy coating and plastic coating

Package Design In Italy
:Agencies
Index

Advance
ph. 0373 256600 fax 0373 257577
advance@advanceitalia.com

Balena Corporation
ph. 051 987279 fax 051 987246
info@balena.it

Basaglia
ph. 059 906582 fax 059 906589
info@basaglia.com

Brunazzi & Associati
ph. 011 8125397 fax 011 8170702
info@brunazzi.com

Carlo Raffaelli Comunicazione
ph. 050 977010 fax 050 3151867
posta@carloraffaelli.com

Carré Noir
ph. 011 5321937 fax 011 538611
carrenoir@carrenoir.it

Casa Walden
ph. 0543 32462 fax 0543 29319
info@casawalden.com

Caseley Giovara
ph. 0423 602077 fax 0423 603226
info@caseleygiovara.com

Charta
ph. 02 6696118 fax 02 6696118
chartast@tin.it

Cilindrina
ph. 0541 635483 fax 0541 635483
info@cilindrina.it

Claudio Cristofori Associati
ph. 0521 272959 fax 0521 774892
info@cristoforiassociati.it

DBV
ph. 055 290505 fax 055 2676309
dbv@dbv.it

Dinamo Project
ph. 0542 25830 fax 0542 619359
961@dinamoproject.com

Equilibri Sospesi
ph. 0544 587252 fax 0544 581149
info@equilibrisospesi.com

Gianni Rossi
ph. 0547 379370
studio@giannirossi.net

Giò Minola
ph. 011 503500 fax 011 505782
info@giominola.it

Grafica BGC
ph. 0542 31269
beatrice@graficabgc.it

Il Telaio Advertising
ph. 0424 521111 fax 0424 521115
welcome@iltelaio-adv.it

Image Studio
ph. 035 4520080 fax 035 4520045
imagestudioagenzia@tin.it

Immedia
ph. 0575 383109 fax 0575 383239
info@immediaarezzo.it

Inside BTB
ph. 0532 769903 fax 0532 769860
inside@insidebtb.it

Isia Faenza
ph. 0546 22293 fax 0546 6665136
isiafaenza@racine.ra.it

Kalimera
ph. and fax 0522 513595
staff@kalimera.it

Le Design
ph. 335 5666238
elenasqualizza@liriosgroup.com

Leonard
ph. 045 8343149 fax 045 8301310
leonard@leonard.it

Marina Turci
ph. 0541 774293
marina.turci@comodosociale.it

Mario Turconi
ph. 031 720994 fax 031 713520
info@turconicompany.it

Matitegiovanotte
ph. 0543 705377 fax 0543 700207
barbara.longiardi@matitegiovanotte.com

Matteo Guidi
ph. 338 6354935
info@matteoguidi.it

Mixage
ph. 051 6019611 fax 051 6012404

Morpheus
ph. 0532 769919
info@aspirine.co.uk

Nedda Bonini
ph. 0532 767537
nedda.bonini@libero.it

no.parking
ph. 0444 327861 fax 0444 327595
inbox@noparking.it

Nouvelle
ph. 051 6611511 fax 051 877837
info@nouvelleadv.it

Officina Comunicazione
ph. 059 822504 fax 059 822504
andreamarchesi@officinacomunicazione.it

Paolo Garofalo
ph. 045 8007951
paologarofalo@paologarofalo.it

Polarolo Immagine e Comunicazione
ph. 011 4371757 fax 011 4371933
polar@polarolo.it

Raineri Design
ph. 030 390120 fax 030 398603
william@raineridesign.com

RBA Design
ph. 02 7608241 fax 02 76082433
rba@rbadesign.it

Ricreativi
ph. 051 6827134 fax 051 6827294
ricreativi@ricreativi.it

Show Box
ph. 02 66302225 fax 02 66302642
mail@show-box.it

SiebertHead
ph. 0044 2076899090
fax 0044 2076899080
satkargidda@sieberthead.com

Skatto.com
ph. 050 580558 fax 050 3138000
skatto@skatto.com

Studio Brozzi
ph. 0521 211500 fax 0521 211500

Studio Estilo
ph. 0547 611039 fax 0547 363105
estilografica@virgilio.it

Studio Knetch Sottile
ph. 0422 379241 fax 0422 436272
daliah@akappa.com

Studio Magni
ph. 0532 766897 fax 0532 761440
laura@studiomagnidesign.it

Studio Padovani
ph. 059 342144 fax 059 350004
padovani@tsc4.com

Tangram
ph. 0321 392232 fax 0321 390914
info@tangramsd.it

Temecula Design
ph. 06 3233410
info@temecula.it

The AD Store
ph. 0521 504345 fax 0521 504376
info@adstore.it

Ubis
ph. 0422 436290 fax 0422 436272
ubis@ubis.com

Unjust
ph. 059 663940 fax 059 663725
francesco@unjust.it

Viabizzuno
ph. 051 8908011
d.paccagnella@viabizzuno.com

Package Design In Italy
:Featured Works Index

Advance
40-88-194

Balena Corporation
179

Basaglia
41-42-43

Brunazzi & Associati
28-29-30-31-100-152

Carlo Raffaelli Comunicazione
89

Carré Noir
24-119-120-121-122-123

Casa Walden
39

Caseley Giovara
32

Charta
116-117-118-165

Cilindrina
154

Claudio Cristofori Associati
33-91-92

DBV
35-88

Dinamo Project
180-181

Equilibri Sospesi
86-87-161

Gianni Rossi
190-191-192-193

Giò Minola
60-76

Grafica BGC
25-58-59-160

Il Telaio Advertising
68-83

Image Studio
61-62-63-64

Immedia
90

Inside BTB
12

Isia Faenza
14-15-16-17-65-112-113-156

Kalimera
67-144-145-146-147-148-149-150
151

Le Design
23-34

Leonard
134-135

Marina Turci
183-184-185

Mario Turconi
110-111

Matitegiovanotte
166-167-168-169-170-171-172-173
174-175-176-177-178

Matteo Guidi
155

Mixage
13

Morpheus
187-188-189

Nedda Bonini
25

no.parking
20-21-22-36-37-57-79-162-163-164

Nouvelle
94-95-96-97-194

Officina Comunicazione
101-102-157

Paolo Garofalo
186

Polarolo Immagine e Comunicazione
69-70-71

Raineri Design
80-81-82-182

RBA Design
44-45-46-47-48-66-131-132-133

Ricreativi
93

Show Box
130

SiebertHead
98-99-100

Skatto.com
139-140-141

Studio Brozzi
52-107-108-109

Studio Estilo
195

Studio Knetch Sottile
114-115

Studio Magni
38-69-124-125

Studio Padovani
49-136-137-138

Tangram
24-53-77-78-79-103-104-105-106

Temecula Design
74-75-158-159

The AD Store
18-19-54-55

Ubis
126-127-128-129

Unjust
56-196-197-198-199-200-201-202
203

Viabizzuno
153

Printed by Grafiche dell'Artiere in December of 2004 in Bologna Italy
Novatech Satin paper 170g distributed by Antalis.

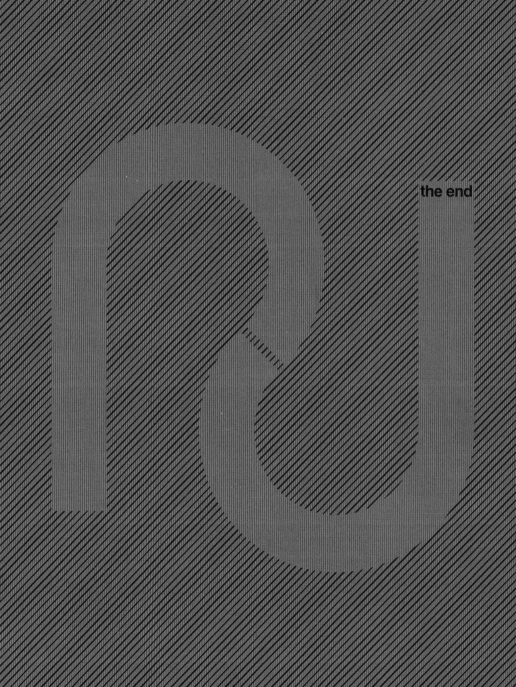

the end